The Ideal Cheese Book

The Ideal Cheese Book

Edward Edelman
and Susan Grodnick

Preface by Barbara Kafka

Illustrations by Ippy Patterson

1817

HARPER & ROW, PUBLISHERS, New York

Cambridge, Philadelphia, San Francisco, Washington, London, Mexico City, São Paulo, Singapore, Sydney

Copyright acknowledgments follow the Index.

FIRST EDITION

Copy editor: Joan Whitman
Designer: C. Linda Dingler

Library of Congress Cataloging-in-Publication Data

Edelman, Edward.
   The ideal cheese book.

   1. Cheese—Varieties.   2. Cheese—History.
3. Cookery (Cheese)   I. Grodnick, Susan.   II. Title.
SF271.E325 1986   641.3'73   85-45996
ISBN 0-06-055073-2   86 87 88 89 90 MPC 10 9 8 7 6 5 4 3 2 1
ISBN 0-06-096116-3(pbk.) 86 87 88 89 90 MPC 10 9 8 7 6 5 4 3 2 1

Contents

Preface

BARBARA KAFKA

Finally, Americans have become really interested in cheese. I remember when it took arduous searching to find a decent Brie or a Camembert that wasn't in a tin. Aside from rat cheese or country store Cheddar, American-made cheeses were virtually unheard of. At people's houses, one was most likely to be given a Gouda or a barely Swiss cheese served up with crackers as an accompaniment to drinks. As the food boom started, a cautious hunt for more interesting cheese surfaced. Supermarkets were still the domain of the processed and the prewrapped. Too many cheeses bought in "gourmet" shops that should have known better smelled acridly of ammonia. Progress once started kept rolling. Today, in most major American cities and by mail order, a better selection of cheeses is available than anyplace else in the world. We have all the best cheeses of the whole world. Supermarkets have extensive cheese selections and there are many stores that specialize in cheese.

Our chief current lack seems to be in the service of cheese in restaurants. Partly, this is due to antiquated American health codes that insist that cheese be refrigerated and, partly, to economic reasons. Restaurants that have tried to present glorious cheese assortments, like the ones that are the pride of good French restaurants, have found that they have to throw out enormous quantities of cheese as Americans do not have the habit of a cheese course. Maybe we are reluctant to pay a restaurant for a bought product or maybe we are just greedy to get on to dessert. This means that cheese is mainly consumed at home and we have to learn how to buy it.

Proliferation has meant confusion. What is the cheese? How do I know when it is ripe or aged or fresh enough? How do I store it? When should I serve it? What does it go with? Can it be used in cooking and, if so, how? And, finally, what are the best recipes using cheese? This seems a particularly relevant subject at a time when there are more vegetarians in this country than ever before and when the rest of us seem to want to eat less meat.

During the first wave of enthusiasm, a wonderful woman named Helen McCully decided to write a guide to cheese with Ed Edelman of Ideal Cheese, a shop in New York that had gracefully evolved from being a simple dairy store to one of the foremost importers and sellers of cheeses from all over the world. Unfortunately, Helen died. Time moved on; the subject became more complex. Susan Grodnick was induced to pick up the task and she has made a glorious job of it. You should be able to find here the answers in crisp, clear, easy-to-understand prose to all your cheese questions.

This is an important resource and is sure to become a standard reference for all of us who love cheese or who write about it.

Acknowledgments

Without Joseph Edelman, Ed's father, there could be no book. He established the original Ideal Farms and taught Ed about the cheese business.

Our heartfelt thanks to Barbara Kafka, first for introducing us to each other, but most especially for her loving help and guidance as we struggled to organize the material and find the right voice for the book.

For having created the predecessor of this book, we owe a debt to the late Helen McCully, extraordinary food editor and friend.

For their help in our research, we thank John Paul Grasmuck, Jen Pederson of Tholstrups USA, André Jaeckle of Otto Roth, Gail LeCompte of the Goat Works inc., and Ann Dixon of Verde-monte.

Many friends contributed favorite cheese recipes. We thank Daniel Bloom of Pizzapiazza, Naomi Chanen, Craig Claiborne, Marion Cunningham, Gael Greene, Jean Hewitt, Sue Huffman, Jane Helsel Joseph, Barbara Kafka, Paul Kovi, Aphrodite Lianides, Jacques Pépin, Seppi Renggli, Richard Sax, Shelburne Farms, Martha Shulman, André Soltner, Jeremiah Tower, Alice Waters, Chuck Williams, and Paula Wolfert.

Introduction

For nearly thirty years, Edward Edelman has been behind the counter at Ideal Cheese (originally Ideal Farms) selling cheese—and a few pâtés and crackers. He started in the business when Brie was considered exotic, working with his father in a dairy shop that sold butter, eggs and cheese, mostly young and fresh. In time more and more customers were interested in finding cheeses they had tasted on trips abroad: soft-ripened Camemberts, creamy Boursault, fresh Mozzarella di Bufalo, rich Explorateur. Edward responded with enthusiasm, working with importers to promote dozens of cheeses unknown to most Americans. In the fifties, he brought in Pont l'Evêque, Boursin, Coulommiers and Valençay, among others. Later he introduced Explorateur, Caprice des Dieux, St. André, Doux de Montagne, Pipo Crem' and Crottin de Chauvignol. He also has recognized the growing interest in American cheeses, being an early supporter of Laura Chenel's as well as those of Sallie Kendell and other young Americans.

When customers asked Edward to recommend a book to help them learn about all the new cheeses piled in his cases, he told them about Pierre Androuët's *The Complete Encyclopedia of French Cheese,* now out of print. That book had many shortcomings for the average customer, however, and it was frustrating to read about cheeses never seen in this country. He began to joke about having to write one himself, but he soon realized it made sense: after years of answering questions and conducting classes and tastings for students, he certainly knew what people wanted to know.

He decided he wouldn't be comfortable writing the book alone, so he enlisted the help of Helen McCully, then food editor of *House Beautiful.* Miss McCully, one of the most respected food editors around, started on the project, but passed away before it was finished. Edward then turned to Barbara Kafka for advice, and she was good enough to recommend me. Long a lover of cheeses, I was delighted with the opportunity to be able to taste many new varieties as well as have unlimited access to Edward's expertise.

Since many new cheeses had come on the market since the book first began, Edward and I started the project from scratch. We have concentrated on those cheeses that are available in the United States, and we've tried to include as many of them as possible. But we've left to travelers the fun of discovering hard-to-find cheeses on their own, since it didn't make sense to describe cheeses sold only in a little town in northern Italy or southern New Jersey.

We started at Ideal Cheese. I examined the forms, squeezing, smelling and finally tasting each cheese in the shop. We then went out to local warehouses to see and taste the cheeses Edward does not carry himself. He told me the questions his customers asked about entertaining, storage, serving, making up assortments. We tried to answer all of them as well as my own.

As we worked, new cheeses came on the market; companies went out of business. Each time we had new information, we changed the manuscript.

As much as Edward likes to eat cheese in different forms, he doesn't cook, so I wrote the recipe section myself. I have tried to combine classic recipes with some new inventions and to use some cheeses rarely seen in the kitchen. In some cases I called on other food writers and cooks to help. Some gave us permission to use recipes they had sent to Miss McCully years ago.

The result is the book before you. Edward and I hope you will use it to learn about cheeses you may already know and to discover the many wonderful new cheeses now available.

SUSAN GRODNICK

April 1986

The Ideal Cheese Book

The Cheeses

This section is designed to help you find your way through the dozens of cheeses you see in your local cheese shop or grocery. We have tried to include every cheese sold in the United States, but every week new cheeses appear and old favorites fade into memory. At no time in history have so many new companies, large and small, been so busy creating new cheeses, often directed at the American market. There are dozens of chèvres and double creams today where once few existed. Old favorites are now flavored with pepper or herbs. The variety can be overwhelming at times and is certainly confusing. In an attempt to create some order out of the seeming chaos, we have divided the cheeses into groups according to what we see as their strongest characteristic. Within these large groups, we have further divided them as clearly as we can, putting together all those cheeses that are close relations, regardless of nationality.

Deciding what characteristic was most important for each cheese was not always obvious. Was it texture, taste, cheesemaking method, milk? After careful examination of all the cheeses, we realized it wasn't clear cut. Each cheese had to be examined on its own strength. In the end, we grouped the cheeses according to different criteria. Since most cheeses are made with cow's milk, that would be too large a category to be effective. Cheeses made with goat and sheep's milk, however, do logically go together. Many cheeses are flavored with herbs and spices, but the flavorings didn't seem to be a strong enough tie to make a group. The exception is blue molds where the changes are quite different than mere flavorings. They, too, make a family. The white mold sprayed on the outside of soft-ripened cheeses also has a strong enough effect to justify discussing those cheeses together. Yet washing those same forms with brandy or salt water changes them sufficiently to make them worthy of a separate grouping. Cheddaring is another method that shaped a group, and Swiss-style cheeses, although not all made in quite the same way, are enough alike to be a family.

It is age rather than technique that sets fresh cheeses apart, and their richness makes double and triple creams special. Largest of all groups is that of the semisoft cheeses. Those we further divided into basic cheeses and dozens of copies. Aging these cheeses and others like them alters them enough to create a family of hard and grating cheeses.

We hope our organization makes it easy for you to find out about cheeses you see and to discover new ones similar to those you like. Most fit very neatly into one of our imposed categories. Others fit two or more, forcing us to make arbitrary decisions. If you don't find a cheese where you think it should be, the index will help you.

Among the hundreds of cheeses we've discussed are some we like more than others, some that are little known in the United States. We've marked them with an asterisk * to say that these are cheeses we urge you to try. They may be old classics that are often forgotten, like Reblochon and Stilton, great cheeses only recently available here, like Mozzarella di Bufalo and Mascarpone, or new inventions, like Huntsman, a combination of Stilton and Cheshire.

Fresh Cheeses

Most delicate of all are the fresh cheeses, just one step removed from cream. Made all over the cheese-eating world from every kind of milk—cow, goat, sheep, water buffalo, sour, skim—most never travel more than a few miles from home. They are simple cheeses, inexpensive and accessible, always soft and spreadable, eaten little more than days old. They are lighter than butter but equally versatile. The most perishable group, fresh cheeses make up in youth what they lack in complexity. They can be memorable, when very young, impressive to serve alone or with a few lightly dressed greens in place of a traditional cheese course.

Cooks never exhaust the possible uses of these cheeses, stirring them into creamy cakes and delicate pancakes, adding their silkiness to spicy sandwich spreads or in dips for fresh tortilla chips, rounds of daikon (Japanese white radish) and baby turnips. They are ideal for salads or light meals, breakfast or snacks. They can be used to stuff crêpes and pastas, cherry tomatoes and fluffy baked potatoes. Served with beautiful berries or melons and a sprinkling of sugar, they make elegant, quick desserts.

Fresh cheeses include those so new the curd still shows, others smooth and creamy, and those made firm because they are kneaded like bread. Often they're flavored with herbs, fruits, garlic, pepper and other spices. Because they are young, they never develop rinds and molds. Although they may have up to 70 percent butterfat, some have surprisingly little. Most also are made with a minimum of salt, and a few are completely salt free. The very rich ones are in the Double and Triple Cream section.

Buying and Storing

Since their youth is what makes these cheeses special, try to buy only as much as you will use in a day or two. They are very moist, sometimes crumbly, and should taste, smell and look fresh and white, not runny and certainly not moldy. All except those hung to dry need constant refrigeration. Remove them from the refrigerator just long enough before serving to take the chill off. Keep them wrapped as airtight as possible, in the container they are packaged in, glass jars or plastic tubs with tight-fitting covers.

Curd Cheese

The simplest is the delicate curd cheese, for centuries the exclusive domain of farm women who gently heated the milk and starter until it separated into curds and whey. The gleaming white curds are drained, often salted, perhaps pressed a bit to make them firmer. They are then ready for breakfast and lunch spread on bread alone or with jam, olives, nuts. They can be added to batters and eggs, used in rich cakes and fruity pies.

In America, we eat more of these cheeses than any other kind, although they are made in factories rather than cottages. The moistest are **Cottage Cheese** and **Pot Cheese.** Made of very soft curds, they should have a delicate sour taste, excellent in place of lettuce in a chunky salad of cucumbers, radishes, red and green peppers. Flavored with fresh herbs, warm spices, garlic or hot pepper, they can make varied spreads and dips or be a creamy addition to scrambled eggs and chives, egg or tuna salad. Strawberry-studded cheesecakes made with Cottage Cheese are lighter than the cream cheese varieties. Cottage Cheese pancakes served with raspberry jam make an incredible breakfast or dessert.

As with other fine cheeses, there are regional variations among these soft cheeses. Federal law requires them to be made with skim milk and have at least 4 percent milk fat. Those made with only 1 percent must be marked "low fat." When the curds are large (about ½ inch), the cheese is called popcorn, large curd or California style. The curd is mashed to make country or farm style. These moist cheeses are sometimes called creamed-style Cottage Cheese. Old-fashioned Pot Cheese is pressed Cottage Cheese, having the same large curds but less moisture so it is drier and firmer. Both are sold in 8-ounce, 1- and 2-pound containers, as well as in bulk in specialty stores. The bulk cheeses are usually superior in taste and texture. Most are made without gums or citric acid, preservatives that detract from the fresh taste. To be sure, check the ingredients on the label.

Farmer Cheese is whole milk Cottage Cheese with almost all the liquid pressed out and some cream added. This firm cheese is popular with home bakers to fill flaky strudels and delicate blintzes. Puréed, it is used for Easter pashka. It is sometimes commercially mixed with berries or raisins and nuts and baked for **Baked Farmer Cheese,** excellent for breakfast. Usually shaped into loaves, this denser cheese can be sliced. The plain cheese comes in 7½-ounce packages and 3-pound loaves.

Cream Cheese

Rich and creamy, as the name implies, **Cream Cheese** is a thick cheese perfect for spreading on crackers, bagels or other breads, to top with smoked salmon and thin slices of Bermuda onion or all-American strawberry jelly. The best is slightly sweet, fluffy and white, made without preservatives. It produces those dense cheesecakes that melt in the mouth. We love to spread it thick on sandwiches and top it with Greek olives, chopped walnuts, spicy salamis or luscious mangoes. It makes flaky pie crusts and delicate nut- and raisin-studded rugelach. To whip up a host of spreads, thin it with fresh or sour cream, milk, mayonnaise or yogurt; flavor with garlic, chopped herbs, hot peppers, nuts. Serve with broccoli florets, haricots verts, fresh mushroom caps, red and yellow pepper strips.

Creme Supreme from California does the flavoring for you, offering all natural Cream Cheese with layers of smoked salmon, pesto and walnuts, or Gorgonzola and almonds. Three-pound pyramid-shaped loaves are perfect at brunch for a crowd. Slices are pretty for smaller groups.

Most cream cheeses are made with vegetable gum (listed on the label), but it is worth paying a premium for the purer cheeses. These natural cream cheeses come from California. A caveat: most baking recipes have been developed for the gummed version and the two are not exactly interchangeable. If you make the switch, be sure to adjust the recipe to make up the differences in sweetness and texture. (Compare the Lindy's Cheesecake recipe on page 206 with that for Preservative-Free Cheesecake on page 207 to get an idea.)

Believing in the importance of American farmstead cheeses, the Dixon family in Vermont began making **Verde-mont,** a wonderfully creamy cheese from their own cows. Softer than packaged cream cheeses, it is ideal spread on toast with onion marmalade, or mixed with whipped cream and a bit of sugar for a fruit topping. Although it seems as rich as Boursin and other triple creams, the butterfat content is less than 20 percent. Both plain and herb-flavored cheeses come in 5¼-ounce packages. We hope other Americans will follow their fine example.

Days often begin in France with **Carré Frais,** also called **Gervais,** a sweet, pure cream cheese to spread on morning toast, plain or sprinkled with nuts. It comes in foil-wrapped squares or cups.

Even milder is Italian **Robiola,** moist, white and creamy. More delicate than most American cream cheeses, it is made plain, with parsley and with Norwegian salmon in paper-wrapped 8-ounce and 1-pound packages. Serve it on dry toast with raspberry jam or with fresh tomatoes and cucumbers, liberally sprinkled with black pepper. There are also Robiolas flavored with pineapples, pears or apples.

Among the many flavored cream cheeses on the market are American **Crème de Neufchatel, Smiling Cheese Man, Alouette** and **Rondelé,** German **Exquisa,** French **Maigrelait** and **le Cremeux,** and **Danish Cream Cheese.** Flavors include garlic, onion, caviar, smoked salmon, pepper, peach melba, pineapple, orange and chocolate. The butterfat ranges from 20 to 70 percent. They are sold in 5-ounce packages, logs or bulk and should last for weeks.

Yogurtelle, made with yogurt culture, is a spread to serve with vegetables and crackers. It comes flavored with herbs, garden vegetables and bacon and horseradish.

Ricotta

Travelers are often surprised to discover that **Ricotta** in Italy is quite different from that sold and made here. As originally conceived, Ricotta was a thrifty invention, not a true cheese but something cheeselike made from the whey given off in the production of Mozzarella and other cheeses. In the United States, the curd is used as well. The result is smoother and moister with the curd evident. A popular cooking cheese, Ricotta is a frequent ingredient in spinach ravioli, meaty lasagne, creamy gnocchi and light cheesecakes flavored with amaretto. Our part-skim Ricotta is drier, closer to the Italian than the fresh, sweet whole milk cheese that is much like Cottage Cheese. Generally low in sodium, Ricotta is sold in 15-ounce and 3-pound containers. Fresh Italian Ricotta, rarely sold here, is quite different from firm Ricotta Romano and Ricotta Salata, discussed in the Hard and Grating section.

Cedulait, a French cheese made without any fat and with 20 percent butterfat, is much like a smooth Ricotta without the curd. Delicate in taste and extremely perishable, it is a superb diet food, especially when mixed with fresh fruit.

Mozzarella and Other Pasta Filata Cheeses

Italy's other famous fresh cheese—**Mozzarella**—is made by a more complex method known as *pasta filata,* "spun paste." The curds are warmed, then kneaded like bread dough. The original Mozzarella, * **Mozzarella di Bufalo,** was made from water buffalo milk. It is still made in Italy's Salerno region either of pure water buffalo milk or mixed with cow's milk (usually one-third buffalo). It is sold here in limited quantities and tastes much like a young goat or sheep's milk cheese. Squeezably soft and white, it is too delicate and expensive to top pizza. Serve it by itself with a light Chianti or in a salad with ripe red tomatoes and fragrant green basil leaves, dressed with virgin olive oil. Individual balls, about 8 ounces, are often wrapped in paper, always packed in their own brine. If kept in the liquid, they will last two to three weeks.

Long before air travel made it feasible to bring in the Mozzarella di Bufalo, Italian grocers began making their own cow's milk Mozzarella, usually from a commercial starter. They gently warm the curds and shape them into soft, chewy balls kept in water or mild brine. Some they roll with thin slices of prosciutto or pepperoni, others they smoke. They make them with and without salt. It is worth traveling across town to get these cheeses, especially if you go to the trouble of making your own pizza. Wonderful in fragrant summer salads with tuna and red onions and on crusty bread with thin slices of prosciutto, they soften beautifully in heat to make oozing fillings for fried sandwiches called mozzarella en carrozza.

The commercial Mozzarellas, sold in supermarkets in plastic-wrapped 8-ounce or 1-pound packages, are firmer and somewhat rubbery, designed for ordinary cooking. This cheese gets stringy when melted on such traditional foods as pizza and lasagne, but adds little flavor.

Scamorza is Mozzarella wrapped in raffia and hung in pairs to age a bit. It may be lightly smoked. If imported, it is called **Scamorza Affumicate.** Some come in 10-ounce forms shaped like animals, usually pigs. **Treccione,** a smoked Mozzarella made from a mixture of cow and water buffalo milk, comes in 5-pound braided loaves that are smoked over hay fires. The domestic cheese, smoked in smokehouses or with a dose of liquid smoke, is simply called **Smoked Mozzarella.** Smoking increases the life of the cheeses. If left to hang at home, they will age and get firmer. Try them in a salad with celery root and prosciutto or in sandwiches with mild ham and tomato.

Other Fresh Cheeses

Soft, fresh and creamy, **Stracchino** is pleasantly tart, good added to a salad of beets in a mustard vinaigrette. It is best in winter, theoretically made from the milk of tired (*stracco*) cows, worn out by their journey down from the mountain pastures and their sparse grazing land.

Fresh white cheese from France, **Fromage Blanc,** is rarely imported. It has a mild taste, making it an excellent base for many recipes. In most cases, puréed Cottage Cheese is an acceptable substitute.

Queso Fresco describes an assortment of fresh white cheeses made around the country in the Mexican/Spanish style. Often saltier than other fresh cheeses, but at times made without additional salt, they are sometimes taken for goat or sheep's milk cheeses. Try them as stuffings for peppers or enchiladas; crumble some over tortillas, run under the broiler and serve with tequila. If you cannot find Queso Fresco, substitute Farmer Cheese.

Soft-Ripened Cheeses

NORMANDY TRADITION

genuine high quality camembert from Normandy

Soft-Ripened Cheese

véritable camembert Normand de haute qualité

Florval Camembert

PRODUCT OF FRANCE

IMPORTED BY ANCO FOODS FAIRFIELD NJ

MADE FROM PASTEURIZED MILK

Soft-ripened cheeses are probably what Clifton Fadiman had in mind when he said that cheese is "milk's leap toward immortality." We never cease to marvel that behind the downy white rinds are wondrous ivory cheeses thick as honey and almost as quick to ooze. We could happily eat these cheeses every day, but we usually save them for entertaining, confident that they will be appropriate at almost all dinners or parties along with a watercress and shiitake salad or in place of dessert. They fit amiably into an assortment and have enough character to star on their own with buttery Chardonnays or aged Burgundies.

Ripe juicy apples, pears and grapes are ideal companions for these soft cheeses. We like them together: a slice of apple topped with a slice of cheese. The French think it is a quaint American custom but recognize the affinity of the two foods. They still insist on eating the fruit on the side, however, spreading the cheese on crusty unseasoned bread that won't interfere with the delicate flavor of the cheese.

There are those who think it is a crime to use soft-ripened cheeses for cooking. Even a sandwich of Westphalian ham and Brie on chewy pumpernickel bread with mustard doesn't sound quite right to them. We're not such purists. These creamy cheeses melt beautifully over pasta or hamburgers, in omelets and crêpes, on top of onion soup.

Serve soft-ripened cheeses on flat plates or boards with a knife. Be sure to leave enough room for the cheese to spread a bit, especially if you start with a wedge. The entire cheese is edible but some don't like the rind and cut it away just as they might cut the crusts from bread. The rind is the first part of the cheese to get overripe, so if it starts to brown, you probably should remove it and just eat the creamy center, which will still be fine.

Although most soft-ripened cheeses are made with cow's milk, cheesemakers use goat and sheep's milk as well. The butterfat content is usually between 45 and 50 percent.

Buying and Storing

Soft-ripened cheeses come in wheels from 8 ounces to 2 kilograms (actually 4½ pounds). Whole small cheeses like Camembert or Chaource contrast nicely with chunks of Fontina and logs of chèvre. If your other cheeses are round, a wedge of Brie might be appropriate. Should the group be large enough, a whole wheel of Brie is always welcome.

Soft-ripened cheeses are said to run when brought to room temperature, but they actually ooze and should never be liquid. Relatively young, they are sprayed with a penicillin mold to form the white rind; they are sometimes called white-mold cheeses. They may also be called bloomy or floury rinds. The cheese develops from the outside in to the middle, opposite from blue molds that develop from the inside out.

While it is not difficult to find a perfectly ripe Brie or other soft-ripened cheese, you should shop with care. Most important is that the cheese be in prime condition, generally fresh and plump, full, with a snowy white rind. A whole cheese should give a bit and be as full on the bottom as on the top. A cheese that is firm when you squeeze it is not completely ripe and will have a dry core running through the middle. Among soft-ripened cheeses that are an inch or less in thickness, the cut wheel should have an even creamy interior through to the middle with no trace of the core. If the core is still there when the cheese is cut, it will never disappear, although the rest of the cheese will continue to develop.

In contrast, thick cheeses always have some core; it makes for an interesting variation in texture. If thick cheeses were left to develop until the core completely disappeared, they would be overripe at the edges. Europeans like cores in most soft-ripened cheeses, even Brie, but Americans prefer them with an even texture. If the rind has started to brown, the cheese may be past its prime, although a reddish cast is fine. Avoid any cheese that has dry edges, smells of ammonia, or is concave.

You can ripen a young cheese or one that needs more flavor by leaving it wrapped in plastic or foil at room temperature for a day or two. Once it is to your liking, keep it wrapped in the refrigerator, removing pieces as you need them and immediately rewrapping and refrigerating the excess. Kept this way, the cheese will be fine for three to four weeks. The fastest way for a cheese to get overripe is to expose it to frequent changes of temperature, letting it warm and then refrigerating it.

Although all cheeses are best with the chill taken out of them, soft-ripened varieties change markedly in texture after warming up, going from firm and salty when cold to supple and luscious when left at room temperature. Be sure to give them four to eight hours to soften. Unless you buy cheese from a shop that keeps them at room temperature ready for that evening's dinner, you will have to plan ahead. If you're not home during the day, take the cheese out in the morning or the night before (unless your kitchen is exceedingly warm). Keep it wrapped until serving time so it keeps its shape and does not dry out.

Leftover cheese that has been sitting out unwrapped will never be wonderful again. Rewrap it and leave at room temperature for a snack the next day, use in a dip, as a topping for a hamburger or sandwich, or in a sauce, anything where taste, not appearance, counts.

French Varieties

The world is indebted to France for developing soft-ripened cheeses, in particular Brie and Camembert, the undisputed monarchs of the group. Virtually all soft-ripened cheeses are variations of these two. **Camembert** comes from Normandy, known for its wonderful dairies. The plump white rounds, a mere 5 inches across, have enthralled cheese lovers since the eighteenth century. The cheese will smell slightly fruity at its peak, fill its box and have just a hint of red in the white rind. Because it is small, a cheese cut before it is fully ripened will never completely develop.

True Camemberts weigh about 8 ounces. They are wrapped in perforated plastic and boxed. Always made in Normandy, the quality varies among the more than five hundred brands. When you find one you like, stick with it. Serve a whole or half wheel with cocktails, hard cider or Calvados to a small group. It makes a satisfying dessert with slices of crisp reddish-green apples and is equally at home with elegant red wines from Burgundy and Bordeaux and soft California Merlots.

To make some unknown white-mold soft-ripened cheeses familiar to Americans, some cheese importers and merchants tag the Camembert name onto large white-mold cheeses, calling them bulk Camemberts. It is unfortunate that in this competitive world they believe, probably with cause, that the cheese would not sell with another name. Many are excellent cheeses, although none is a true Camembert.

Titles may be bestowed too freely on cheeses but few would argue about the worthiness of Camembert, the queen, and Brie, her honored consort. One of the most popular cheeses both here and in its native land, **Brie** was officially declared the King of Cheeses at the Congress of Vienna in 1815 when the representatives had an argument about which country made the best cheese. To settle it, each delegate brought his country's finest example to a dinner. The Brie that Monsieur de Talleyrand submitted won the crown.

Much larger than Camembert, Brie comes in thin wheels that are equally white with honey-thick interiors that ooze at room temperature. They have a milder flavor and an aroma reminiscent of Anjou pears, with which they are often paired. Like all white-mold cheeses, the ideal Brie in America is plump and full, the rind downy white. There is no core. Some people, usually Europeans, prefer a cheese no longer snowy white, one that has a reddish tint because it has aged longer and developed a more pronounced taste. Since few shops sell the cheese that way, you will have to age it yourself.

In searching for the Brie you like best, look to brand names. The best are consistently good. The same Brie may be sold under two or more different names, made by the same manufacturer for different importers. **Brie de Meaux,** for example, is an excellent Brie made by H. Huntin. They also make Brie under the Couronne label. Originally, all Brie was made in the Île-de-France, near Paris. Later, the city of Meaux became famous for its fine Bries. Today, both are brand names, telling nothing about where the cheese was made.

There is a perfect size Brie for just about any party. Rounds the size of service plates are usually sold by the wedge; smaller, salad plate-size rounds are sold in whole or half wheels. They look attractive alone on a buffet table, or with an assortment including a chèvre, Tamie and aged Gouda. After dinner, we like Brie with fruity Beaujolais and soft Burgundies or an icy glass of poire. If you are serving a whole cheese, keep it in the perforated plastic wrapping and wooden box it comes in until just before serving.

Although Brie is best plain, it is also made flavored with herbs and with coarsely ground black pepper. Both are popular. Since the flavorings overpower the basic taste of the cheese, we serve these at cocktail parties.

The finest, most flavorful Bries are those made from unpasteurized milk. Unfortunately, United States Customs regulations prohibit the importation of any unaged cheeses made from unpasteurized milk. Once in a while, however, an importer quietly sneaks a few unpasteurized Bries past Customs. They are thinner than the pasteurized varieties and their flavor is more distinctive and a bit saltier, since salt is rubbed into the rind. Pasteurized cheeses are just dipped into a salt-water brine. The rinds of unpasteurized Bries are slightly brown and the cheese oozes a little more. Shipped out younger, these cheeses still have cores. They are brought in by air because they are more fragile and wouldn't stand up to the typical sea voyage. Even so, there is a strong possibility that the cheese you find will be past its prime. If it is in good condition, get it for a memorable experience.

As with Camembert, importers put the Brie label on cheeses that, while related, are not true Bries. Most common among these are the 60 percent Bries discussed in the Double Cream section. Check the label. Increasingly, cheeses sold as Brie are actually double creams.

Made like Brie, **Coulommiers** is smaller and thicker, between Brie and Camembert in flavor. The 12-ounce round is attractively packaged on a straw mat wrapped with a red ribbon. Serve it by itself with grapes for dessert.

Chubby **Chaource** has such a rich, creamy texture, many mistake it for a double cream. It has the characteristic core of thick cheeses and tastes much like Camembert or Coulommiers. It develops an aroma of mushrooms that is enhanced when served with a salad of fresh chanterelles and thyme. The 20-ounce round is 5 inches in diameter; the 8-ounce is a mere 2½ inches across.

To make them less temperamental, some cheeses are stabilized. While they won't run like Brie nor have its finesse, you can be assured of a good soft and buttery cheese that keeps well. **Valembert, Belle de Champs, Clair de Lune, Dauphine** and **Chamois d'Or,** all available in 4-pound wheels, are essentially the same. Valembert, made with partly skimmed milk, has less butterfat than most soft-ripened cheeses. It is also aged longer so the rind is a little thicker.

The cheeses called "bulk" Camemberts include **Délice de France** and **l'Artisan Fromager** from Normandy. Good quality cheeses, although not true Camemberts, wholes or halves are fine for large groups, especially when they are well priced. Délice de France comes plain or herb-flavored in 3-pound ovals. L'Artisan Fromager, which tastes like an unpasteurized Camembert, comes in 2½-pound wheels.

A most interesting addition to this group is **St. Albray,** shaped like a thick, scalloped doughnut. Mild when young, it gets stronger with age. The 4½-pound cheeses are foil-wrapped.

American Varieties

While American soft-ripened cheeses will always be overshadowed by the French, they are often as good. Californian **Rouge et Noir** (red and black) is our answer to Camembert. It can nobly end any meal, mated with crisp New England apples, as can **New York State Camembert.** They are the same size and shape as the French cheese, but the quality is not always consistent. Both are available by mail. **Cheese Taster's Choice,** made in Ohio, is not as good. It comes three pieces to a 4-ounce, half-moon box.

Tradition de Belmont is a new American-style Brie from Wisconsin. Although younger and milder than the French, it shows promise of being a worthy rival. It is packaged in the same 1- and 2-kilogram wheels, wrapped in perforated plastic and boxed. The oldest domestic Brie comes from Illinois under the **Delico** name. These 2-pound wheels, sold primarily by mail, are generally excellent.

There are many small cheesemakers around the country working to make excellent, full-flavored soft-ripened cheeses. We predict the number and quality will continue to improve over the years, although it will always be on a limited scale. Whenever your local cheese shop has one, try it. You'll probably be glad you did.

Vacherin Mont d'Or

Known mostly for large firm cheeses, the Swiss once a year make an incredible soft cheese, ***Vacherin Mont d'Or.** Shaped by a thin birch mold, it develops an uneven top and runs like Camembert. Most often it is served with a spoon. Although not sprayed with white mold, the top is powdery white; the interior, ivory. It should easily come away from the birch, revealing brown sides. Wheels are 1¼, 3 and 5 pounds. Made in mid-October, it is available only in November and December. It starts out very mild but will become fairly strong as it ages.

As the supreme compliment to the Swiss, the French have copied this special cheese. Available all year, **Tourée** is an excellent substitute, although it will never get quite as runny and spoonable. Also shaped by birch, wheels weigh about 4½ pounds.

Italian Varieties

Not known for white-mold, soft-ripening cheeses, the Italians have recently developed some excellent examples, usually mild but not bland. **Formaggio Granduca,** a lovely cheese, is delicate in taste and creamy throughout with a few small holes. It never oozes as much as Brie but it gets nicely buttery. The wheels weigh 3½ pounds.

Mario Blanco, from Piedmont, is another pleasant soft-ripened cheese. Serve it with pears and pear brandy. There are 10-ounce, 3-pound and 4-pound rounds, all wrapped in plastic.

Toma di Carmagnola, a 12-ounce buttery cheese also from the Piedmont area, has a mildly nutty flavor. **Vecchio Mulino** from Acqui Terme is a stronger, very pleasant cheese with a brownish-orange rind.

Another cheese from Piedmont, **Paglietta** is a thin 5-ounce round with a fruity, lactic taste and pungent fragrance. Properly ripe, it will run like Brie. Serve it with a Piedmontese red.

Double and Triple Creams

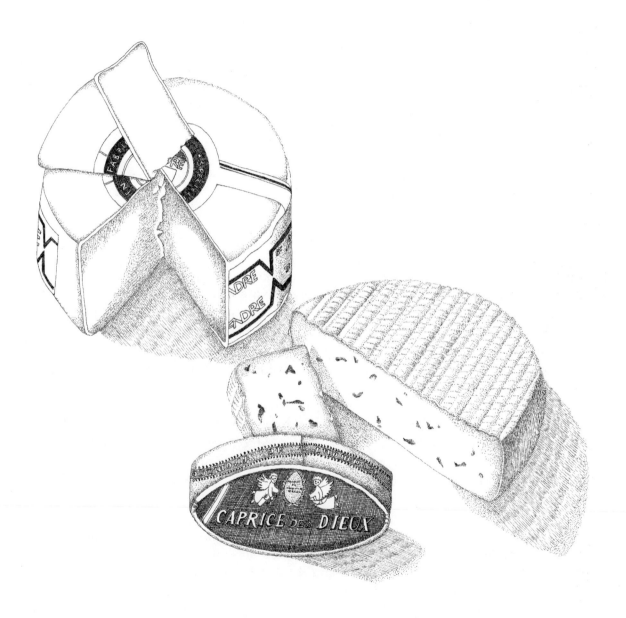

When it comes to lush cheeses, nothing compares with the thick, buttery double and triple creams. Most luxurious of all, these are extravagant cheeses made from enriched milk. Because they are too special for everyday eating, we serve them at grand parties when we bring out our best silver and crystal, the finest wines. In the past, these rich cheeses, made with extra cream, were too expensive to manufacture in quantity and too fragile to ship. Now cheesemakers around the world spend years developing new cheeses to enthrall us.

The flavors are clean, ranging from extremely mild to wonderfully tangy. Some cheeses are fresh; others are soft-ripened. None is meant to age or get hard. Like the less fatty soft-ripened cheeses, many are sprayed to form a white-mold crust. They get spreadably soft, but will not ooze as much as Brie or Camembert. Those not sprayed with mold form natural, barely noticeable crusts. Some are flavored with blue mold, others with herbs or spices. All are made from cow's milk.

These cheeses appeal to most cheese lovers. They are so rich, we rarely serve them before dinner, including them instead as part of a meal with or after salad, in place of dessert. The double creams enhance salads of just-picked summer greens. We plop spoonably soft triple creams onto ripe berries or tropical fruits for dessert. The flavored cheeses, especially the blues, are best alone or as part of a cheese course. The subtle flavor calls for plain crusty baguettes or crackers. To drink, we like the soft reds of Bordeaux or California Merlots.

Cooking with these cheeses is difficult because they break down when exposed to much heat. They make luscious fillings for crêpes with orange-cranberry conserve, however, and can be added to onion soup at the last moment or run quickly under the broiler to melt over tiny new red potatoes still in their skins.

The term "double cream" was coined by the French to distinguish between the very rich and creamy cheeses with butterfat contents exceeding 60 percent and those soft-ripened varieties, like Brie and Camembert, with less than 50 percent butterfat. While the numbers sound high, a double cream, being about half liquid, is actually 30 to 35 percent fat. The percent of butterfat, expressed in French as *matières grasses,* refers to the amount of fat in the theoretical dry weight of the cheese. In France, the law decrees that any cheese over 60 percent is a double cream. In other countries, the term is used more loosely. Triple creams are an informal subgroup of those cheeses with at least 70, sometimes up to 75, percent butterfat, as close as cheese can be to pure butter. Some cheeses high enough in butterfat to be technically double creams are like semisoft cheeses in texture and appearance. Those cheeses are discussed in the Semisoft section.

Buying and Storing

Since these rich cheeses are delicate, make sure they are in excellent condition when you buy them. Taste them if you can. They should be smooth and creamy, usually even in texture, with a fresh and light aroma, ranging from very mild to fuller in flavor. Keep in mind that they will be firmer and a bit saltier straight from the refrigerator than at room temperature. The only mold should be that characteristic of certain cheeses. An overripe cheese can get so soft it almost turns to liquid. Pale in color, spring to autumn cheeses are usually more yellow than winter cheeses. The warm-weather grass diet gives them more carotene, which brings out the yellow color.

The cheeses are at their peak when young and may be fine for weeks. Ideally, buy them as you need them, allowing enough time, of course, for them to warm up and get buttery soft. Unless your kitchen is very hot, take the cheese out in the morning for that evening. If you purchase it one afternoon for the next day and your kitchen is cool, you can leave it out overnight. Frequent change in temperature is much more harmful to the cheese than a long exposure to a 60° F. room.

Many cheeses are sold whole, running from 7 ounces to 6 pounds. If you buy one wrapped to protect it from the air, leave it wrapped until just before serving. If not, seal the cheese in plastic or foil. Rewrap it if it gets wet and scrape off any unpleasant mold. Because they get so soft at room temperature and are not evenly cut into, leftovers are usually misshapen. They still taste fine, and your family probably won't mind the messiness.

Double Creams

Like soft-ripened cheeses, most double creams have white-mold crusts, which confuses many people. Although similar, the double creams do not ooze as much as soft-ripened cheeses, are not as temperamental, ripen faster and stay fresh longer. At the moment, almost all come from France.

Caprice des Dieux, "whim of the gods," is a very mild, snowy-white double cream, one of the first brought into the United States. Packed full and plump in its box, this soft and creamy cheese is a safe choice when you're not sure what your guests like. Its pleasant flavor is appreciated by timid and adventurous cheese eaters alike. A 7-ounce oval is a fine way to end a late-night supper for four. The 3-pound oval ring will serve many more.

Most confusing of all the double creams are those called **60 percent Brie.** An excellent cheese with a fruity Beaujolais, it is unfortunate that its name was chosen deliberately to confuse customers who know and like Brie and might not be interested in trying this cheese if it had another name. Like Brie, it is made in 2½- and 5-pound wheels, either plain or coated with herbs or peppers. We serve it with salad or bread before dessert.

In taste and texture, most double creams are alike, although they vary in size and shape. Some have proprietary names, and the same cheese may be sold under two or more different brands. No cheese shop will carry all of them because of the obvious similarities. The larger cheeses, from 2½ to 4½ pounds, have more flavor. Among this ever-changing group are French **Crème des Près, le Petit Délice, Suprême** (plain, with basil and thyme, or with fennel), **Premier, Tendresse** and **Delicadou,** as well as Danish **Blanc de Blanc.** Plump and white, they come in rounds or ovals. Like other double creams, these are fine with salads of mixed greens or as part of an assortment with an aged Cheddar, a fresh chèvre and a Saint Paulin.

Look to **Père Michel** if you want neat slices for a sandwich with thin rounds of cucumber and watercress leaves. The 3-pound rectangular loaves have a light white rind. Even more interesting in form are the clover-shaped **Quatrin** and the hexagonal, 7-ounce **Revidoux.** They can stand by themselves after dinner with a young Chénas or as part of an assortment with an aged Gouda, a peppered chèvre and Maytag Blue.

Most distinctive of all double creams is **Corolle.** Shaped like an oversized, squared-off doughnut, the center remains drier, almost chalky in contrast to the creamy edges. We like this variation in textures and its tangy taste. Serve some with a spicy Zinfandel and skinny baguettes. Let thin slices melt over steaming fettuccine tossed with hot pepper flakes. Whole 8-pound forms are wonderful for large parties; slices are fine for smaller groups.

Don't be put off by the packaging of French **Petit Suisse.** What look like 1-ounce containers of ersatz cream are actually lovely, fresh, unsalted double creams usually served with fresh or poached fruits and a gentle sprinkling of sugar.

Of the flavored double creams, the prettiest are **Le Roulé,** delicate 3½-pound jelly rolls spread with herbs and garlic, pepper and strawberries. They are attractive at brunch spread on toasted brioche.

Triple Creams

French Varieties

It seems that every time we turn around there is a new triple cream on the market ready to entice us. It's a major change from the sixties when only three, all essentially the same, reached our shores. We did not then know the delights of ***Explorateur,** one of France's most sophisticated cheeses. Made in the same region as Brie, it is rich and buttery, almost as white as Cream Cheese. The flavor is complex, slightly tart; the rind, thin and supple. Serve it at the end of a gala meal with a bottle of fine Burgundy when you want to indulge or impress your guests. Shop carefully; not every wheel is ideal. The best weigh 1 pound and are about 1½ inches high. If a pound is too much, buy half. You can cut pieces from a whole wheel as you need them, keeping the rest well wrapped in the refrigerator. It will be good for up to six weeks. The 3½-pound, 12-inch wheels are difficult to work with because the individual pieces are long, thin and messy. A ½-pound Explorateur sounds convenient, but it is rarely superb. Because it is almost as high as it is wide, the outer edges are overripe and unpleasantly strong by the time the center is ripe and creamy.

Boursault, a rich and extremely creamy cheese, is slightly sour with a hint of the freshness of goat cheeses. Each 5-ounce cheese should be firm and full, never sticking to its parchment paper covering. As the cheese ages, the air dries the paper, which then sticks to the cheese forcing it to ripen too fast. Many cheese shops replace the parchment with plastic wrap to eliminate the problem. If you come across a cheese that is very soft, it is at the peak of ripeness and must be used immediately. A firm cheese will last longer. Leave it at room temperature for a day to develop its full flavor. Include it in an assortment with Parmigiano-Reggiano, a sheep's milk Fromage des Pyrénées and Livarot.

Originally, **Boursin** was like Boursault. When the companies making the two cheeses merged, Boursin was flavored with herbs and garlic or coated with black pepper, turning it into a less serious cheese, but a pleasant choice with cocktails, spread on crackers or sections of red and green peppers. The 5-ounce rounds are handy for unexpected company. Well wrapped in foil and boxed, they last for months, unchanged even after the expiration date on the box has passed. **Tartare** is similar in appearance, taste and packaging.

St. André and **St. Martin** are rich and buttery with a tangy flavor much like Boursault. A whole 4½-pound cheese, looking like a giant cheesecake, is well suited for a large party. Almost identical, except for its fluted edge, is **St. Honoré.** Unlike the small Explorateurs, these thick cheeses are perfectly proportioned and ripen evenly. If you buy from a cut cheese, as you usually will, you can see if the cheese is ripe. The center will be whiter than the ivory edges and the texture there slightly crumbly. Like other triple creams, these develop natural white crusts. At the proper temperature, they get soft enough to spoon. Use them for dessert with mangoes, papayas and other tropical fruits.

Some St. André has two thin lines of pepper or herbs and garlic running across the cheese. Try the herb-flavored cheese with a salad of mâche and endive. The peppered cheese is fabulous with juicy red strawberries. For an impressive dessert, make the ultimate cheese and fruit cake. Divide a chilled, firm St. André into three layers. Place one on a flat plate and top with sliced peaches, oranges, kiwis or other lush and colorful fruit. Place another cheese layer on top, followed by a layer of fruit and the last layer of cheese. Make concentric circles of blueberries and raspberries over the top. Chill the cake to set it. Leave at room temperature for an hour or so before serving to soften a bit but still hold its shape.

Petitcrem', packaged like Boursault, is a mini (7-ounce) St. André, sometimes made without salt. It is a convenient size, as are 8-ounce rounds of **Belletoile,** a mild white-mold cheese from Normandy. Serve either with blackberries, raspberries and clementines laced with Cointreau. Belletoile also comes in 6-pound wheels.

One of the mildest and sweetest triple creams is **Brillat-Savarin,** named for the famous French gastronome. He would surely be pleased with his namesake. With its soft, downy white crust, it is excellent with fruity Beaujolais and as a companion to Bosc pears. The 1-pound wheels are perfect for six to eight friends; for large groups, there are 3½-pound wheels. Usually in excellent condition, the cheese will separate from the crust if it is overripe.

Le Délice de Bourgogne, made with less salt than most triple creams, is similar to Brillat-Savarin. End dinner with a 1-pound round and a fine Burgundy.

Very much like Brillat-Savarin and Explorateur in appearance, **Pierre Robert** is a little stronger than the former, not as distinctive as the latter. Unfortunately, this Norman cheese is not widely distributed here.

***Gratte Paille,** made in the same region as Brie, is the fullest flavored triple cream. The thick 14-ounce rectangles make a delightful end to a meal with a fruity red wine. The crust is pale yellow, the inside almost crumbles.

German Varieties

Bonifaz, made plain and with green peppercorns, is a mild white-mold cheese. ***Bonchampi** is the same cheese flecked with pieces of fresh Bavarian mushrooms. The unmistakable flavor of these fungi will intensify as the cheese ages and browns. Bonifaz remains white and a bit milder. We serve the flavored cheeses on bread with crunchy celery and radish salads. The plain is fine after a meal with red wine. Foil-wrapped wheels weigh about 3 pounds.

Danish Varieties

The Danes have invented some fabulous cheeses including Saga, a blue-mold discussed at the end of this section. They also make buttery **Crèma Dania** (originally called Crèma Danica). It is a full-flavored white-mold cheese, either plain or coated with chives, excellent at the end of meals or with lightly dressed greens. Put some of the chive-flavored cheese in a baked potato instead of sour cream. The manufacturers have experimented with the sizing and packaging in recent years. At present, it is made in 3-pound wheels.

The people who make Saga now produce a line of triple creams including plain cheeses and those flavored with chives, both like Crèma Dania, and one flavored with mushrooms like Bonchampi. Made by the same manufacturer as Crèma Dania, they are all packaged like the original blue-mold Saga.

Italian Varieties

*Mascarpone (sometimes spelled Mascherpone) is one of those sinfully rich foods that people go into ecstasy over, eating more than they should and loving every bite. Unlike most triple creams, it is a fresh cheese that looks like very thick sour cream but tastes considerably sweeter. In Italy Mascarpone is served after only a day or two, but here it is older and, therefore, fairly solid. It gets soft enough at room temperature, however, to spoon over berries or other fruit. It is a key ingredient in tiramisu, a delicate dessert of espresso-soaked ladyfingers topped with Mascarpone and grated chocolate. Since it is fresh, it lasts only about two weeks, starting to sour after that. There are 8-ounce individual packages, and 1- and 4½-pound tubs.

Cheese has been used as a first course in many countries over the centuries. Modern cheesemakers make layered cheeses, often using herbs, nuts and other non-cheeses. These can be instant, elegant first courses served by themselves, with greens or melted over hot, julienned vegetables. Most interesting of these are the *tortas* (cakes) made in Italy with Mascarpone. **Torta Gorgonzola,** also called **Dolcecasa** or **Cremazola,** has alternating thin layers of Mascarpone and Sweet Gorgonzola, a remarkable combination. Others include layers with basil and pine nuts, garlic, onions, mushrooms, olives and smoked salmon. Because the flavored layers protect the delicate cheese, the tortas will last a week or two longer than plain Mascarpone. All are made by hand and, consequently, are quite expensive. You're paying more for labor than for cheese.

Blues

Cheesemakers sometimes get carried away and create disasters. Every now and then, they create sensations. The Danes did just that in 1978 with *Saga, a rich white-mold triple cream flavored with blue mold. The cheese is not aged and the blue taste is muted. Those who don't like most blues find this one enchanting. Blue cheese lovers are delighted with its creaminess and subtle flavor. The white mold conceals an ivory-gray interior with fine greenish-blue veining, more evident in some wheels than in others. It is a luscious end to a meal by itself or with a salad of buttery greens. Served with pears, it is a satisfying dessert. It does well with full-bodied reds from Burgundy and California. Three-pound wheels are wrapped in foil and a cardboard ring.

Saga was such an immediate hit in the United States and abroad, cheesemakers in many countries began making copies, similar in appearance and packaging. Most have less blue mold and may be made with or without white mold. German **Cambozola, Bavaria Blu,** is virtually identical as is **Opus '84,** made by a Danish rival. French **Sacré Bleu** has a little less blue. *****Blue Castello,** from the same Danish company, comes in 5-ounce gold foil half-moons, perfect for a small group, and 2½-pound half-moons. English *****Lymeswold** stands out as the only white mold made in the British Isles. Add some to salads of poached chicken and avocado or serve in an assortment with Gruyère, Ste. Maure and Port-Salut. They can be creamy spreads with crisp cucumbers and zucchini.

Washed Cheeses

Most cheeses pale beside the demanding, dominant washed forms. Memorable and assertive, this group includes some of the world's most extraordinary cheeses: Epoisses, called the "king of cheeses" by Brillat-Savarin, the noted gastronome; delicate Pont l'Evêque; lusty Limburger. We serve these provocative cheeses often during the winter when their aromas mingle well with those of mulled wine and cider, warming cassoulets, spicy sausages, pepper-coated loins of pork, chunky white bean and lamb stews. They make superb sandwiches on whole-grain breads with country ham and chutney, wonderful snacks with crunchy apples. With the stronger cheeses, we serve hearty foods: dark pumpernickel and rye breads, raw onion slices, thick, salt-flecked pretzels, green peppercorn mustards, garlicky salamis, and lots of icy beer or ale, hard cider or jug wines.

For years, Americans traveling abroad have known the pleasure of these fragrant cheeses. Their demands for the same satisfying tastes at home has made it easier for all of us to get once uncommon varieties. It is particularly heartwarming to see this growing trend at a time when the market seems overrun with light beers and salt-free foods. Washed cheeses, ideal companions for aged Burgundies and draft ales, seem to know their mind and speak it. Some of the robust forms are belittled by timid eaters who call them "smelly," as if foods shouldn't have aromas. They forget that tantalizing scents—freshly baked ginger cookies, hot chicken soup, spicy chili, sizzling hamburgers—are the great joy of eating. They would be surprised to learn that full-bodied cheeses are often far milder than their aromas suggest.

Serve them singly or with others in this group. Eating a washed cheese and a mild double cream at the same time is like having Château Lafite and Tavel at a wine tasting. Both superior wines, the rosé will seem tasteless next to the richness of the Bordeaux.

Washed and soft-ripened cheeses start alike in the creamery. Once formed, the soft-ripened are sprayed with mold and aged in dry rooms. The others, not sprayed, are aged on beds of straw in warm, very humid rooms where they pick up molds naturally growing in the damp air or clinging to the walls. Later they are washed with salt water, brandy or beer to make them more assertive in aroma and taste. The thicker rinds, usually pale brown, often hold the imprint of the straw mats.

Never more than 4½ pounds, most washed cheeses are still made from centuries-old recipes by small dairies where they are wrapped in paper or foil and then boxed. They are always made from cow's milk, and have a butterfat content of 45 to 50 percent. Give them at least four hours at room temperature before serving so they are almost spreadably soft and cling to the knife when cut.

Buying and Storing

Although sold all year, washed cheeses are at their best in the cooler weather when they are fully developed, the supply is greatest, and turnover is rapid. Judge them like most other cheeses. The best are firm and plump with slightly tacky brown or orange rinds and a strong and enticing aroma. Before tasting, let the cold cheese warm up in your hand or mouth. It may be mild or robust. Let common sense be your guide. If you like the cheese, buy it. If it seems off to you, pass it by. It may be the way it's supposed to be; it may be past its prime. Some people have been put off these flavorful cheeses forever because they believed an ill-informed salesperson who assured them that an overripe, ammoniated, acrid cheese was "the way it's supposed to be." Unless serving the cheese right away, keep it well wrapped in foil in a sealed container in the refrigerator. It will become more piquant as it ages.

French Varieties

Along with Roquefort, Camembert and Brie, **Pont l'Evêque** is one of France's greatest cheeses. Directly descended from thirteenth-century Angelot, it comes in plump, 8- or 12-ounce squares with smooth, light brown rinds and supple, yellow interiors. The scent is savory; the flavor, zippy. Made in apple-rich Normandy, Pont l'Evêque has an affinity for hard and fresh cider. We serve it after creamy, Calvados-scented chicken Vallé d'Auge, garnished with sautéed apple rings.

Sometimes a whole Pont l'Evêque is too much. The amenable French solved the problem by creating **Vieux Pané.** Squares look and taste like Pont l'Evêque but weigh 4 pounds. We can buy cut pieces of just a few ounces, enough for that day, and serve them with golden delicious apples or juicy pears in the afternoon; with vintage Calvados or a buttery California Merlot after dinner.

A copy of Pont l'Evêque made in both small and large squares, **la Varinière** is an excellent substitute with fruit or in sandwiches with lightly smoked chicken.

Made in the same region, **Livarot** is heartier than Pont l'Evêque, and is one of the oldest and most respected French cheeses. It is our choice for grand dinners when we want to impress our guests, serving a cream of wild mushroom soup followed by duck breasts with juniper berries and a fine Cabernet Sauvignon or Burgundy. The climax of the meal is a dark brown Livarot, still girdled in blades of marsh grass, crusty baguettes and an even bigger wine: an aged Mondavi or BV Reserve Cabernet, a fully developed Latour. On simpler occasions, Livarot is just as splendid on firm-grained breads with hard cider, Calvados and spicy Zinfandel. Because the 1-pound rounds typically have five blades of grass, matching the number of stripes on a colonel's cuff, Livarot is often called "Le Colonel." Peeling the stripes off is the hardest part of serving the cheese.

Savory orange **Chaumes** is milder in scent than most in this group. Also called **Buron,** it is a fine cheese to serve a crowd after a steaming pot au feu.

From the Monasteries

Monks, known for their discerning palates and meticulous ways, have been making wonderful washed cheeses for hundreds of years. The best develop in damp cellars until ready to be shared with special friends at Christmas dinner or on New Year's Day. The tradition continues with superb cheeses like **Alsatian Muenster,** first made in the Middle Ages in France near the German border. Having little in common with American Munster, the Alsatian cheese tastes peppy and spicy with a strong scent much like Pont l'Evêque. It's a favorite after a tiring day of cross-country skiing when split pea and eggplant soup and slabs of dark pumpernickel bread make a satisfying meal with ale, a rich Côtes du Rhône, or a spicy Alsatian Gewürztraminer. Of the 8-ounce, 1-pound, and 2½-pound (1 kilogram) forms, the largest is the best.

Maroilles, fondly called "vieux puant" (old stinker), was first made in a monastery in the tenth century. The square cheese is brushed with beer rather than salt water, and develops a smooth, shiny, reddish-orange rind over its creamy, ivory interior. With age, it becomes more vigorous, perfect with icy draft beer and casseroles of thick, country sausage and sauerkraut cooked in more beer.

Brushed with Brandy

Burgundians prefer their local brandy, marc, to the finest Cognacs. An invigorating after-dinner drink, it is also used to wash local cheeses like **Epoisses** and **Ami du**

Chambertin. The brandy gives these flat rounds unusually delicate flavors and scents, excellent with pears poached in spicy red wine. Try them with a well-balanced Burgundy after a stew of chunky fork-tender beef and carrots simmered in the same wine. Burgundians often macerate the hearty Epoisses in marc before serving.

North of Dijon, in the little Burgundian town of Poiseul, they still make **Langres** in small farms and dairies. Looking something like a crater, each flat-bottomed orange cone is carefully washed by hand, leaving a thumb print on top of the soft, mild cheese. Some pour brandy into the indentation and let the cheese absorb it before serving. We prefer it on light rye or whole grain bread with a full-bodied Burgundy. At 11 ounces, it is ideal for a small group.

German Varieties

Limburger seems destined to live down an unjust reputation. To some who have never even tasted it, the name conjures up images of horribly smelly, almost rotting cheese, cheese so overwhelming it can be detected for miles. We have a friend who changed his name from Limburger because strangers sometimes extended their opinion of the cheese to him. We've never understood what all the pooh-poohing is about. Many skeptics have been won over by the young cheese when they've had it at informal parties with German beer, soft pretzels and mustard, slices of black radish, spicy salamis. The older cheeses, heady and strong, are popular with those who savor stews and roasts of well-hung game. Covered in brown rind, most of the smooth yellow cheese is made in Germany and the United States. The imported, usually found in cheese shops, is stronger.

Limburger's reputation really belongs to German **Hand Cheese—Handkäse** or **Harzer Käse.** With a sharp and pungent flavor and aroma, a dark heavy rind and thick, gelatinous interior usually flecked with caraway seeds, it is truly a cheese for the brave. Try it, if you dare, with slices of raw onions, black bread and beer. Originally shaped by hand, it is now machine made in Germany and the United States in 2-ounce rounds, three to a package.

American Varieties

Liederkranz, one of the few cheeses developed by an American, is our most popular washed cheese. Through one of history's fortunate accidents, Emil Frey, a German immigrant, tried unsuccessfully to create a copy of German Bismarck Schlosskäse. He made instead a totally new cheese with a rust-colored rind and buttery smooth white interior. As it ripened, it became golden and soft, picking up a distinctive, zesty flavor.

The members of his choral group at Liederkranz Hall liked it so much it was named for them. As ultimate proof of its success, Liederkranz now has a following abroad. Try it in grilled sandwiches with turkey and bacon on caraway rye; use slices in a salad with julienned Virginia ham, crunchy celery, walnuts and tomatoes.

Today Borden in Ohio makes Liederkranz in convenient 4-ounce rectangles. The boxes explain, through words and pictures, how to judge the relative strength and ripeness of the cheese. Dated to show its age, the cheese is removed from shelves if not sold while still young. It will continue to develop in the refrigerator.

American Limburger is made in New York and Wisconsin. Milder than the German, it is rugged enough to enhance a roast beef sandwich on pumpernickel bread with horseradish-flavored mustard, or to melt on top of pork chops and tomatoes.

Brick, also called **Bierkäse** (beer cheese), is an excellent companion to frosty mugs of draft beer. The brick shape makes it perfect for rye bread sandwiches of honey-glazed ham, mustard and lettuce. A bit milder than Limburger, this German-style cheese is also terrific shredded over bratwurst and sautéed onions.

Belgian Varieties

*Wynendale, made from raw milk and aged at least two months, is a creamy, soft-ripened cheese relatively new to the American market. It is steadily being discovered as a fine cheese after dinner with fruit, on its own with a zesty red wine. We also like it cubed in a salad of poached chicken and red onion or melted on top of creamy vegetable soup. Serve it to friends who claim to know all cheeses. This is one they may have missed. If it isn't, they will still appreciate your choice.

Semisoft Cheeses

Most cheese is semisoft, firm enough to slice, yet still soft and buttery. This vast array of cheeses may be full-flavored or mild. Some have a pleasant nuttiness. They are good for early morning breakfast, a midnight snack and on into the wee hours of the day, plain or melted over toast, in a simple sandwich of fresh buttered bread or the most elaborate hero. They can top hamburgers, fill crêpes, stuff chicken. Grated or cubed, they turn eggs into fabulous omelets with some fresh parsley and oregano. Pair them with ham and salami, roasted peppers, freshly grilled bacon, beefsteak tomatoes, hot and sweet mustards to make dozens of sandwiches. Deep-fried cubes are great with cocktails by themselves or dipped into a spicy salsa. Let these cheeses melt into white sauces to subtly enhance poached bass or steamed broccoli. Serve them with French Beaujolais, California Cabernet Sauvignons, Italian Barolos or frosty bottles of beer.

This group includes some of the world's finest cheeses: Fontina Val d'Aosta, Port-Salut, Reblochon, Farmer's Gouda, Tilsit. Many can trace their histories to the monasteries of France and Germany. Others come from small European villages. Compared with other cheeses, they are easy to make and transport.

Semisoft cheeses are pressed to eliminate much of their moisture, then aged for a few weeks, so they are firmer than soft-ripened and full-bodied varieties. Usually rindless, most are either coated with a layer of wax or paraffin or rubbed with oil. They continue to breathe and age, losing moisture and becoming firmer. Some get as firm as cheeses in the Hard and Grating section. We're discussing them here because their textures are typically semisoft. Lesser cheeses are wrapped in plastic when young, stopping their development.

More than any other group, semisoft cheeses cross national boundaries. Those made in neighboring villages or the same factory may have little in common with each other and be almost identical to some made hundreds of miles away. Consequently, we have grouped the cheeses in this section by type rather than nationality. In some cases the cheeses of a particular region are enough alike to discuss as a unit.

Buying and Storing

Semisoft cheeses are relatively hardy. They should smell fresh, be smooth and full, never cracked, dried out or moldy. It is rare that one will arrive here in less than optimal condition. If it does, or if it was poorly stored on our shores, it is easy to spot. Often, importers and cheese shops cut these large cheeses—3 to 15 pounds—into wedges, weighing and packaging them ahead. Ideally, they should be cut to order.

Like all cheeses, these taste best when left at room temperature. They retain their shapes as they warm, but become more supple. If you like to have cheese ready for snacks, leave a wrapped wedge at room temperature. Unless the room is very warm, it should last for a week or so. Keep refrigerated cheeses tightly wrapped in foil in the vegetable bin to insulate them from extreme cold. If you use plastic wrap, replace it every few days as moisture appears. The cheeses should be good for weeks; they may get stronger and firmer. Should any begin to mold, just scrape away that part. The rest of the cheese will be fine. There is no reason to throw away old cheese. If it gets too dry for pleasant eating, grate it and sprinkle into omelets, casseroles or soups or mix it with a softer cheese or butter for a spread.

Goudas and Edams

Gouda and **Edam,** Holland's best-known cheeses, are often taken one for the other. Coated in wax, both are mild, smooth and pale yellow. The most apparent difference is the shape. Traditional Edams are nearly perfect rounds, close enough to balls that aged Edams were used in place of cannonballs in 1841 to help the Uruguayan fleet under United States command defeat the British-led Argentine navy. Other Edams are made in loaves. Gouda, made with a little more butterfat, ends up as a wheel, convenient for rolling down the street to trucks and ships.

The best of the Dutch cheeses is aged *Farmer's Gouda,** made from raw milk and excellent with bowls of thick, steaming vegetable soup. As it matures, it changes from semisoft and creamy to firm and crumbly. The older the cheese, the more distinctive the taste. Some Farmer's Goudas, called superaged, are nearly three years old. Firm enough to grate and quite salty, they are superior eating cheeses. Most come here when they are nine months old, still rich, creamy and mild. The 20-pound wheels, covered in pale yellow wax, are marked "boerenkaas" to distinguish them from commercially made Gouda. To age some yourself, wrap a piece in foil and leave it at cool room temperature for weeks or months.

Among the commercially made Goudas, the older cheeses are best. Sharp and a little salty, **Aged Goudas** are wonderful in omelets with chunks of mushrooms and tomatoes. Use some in a roast beef and mâche salad, sprinkle it over spinach fettuccine, stuff it in brook trout. Nine-pound commercial rounds are coated in red or yellow wax.

Since cheesemakers use little salt to make Goudas, they have been very successful in making cheeses without adding any sodium to that naturally in the milk. These so-called **Salt-Free Goudas** are said to be the tastiest and truest of all the no-salt-added cheeses.

One of the best Goudas we've ever had is **Boerkäse** made by Caleb Williams in Pennsylvania. Convinced that Americans can make cheeses as full-flavored as Europe's best, he has perfected a buttery cheese made from the raw milk of his own cows, either plain, with caraway or naturally smoked. He loves it with corned beef and sauerkraut in a grilled Reuben.

Mildest in this group are the buttery soft, unaged Dutch Edams, followed by the still mild aged cheese, about as strong as a medium Gouda. Edams come in 2- and 4-pound balls and 5-pound rectangles covered in red wax and cellophane. For the holidays, they are wrapped in festive silver foil. In Curaçao, they use them to make keshy yena: the round Edams are hollowed out, filled with spicy meat stews and baked, giving the meat an unusual casing.

An excellent British cheese is that of **Curworthy Farm** in Devonshire, a county renowned for its rich cream. Based on a seventeenth-century recipe, these 12-ounce and 4-pound waxed rounds resemble a medium Gouda in taste and texture. Thin slices of the ivory cheese are delicious on sandwiches with rare roast beef and green peppercorn mustard.

With 60 percent butterfat, **Roomkaas** is richer and smoother than most Goudas, excellent for melting in sandwiches with smoky bacon. Wheels are coated in red or yellow wax.

Pompadour is a flavored Gouda from Holland, fine on crackers, to melt over hamburgers, or layered on hero sandwiches. The herb-and-garlic cheese has a green wrapper; the pepper's is blackish-brown.

Similarly, there is Dutch **Leyden,** an aged cheese flavored with cumin seeds, a warm spice often used in chili. The flavor dominates the cheese itself and the aroma of the spice is distinctive. Add some to omelets or sandwiches on caraway rye. Like Edam, wheels are coated in red wax and red cellophane.

Commercially made **American Goudas** are sometimes excellent, occasionally poor in flavor and texture. They come in large and "baby" packages, either plain or flavored with caraway seeds.

For picnics and other casual occasions, wheels of **Baby Gouda,** less than a pound, are convenient. They are very mild, like unaged Edams with slightly more butterfat. **Baby Samsoe,** which comes in 8-ounce red-waxed rounds, is similar. Danish Edam, called **Tybo,** is a smooth mild cheese made in square waxed forms, sometimes flavored with caraway.

French Port-Salut

Mild, creamy **Port-Salut** is an excellent French cheese with a long history. First made by Trappist monks in the monastery of Port-du-Salut, it has spawned an impressive family of cheeses. We like Port-Salut on chewy baguettes with light fruity wines or in sandwiches with smoked ham, turkey and tomatoes. The pale yellow cheese, from 3 to 4 pounds, develops tiny holes from fermentation. Once shaped, it is washed and coated with edible orange food coloring.

Although the monks no longer make Port-Salut, they control the name. At the moment, SAFR, a French company, has the exclusive right to manufacture the cheese, which is aged about two months. The Port-Salut wheels are identified by the words "Fermiers Réunis" on the label.

Most other cheeses in the family are called **Saint Paulin.** They are similar to each other and to Port-Salut. Among those sold here, **Abbey** is the best known because the company once had the license to make Port-Salut. Both Abbey and Port-Salut often cost considerably more than other Saint Paulins but are usually not worth it. Like Port-Salut, most Saint Paulins, wrapped in cryovac, have orange rinds.

Bonbel, a well-known brand, comes in firm rounds coated in yellow wax. The mildest of all Saint Paulins is **Pré Clos.**

Port-Saluts from Other Countries

Just about every country that had Trappist monks makes a copy of Port-Salut. Sometimes, to get around the law, cheesemakers use creative spellings for the name. In the United States, it may be called "Port-du-Salute." Like Port-Salut, these cheeses add interest to sandwiches with chicken and sweet onions or grated over pasta shells or blanched cauliflower. Serve them with light and fruity wines from Alsace or Napa Valley.

Among the more flavorful monastery cheeses is **Oka,** made by Canadian Trappist monks since 1880. Still following the old methods, which include washing and turning the forms by hand, they have expanded the facilities to meet the growing demand. Oka has a slight brownish crust that is floured to absorb moisture. The young cheese is mild; the older, stronger and a little nutty.

From Austria comes **Thomasino Trappist,** a firm, mildly piquant cheese made by Trappist monks. The 3-pound wheels are coated in yellow wax. The Austrians also make **l'Amour** in 4-pound forms, as well as **Mondseer.** Stronger than other monastery cheeses, they are semisoft when young, and get firmer and stronger as they age. The yellow wheels are wrapped in cellophane.

One of the best-known cheeses in this group is Denmark's **Esrom.** Somewhat stronger and more aromatic than the French cheese, it is coated in yellow wax, then in foil. American **Port-du-Salute** can be strong or mild, depending on the brand and the age. The best-known brand, **Lion,** has a damp crust.

Also like Esrom are the German **Biarom** and **Jerome.** Biarom is slightly sour, made plain and flavored with herbs, green pepper or red pepper. The smoked version, called **Bruder Basil,** has a completely different character as does **Mamsell Babette,** flavored with ham. All are coated in brown wax, then wrapped in foil. Jerome is made plain and flavored with caraway, pepper or French herbs. Use the flavored cheeses for snacks and sandwiches.

St. Bernard is a Belgian cheese with an orange interior and dark rind. It is sharper than some in this group, and comes in 11-pound wheels. Its compatriot, **Père Joseph,** is creamier and milder and comes in 4½-pound wheels.

Trappists at Gethsemani Farms in Trappist, Kentucky, make mild and aged **Trappist Cheese.** The mild, much like Monterey Jack, is young and delicate in flavor. The aged, more like a strong Esrom, has a definite aroma. There is also a smoked version. The cheeses will last several months in the refrigerator. The Trappists recommend serving them for dessert with apples and tea.

Savoy Region Varieties

Some of France's greatest cheeses come from the mountainous Savoy region near Switzerland and Italy. The best, ***Reblochon,** is a flavorful cheese, the softest of the semisofts, unfortunately underrated in America. Peel away its paper and wood wrapping and relish this fine cheese at the end of a meal with tart apples and hard cider or a Beaujolais-Villages. If you find that the strong flavor of the brown rind masks that of the cheese, especially possible when the cheese is aged, cut the rind away and concentrate on the smooth ivory center. Reblochon is smooth and firm in its prime, not wet and wrinkled, an indication that it is probably bitter. Buy whole or half 1-

pound farm-made rounds if you can. The 8-ounce commercial forms, sometimes called **Reblochonnet,** are not quite as good.

Beaumont, similar to Reblochon, is a mild, creamy, supple cheese with a light yellow rind. As it ages, the flavor and scent develop harmoniously: it is at its best in summer and autumn. Serve Beaumont after dinner with a young red Corvo or Rhône wine.

The original **Tomme de Savoie,** a semisoft cow's milk cheese, has a pronounced flavor and aroma with a trace of mold, but it is not as strong as the aroma might hint. Serve it with a light and fruity wine from Savoy if you can find one, or something unassuming from Alsace. It rounds out a meal of chicken with raspberry vinegar or duck breasts with melon. The cylindrical form should have a grayish rind and feel supple. Since it does not travel well, only a small quantity comes into the United States. Avoid any with cracked rinds that are reddish around the edges. These are past their prime.

The most flavorful of the Savoy cheeses is **Tamié,** made by Trappist monks in the monastery of Tamies. This mild skim-milk cheese with a somewhat elastic texture is fine on its own with a young Beaujolais. We also use it in the kitchen where it can transform an ordinary gratin of potatoes into something memorable. The ivory interior has some small holes in it. When it is young, it is firm in the center, almost having a core. As it ages, it becomes softer and pastier.

Italian **Reblodor,** similar to Reblochon, is not as interesting. The 20-ounce and 4-

pound wheels have orange rinds and a supple texture. Use it in the kitchen to flavor omelets and rye bread sandwiches with spicy salami.

Fontinas

Fontina Val d'Aosta from the Valley of Aosta, just across the border from Switzerland, is another controlled name. The Italians use this buttery semisoft cheese for their finest dishes like fonduta, an incredibly creamy rarebit poured over polenta and flavored with white truffles. They add cubes to rich pasta sauces made with Gorgonzola, Bel Paese, cream and butter, served with lots of fresh pepper. Fontina Val d'Aosta adds class to any assortment of cheeses and is graceful alone with a full-bodied Chianti Classico.

Made with raw milk, Fontina Val d'Aosta gets tastier and more aromatic as it ages. Wheels, which have a thin brownish rind, are stamped with their name and have round FonTina labels in the center with the seal of the local cooperative. Most weigh about 25 pounds. Unfortunately, all these controls make the cheese cost considerably more than other cheeses made like it. Although the original is still the best, it is not always worth the difference in price.

Regular **Italian Fontina,** sometimes called **Fontal,** is the finest of the copies. Made in a neighboring region, it looks exactly like Fontina Val d'Aosta except for the stamp and label. It is generally mild and gets pleasantly nutty as it ages. It is an excellent value.

The Scandinavian Fontinas and those from Argentina, called **Danish, Swedish** and **Argentine Fontina,** are less complex and less expensive than the Italian. Fine for sandwiches, snacks and cooking, they are firmer and sharper. Some have the characteristic tiny holes from fermentation. The Danish is the best, creamier than its neighbors, but firmer than the Italian. Made from part skim milk, all are slightly less fattening. These copies, coated in red wax, are usually a bit smaller.

Morbier, also called **Royal Morbier,** has a regal grayish-black ash stripe through the middle of its pale yellow body. Always attractive in an assortment, Morbier makes a distinctive-looking cheeseburger or topping to open-faced sandwiches. It is similar in texture to Fontina, but the flavor is slightly more pronounced, although still mild. The ash has no particular taste. There is a raw-milk Morbier that looks the same as the pasteurized variety but is slightly sharper.

Blarney, one of the few Irish cheeses sold here, has a nutty flavor similar to that of Fontina. A pleasant, all-purpose cheese with occasional eye fermentation, it is an appropriate choice after an Irish stew, and is also good for sandwiches. The wheels are coated with red wax and sport labels showing one of Ireland's beautiful castles.

Swiss **Belsano** has a nice flavor, good texture and no discernible aroma. Priced like Italian Fontina, it is an excellent substitute.

French Pyrénées Varieties

The French Pyrénées, well known for wonderful sheep and goat's milk cheeses, is also home to some agreeable commercially made semisoft cheeses. Manufactured in different shapes, they are given importers' brand names or named for the region. Bring them to picnics with chilled Rieslings or rosés. Add them to sandwiches with spicy salamis and pickled tomatoes. Melt them over buttered muffins to start the day.

The original is **Fromage des Pyrénées,** sometimes called **Tomme des Pyrénées,** a fine, mild cheese. Made in pale yellow, smooth rounds with tiny eye fermentation, the cheese comes in 9-pound forms covered in black wax when plain, brown wax when flavored with cumin or caraway, and green when pepper-flavored. Try the caraway on pumpernickel with mustard and Virginia ham; the peppercorn on a baguette with egg salad and black olives. Most often it is imported under the specific brand names discussed below—Mantanou, Royal Pyrénées or Capitoul—rather than as Fromage des Pyrénées. (Do not confuse these cheeses with the sheep's milk Fromage des Pyrénées, discussed in that section.)

Mantanou and **Royal Pyrénées** are made plain (black wax) and flecked with green peppercorns (green wax). With about 50 percent butterfat, they are creamy and mild. **Capitoul** comes plain (black wax), with caraway (brown wax) and with green pepper (greenish-brown wax). **Le Champêtre** is similar. Most flavorful is **St. Gauloy,** made from raw milk. It has a dark brown rind.

Among the Pyrénées cheeses is a popular group that includes **Doux de Montagne, Pain des Pyrénées** and **Fropain des Mages,** essentially the same mild cheese made by different manufacturers. The cheeses are pale yellow with irregular eye formation, similar to Cream Havartis. Like the other Pyrénées cheeses, these are fine with cocktails or light wine, at breakfast, lunch and between-meal snacks.

Doux de Montagne is shaped like a round cottage loaf of bread, while Pain des Pyrénées looks like a standard loaf. Keeping with the bread theme, the manufacturers of Fropain des Mages make their cheese to resemble a braided loaf. All are covered in a thin layer of brown wax. Doux de Montagne also comes flavored with green peppercorns. **Valmage** is similar to Doux de Montagne, but the wax is yellow. Even milder is **Tomme de Rouergue** from the southwest of France. Those wheels have grayish rinds.

From Belgium come two unwaxed cheeses in this group, the hexagonal **Beavoorde** and the bread-shaped **Passendale,** both in 7-pound forms. They are excellent in sandwiches with smoked turkey or melted over hamburgers.

Cream Havarti

Danish **Cream Havarti** is a completely rindless, semisoft, fairly smooth cheese with some eye formation. It is an excellent cheese, much like the Pyrénées cheeses in taste and appearance, made plain, as well as flavored with dill, chives and herbs, mustard, caraway seeds and jalapeño peppers. A pleasant breakfast and snack cheese, Cream Havarti is marketed as **Dofino, Jackie** and **Grand Ost.** The Swedish version, **Graddost,** is made in 1-pound rounds, as is Norwegian **Cream Nøkkelost,** which has more butterfat than regular Nøkkelost. The Finnish Cream Havarti is **Turunmaa.**

German **Butterkäse,** literally butter cheese, comes in 6-pound loaves, making perfect slices to add to a sandwich of watercress and tomato. It looks and tastes like Cream Havarti as does Scottish **Dunlop,** a creamy, mild, white cheese made in rounds.

Tilsit

Sometimes an attempt to recreate a cheese in a new climate leads to the discovery of a completely different cheese. That happened when Dutch farmers living in East Prussia tried to make Gouda. They ended up with a semisoft, strong cheese with cracks that they named **Tilsit** or **Tilsiter.** Closer to Danish Port-Salut than Gouda, it is decidedly stronger in taste and has a definite aroma that increases as the cheese ages. When you want a semisoft cheese with a little more character, look to Tilsit. We include it in an assortment with Saga, Montrachet and Coulommiers. It is good in an omelet with Black Forest ham and green peppers, in a chef's salad with turkey and spinach, served with light and fruity Chiroubles or beer. Firmer than most semisoft cheeses, loaves are usually foil wrapped.

Havarti, the Danish Tilsit, is the favorite this side of the Atlantic. Drier, stronger and smellier than Cream Havarti, it is close to Danish Esrom in flavor and aroma, although firmer in texture. It gets stronger as it ages, while the texture remains the same. Kept wrapped, it can be aged at home at room temperature. The loaves are wrapped in wax and foil.

German Tilsiter, creamier than Havarti, can be quite strong and smelly, a good mate for smoked and spiced meats, thin slices of raw onion and cold beer. The loaves are coated in yellow wax, then wrapped in gold foil or red paper. **Bianco** is a milder, buttery German Tilsit.

Swiss Tilsiter, called **Royalp,** is not as strong as the Danish. Firmer than most semisoft cheeses, the 15-pound rounds have thick crusts and a pleasant flavor and aroma. Add slices to beef and endive salads. There are also **Finnish, Polish** and **Norwegian Tilsits** as well as the Swedish version, round **Ambrosia.**

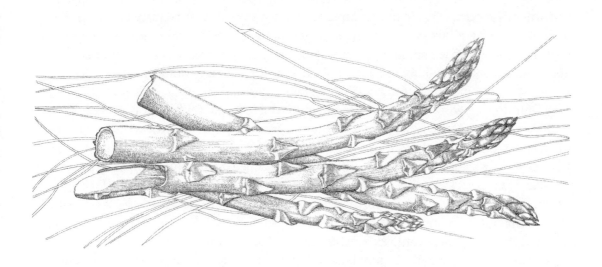

Provolone

Provolone was originally made from buffalo milk, like Mozzarella, but today is produced from cow's milk. The cheese is mild and semifirm when young, getting sharper and drier with age, developing a biting aftertaste. Provolone is a classic ingredient in antipasti of roasted bell peppers, thin slices of pepperoni and marinated mushrooms. We also add it to hero sandwiches with Genoa salami, ham and tomatoes, all dressed with olive oil. Molded by hand into different forms, the cheese is dipped in brine and aged, then dipped in wax and bound with raffia. It is suspended from the ceilings of kitchens and grocerias where it continues to develop. The giant salami shape is the most common. Auricchio, the major importer, also makes **American Provolone.** The domestic cheese, while not quite as good as the imported, can be a better value. The 1- to 5-pound balls are called **Boccette, Provoletti, Provolotini** or **Provoloncini.** The imported salami shape is about 35 pounds; the domestic is 9 to 10 pounds. There are pear-shaped forms weighing 25 to 35 pounds, and 5-, 100- and 200-pound **Giganti.** Some cheeses are smoked. Others, called **Mantecche,** are wrapped around balls of butter.

Monterey Jack

Monterey Jack was first made in the eighteenth century in Monterey, California, by Spanish missionaries trying to develop a simple white cheese. A century later, a Scotsman named David Jacks came to the area and bought fourteen dairy farms. Realizing that the Spanish-style cheese had a strong following, he increased production and set about, quite successfully, to market the cheese. Somewhere along the way, the "s" was dropped from his name. Today it is called Monterey Jack or Jack Cheese.

With the growing interest in American produce, Monterey Jack, once rarely seen outside its native state, has become ubiquitous in sandwiches of avocado and sprouts on grainy whole wheat bread, in salads with smoked chicken and artichokes, stuffed into enchiladas and peppers, sprinkled over poached eggs and salsa, melted over tortillas. The best Jacks are still made by relatively small companies in California— Monterey as well as Sonoma (north of Monterey). They also are made in Wisconsin, Illinois and other states. Mild and creamy cheeses relatively low in salt, most are labeled with their place name as **Sonoma Jack, Wisconsin Jack,** and so on.

California Jacks, made from whole milk, are creamier than those from Wisconsin made with part skim milk. Wisconsin Jacks are not as consistent in texture as Monterey Jacks, but the cheeses have a little more taste. Jacks may be flavored with bits of hot jalapeño pepper (to make **Pepper Jack**), salami, onion or chives. The rindless cheeses are shaped into blocks and wheels. Aged Jack, called Dry Jack, is discussed in the Hard and Grating cheese section.

Similar to creamy Monterey Jack, **Teleme** is another West Coast cheese of small production. Very rarely found away from California, it is extremely mild, a good complement for peppery sausages.

Bel Paese

Bel Paese, Italian for beautiful country, is a mild, versatile cheese, lovely as part of an assortment, terrific at picnics with grapes, plums and other juicy fruits. Good to cook with, the creamy ivory cheese melts easily and smoothly. Whole slices, breaded, fried in butter and topped with a spicy tomato sauce, make a satisfying meal served with Valpolicella. The wax-coated rindless wheels proclaim their nationality with the map of Italy on the cellophane wrapper.

Somewhat deceptively, American Bel Paese has a map of the United States on it with colors and lettering similar to the Italian. It does not have the consistent high quality of the original.

Italian **Italico,** similar to Bel Paese, is mild in flavor, rich and buttery, even creamier than Bel Paese. It is usually made from whole milk in Lombardy and sold under the brand name of the dairy.

Taleggio

*Taleggio, one of Italy's finest cheeses, has a tradition dating to the tenth century. In the United States, it is all too often passed over for better-known forms. Ranging in texture from soft to semisoft, the tart flavor resembles that of a goat's milk cheese. As Taleggio gets older and firmer, it becomes more flavorfully tart and plump. It is traditionally made from stracchino, the whole milk of supposedly tired cows. Unlike most semisoft cow's milk cheeses, Taleggio may have a washed rind. The 7-inch squares have a soft crust coated with paraffin imprinted with the name and a paper label. Not all brands are equally good. One of the best is **Tal-fino.** Serve this special cheese with crusty baguettes and a Moulin-à-Vent, or on a platter with Brillat-Savarin and an ashed Pyramide.

String Cheese

No cheese is as much fun to eat as **String Cheese,** also called **Braided, Rope** or **Syrian-style.** Originally made in Syria from sheep's milk, the String Cheese sold here is all domestic, made from cow's milk with salt added. Manufacturers use a Mozzarella type of base. Some add black caraway seeds. The soft cheese, weighing 8 to 12 ounces, is often braided and packed in cryovac. Before serving it, soak in water to separate the strands and eliminate some of the salt. Guests can take thick strands and pull them into strings. Big chunks are less interesting and intensely salty.

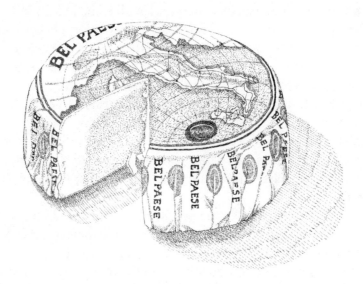

Munster

American **Munster,** made in Wisconsin, New York and Kentucky, is a very mild, semifirm cheese with some small eye formation. It is a rindless cheese, the outside rubbed with yellow food coloring. Made from sour cow's milk, it has a slightly tart, sour taste, pleasant for breakfast on buttered caraway rye bread. Whole cheeses are made in blocks and wheels; it is often sold in thin slices.

Other Semisoft Cheeses

* Saint-Nectaire, an ancient cheese from Auvergne, is a nutty tasting, somewhat rubbery cheese with a high aroma. The natural rind is brownish, showing traces of its straw bed. The cheese should be supple, never sticky or dried out or concave. Use it for open-faced grilled sandwiches or with a thick vegetable soup.

Gaperon (Gapron) is a low-fat garlic-flavored cheese shaped like a baseball with a flat bottom. A soft, supple cheese, it is usually wrapped with cord and hung in the kitchen or cellar where it develops a natural rind. There was a time when a French farmer's wealth was judged by the number of 1-pound Gaperons he had hanging in the kitchen. It affected the marriageability of his daughters. It was originally made with buttermilk, but cheesemakers today use whole or skimmed cow's milk. Serve Gaperon with robust, full-bodied wines able to take the garlic flavor.

Scandinavia is a prosperous cheese-producing area, known primarily for pleasant everyday eating and cooking cheeses to put in lunch-box sandwiches. **Danbo,** a yellow cheese with an orange rind, usually comes here with some age on it. If it is young and moist, it molds quickly. When older, it is drier and sharper, almost with a bite. Some squares are flavored with caraway. **King Christian IX** is the original cheese, made with part skim milk and with caraway seeds. **Danish Mynster,** smooth, supple and semifirm, comes in wheels wrapped in gold foil.

Sweden makes **Riksost,** also called **Swedish Farmer Cheese.** Firmer in texture and milder in flavor than American Farmer Cheese, it comes plain or spiced.

From neighboring Norway comes **Nøkkelost,** like Cream Havarti but strongly flavored with cloves and caraway. More popular in its native land than in America, it makes an interesting quiche with country ham and mustard. Seven-pound loaves are wrapped in red cellophane.

St. Michael Steiermark is a pale yellow, semifirm cheese from Austria. Somewhere between Fontina and Gruyère in taste, it is less expensive than either.

Wisconsin's **Gold-N-Rich** is a mild cheese resembling Fontina and Port-Salut. A fine yellow cheese when in good condition, the texture may be granular instead of smooth. Four-pound rounds, coated in red wax, are wrapped in cellophane.

Goat Cheeses

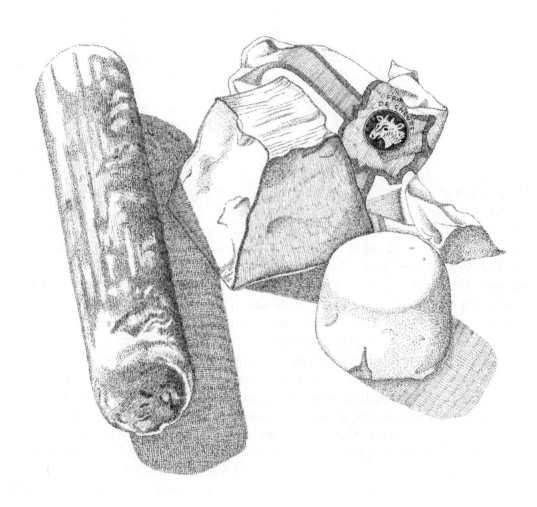

The pleasure of glistening white goat cheeses (chèvres) is in their fresh, mild scent and slightly sharp, lightly acid flavor. They were virtually unknown in the United States a few years ago, but customers now eagerly await the arrival of each new shipment, especially in spring and summer when the cheeses are rarely more than three weeks old. Still so new they barely hold a shape, they are refreshing with uncomplicated warm-weather foods: a salad of arugula, red-leaf lettuce, endive and walnuts; barely cooked linguine tossed with a raw tomato sauce; tarragon-flavored lentils. When left to age, the cheeses lose some of their youthful brilliance, becoming stronger in taste and firmer, better with assertive Zinfandels and the summery room-temperature minestrones of Milan, rich with peas, beans, rice and tomato chunks, flavored with thyme.

There seems to be a goat cheese for almost any occasion, whether with chilled apéritifs on a hot afternoon, alongside a lemony salad of bitter greens at the beginning or end of a meal, or with ripe mangoes for dessert. Some are marvelous spread on the morning's toast or muffins. Most are enhanced by breads made with olive oil or with some oily nuts in them. If the cheeses are herb-flavored, they make instant dips for crisp spears of cucumber and carrot, mild baby radishes and colorful bell peppers. Young chèvres are wonderful in place of cream cheese with date and nut bread or with slices of delicately smoked salmon.

We often serve chèvres before dinner or in the afternoon. Because of their tangy, fresh flavor, they do well with the chilled white wines and wine spritzers so popular today. Their varied sizes and shapes make them attractive choices any time. Some weigh a mere ounce or two, perfect for romantic tête-à-têtes. For less intimate parties, a whole Pyramide is enticing in an assortment and even a half will do nicely. On lazy afternoons, we sometimes have an array of chèvres: Pyramides with different coatings, a dome-shaped Taupinière, nut-studded ball, ash-coated log, leaf-wrapped Banon.

If foreigners, especially Frenchmen, are coming, we always show off at least one native chèvre accompanied by a dry California Chenin Blanc or pink Blanc de Pinot Noir. We hold onto the wrappings in case our guests' pride doesn't let them believe our cheeses can really rival their own.

Goat cheeses can be essential ingredients in cooked dishes as well. When exposed to low heat, they soften rather than ooze, never getting stringy or gooey like Swiss and Cheddar cheeses. The young, moist forms dissolve as beautifully into sauces as butterier cheeses. The firmer cheeses retain their shapes, becoming warm and creamy. In California's new cooking, tangy chèvres have replaced Mozzarella on pizzas made with duck sausage, sun-dried tomatoes, fresh basil or other unusual ingredients. They are also ideal for filling calzones because they don't leak out the sides.

Which cheese to use depends on the recipe. For pasta tossed with dainty zucchini blossoms, butter and cheese, keep it young and light. With anchovies or hot peppers or in a salad of white beans, olives, red onion and shrimp, use an emphatic cheese. Messy leftovers are fine on sandwiches or in spreads, added to casseroles or omelets.

It is only recently that we've been fortunate enough to have all these choices. In the past, most goat cheese was made strictly for domestic use. Families had a goat or two and made just enough cheese to eat. Since goats give only about three quarts of milk a day, they were of little interest to major cheese producers. Cows yield ten to twenty quarts. It was when urban dwellers discovered goat cheeses in their travels and requested them at home that the demand made greater production economically feasible. Unfortunately, it has also virtually outstripped supply, leading some cheesemakers to mix the scarce goat's milk with that of cows. It explains, in part, why goat cheeses are so expensive.

Although goats have been in America since the Pilgrims, native chèvres were virtually nonexistent until recently. The back-to-the-land people of the sixties had goats because they are relatively easy to keep and don't need expensive feed. Interested in foods that seemed lighter and healthier, and influenced by their own trips abroad, some of them made cheese with the milk. Innovative chefs, looking for new American products, used the cheese in pastas, salads, pizzas and other dishes. They soon became a favorite ingredient.

Much of the appeal of goat cheeses comes from the milk. Snowy white, light and fresh with a very slight sour aftertaste, goat's milk tastes and feels more like skimmed than whole cow's milk. Its smaller fat globules, which make it seem less fatty, are easier to digest. It may explain why many people who cannot digest cow's milk in any form have no trouble with goat's milk products.

Rather than imitate cow's milk cheeses, most cheesemakers accentuate the virtues inherent in goat cheeses. None of the enriched double and triple creams are made with goat's milk. Only a few cow's milk knock-offs exist: goat Cheddars and soft-ripened cheeses that resemble Brie and Camembert.

Most chèvres are seasoned only with salt. Some are sprinkled with dried green herbs or dusted with orange paprika or annatto; wrapped in grape or chestnut leaves; or sprayed with mold to form an uneven crust. Cheesemakers may rub black ash from burnt vegetables or coconut shells over certain cheeses to inhibit the growth of mold. The ash doesn't change taste or texture. Since salt is usually mixed with the ash to make it more spreadable, the *cendré* cheeses taste saltier. If the cheese is very soft when the ash is added, it smears, turning the cheese gray. On firmer cheeses, the ash stays black.

Buying and Storing

When buying a goat cheese, keep in mind how you plan to use it. Most are made to be eaten fresh or allowed to drain naturally in molds for a few days, carefully turned by hand. The curds are very white. The newer the cheese, the milder and softer, even softer than an equally fresh cow's milk cheese. The cheeses have a characteristic graininess that increases with age. It makes them crumble rather than spread smoothly. Their sour taste ranges from barely perceptible to quite strong. Only a poorly made cheese burns the throat or smells nasty. As the cheese ages, it gets firmer, saltier and sharper. Some aficionados think the cheeses are at their best after aging. If you have never tasted any, start with the mildest.

Goat cheeses are usually sold wrapped in plastic. Rewrap the cheese every few days in aluminum foil or fresh plastic as it gets wet. Be careful not to break the softer forms. Keep the chèvres refrigerated until four to six hours before serving time. If one gets too strong or dry for your taste, blend it with yogurt, Cottage Cheese or cream, stir in chopped scallions or fresh herbs, and use it as a spread.

French Varieties

Nearly two-thirds of the world's goat cheeses come from France. Learning about all of them can be confusing because the cheeses change as they go from young and moist to old and firm. You will find cheeses almost identical except for their shape and those that look alike but taste quite different. Some have brand names; others are named for their shapes.

Pur chèvre on a French label should mean it is made from pure goat's milk. The labeling is not strictly enforced, and some contain some cow's milk.

Fresh

Young and creamy, fresh goat cheese, called **Fromage de Chèvre Frais,** is a treat not often available in the United States. With a texture like sour cream and just a hint of the sour taste, this is a cheese to spoon over ripe sugared raspberries for dessert or to mix with tarragon, thin with cream and dribble on a salad of poached chicken, radicchio and watercress. Fresh chèvre is sold here in 4-pound pails or crocks.

Logs

Montrachet, a young, delicate, creamy cheese, milder than most, is very popular and readily available. We recommend it to first-time goat cheese eaters. Try some with apricot jam at breakfast or spread on warm scones with mango chutney for afternoon tea. It works in most of the newly created recipes calling for goat cheese, be it tossed with angel hair pasta, tiny peas and oregano; crumbled over chunks of ham on crusty bite-size pizzas; or as the base for a soufflé made with a purée of roasted red peppers. Montrachet is sold in individual 11-ounce logs, either pure white or covered with a light layer of ash, even throughout with a slight characteristic graininess. Even younger Montrachets, much like Fromage de Chèvre Frais, are packed in squat 3½- and 7-ounce plastic containers.

Bucheron, a large, stubby log, definitely tastes "goaty" but not strong or bitter. Some call it **St. Saviol,** the manufacturer's name. We use it in rich pasta sauces flavored with mint and walnuts as well as to fill flaky filo pastries. Moist enough to blend with other ingredients, it has enough flavor to be noticeable. Serve it with grapes for dessert. As Bucheron develops, the center, still moist and spreadable, remains drier and crumblier than the rest. The edge forms a light, creamy, barely perceptible crust that may get to be ¼ inch thick. Bucherons weigh 4 pounds.

An excellent substitute for Bucheron is **Buche,** or **Petite Cabrette,** a smaller log that has a fresh taste with just a hint of salt. Like Bucheron, it is semifirm in the middle and creamy toward the outer edges.

Ste. Maure, one of the first goat cheeses to come into the United States, is a flavorful 8-ounce log. It has a delicate rind, creamy edge and firm, crumbly center core. Many commercial creameries make copies and give them proprietary names. We often cut logs into neat rounds to put on top of still-warm garlicky croutons made from skinny French baguettes. They are perfect with green salad dressed with a fruity vinaigrette.

All-purpose **Logs (Buches)** are cheeses to buy by the piece when you want an uncomplicated goat cheese to cook with, eat for a snack or serve with ripe papayas. Most are a bit more acid than Montrachet. Along with the plain and ash-covered varieties, there are logs coated with annatto and with herbs. The herbs mask the goat flavor so we save them for cocktail parties. Two-pound logs are about 8 inches long and 2 inches wide; 4-pound logs are 4 inches wide.

Hearts, Bells, Balls and Buttons

Mild, but aged enough to hold their enchanting shapes, are some small cheeses great for quick snacks or packed in picnic baskets with firm whole wheat bread, oily black olives and lush beefsteak tomatoes. Cone-shaped **Chabichou,** called **Chabis** for short, are creamy 3-ounce cheeses. Slightly larger are the ash-coated **Selles-Sur-Cher,** 5-ounce rounds the size of thick silver dollars. They have a gentle goat smell and taste. Most romantic of all is **Coeur de Périgord,** a charming heart-shaped chèvre much like Selles-Sur-Cher. These 6-ounce forms, made plain and ashed, taste much like the young, hand-formed, bell-shaped **Clochettes,** weighing 8 ounces.

Crottins are oversized buttons of farm-made goat cheese weighing 2 to 3 ounces. They are sold in France still spoonably soft; here they are a bit firmer. The best-known are the **Crottins de Chauvignol.** Cooks often keep the firm Crottins in a bath of olive oil and herbs. They are superb breaded and baked, then added to salads dressed with vinegar and some of the flavored oil. Some prefer to leave them exposed to the air until they develop a darker crust and are firm enough to grate. Certain fresh Crottins kept in oil are called **Rigotte.**

When serving cheese with summery chilled Lillet or Campari and soda, **Boules de Périgord,** baseball-size goat cheeses flavored with the extravagant truffles of Périgord, are a good choice. They are very mild and creamy. These 8-ounce balls also come plain and flavored with chopped walnuts; some are wrapped in leaves.

Pyramids

There is something visually satisfying about chèvres shaped like flat-topped pyramids. Usually coated with ash, they are sold when firm enough to hold their shape but still moist in the center. The best known is *Valençay from Berry. When having apéritifs for six, we use it with pear-shaped yellow tomatoes and baguettes or country bread. Valençay or another pyramid is also delightful in an assortment with round Camembert, a chunk of aged Cheddar and some blue-veined Saga. Almost cubes, 9-ounce forms are 3 inches high with a 3-inch square base.

The pyramid shape is so appealing it has spawned numerous copies called simply **Pyramides,** made with and without ash. Usually milder and smoother than Valençay, most are well made and less costly. **Pouligny St. Pierre,** with a pointed top, is one of the best. It is sold younger than moist Pyramides, and is slightly salty with a pleasant, pronounced tang.

The same shape is successful when made in 2½-pound cheeses, great for crowds. Wholes or halves are fine with wine and assortments of crisp and colorful crudités. Most readily available are **Pavé Jardin, St. Chevier, Fromage de Rourgue, Lingot de Poitou** and **Fromage de Chèvre Cendré,** all ash coated, with a mild sour tang, slightly stronger than Montrachet. **Pavé Pepper** is coated with ground black pepper instead of ash. Other variations include the uncoated Lingot de Poitou as well as square, ash-coated **Pavé Gençay.**

Domes

More rustic looking is the dome-shaped **Dolmen de Bougon,** a firm, dry cheese from Burgundy. Most prefer it when young and smooth with a sharp, slightly salty taste, perfect with tiny red seedless grapes. More assertive as it ages, the 2½-pound

Dolmen gets creamy and a bit darker around the edges but stays firm in the middle, excellent on firm pumpernickel bread with olive purée.

Taupinière is a smaller dome, still made and aged by individual farmers. Serve this 11-ounce ashed form with rough-textured country breads.

Doughnuts

The attractive cloverleaf doughnut shape makes **Tome Verte** a fine choice for a cocktail party. Coated with pretty green herbs, this 4-pound farm-made form is much like Montrachet. **Chevrolle,** a round 6-pound doughnut, is also very mild and creamy. A whole or half can grace a buffet with a salad of summer greens tossed with a lemony vinaigrette.

Mi-Chèvres

When cow's milk is mixed with at least 25 percent goat's milk, the cheeses, called *mi-chèvres,* are less energetic and a bit smoother. They are often wrapped in leaves to compensate for the loss of flavor. Best-known among these is **Banon,** a charming 4-ounce disk, about the width of a half dollar, wrapped in a chestnut leaf and tied with raffia. The young cheeses are sometimes flavored with herbs, pepper or paprika and are good with drinks. As they age, the flavor becomes more pronounced and nutty. For a few friends, serve one Banon with a wedge of Brie and a piece of Port-Salut. If it's a large group, pile three or five Banons on each other to make a wall, or have a single 1½-pound **St. Marcellin,** wrapped in chestnut leaves. Also known as **Bruleur de Loup,** the larger cheese is quite mild when fresh. If it sits, remove the leaves. They get damp and give the cheese a winey taste.

Soft-Ripened

As goat cheeses grow in popularity, manufacturers continue to experiment with shapes and techniques, sometimes making traditional cow's milk cheeses with goat's milk. We now have **Goat's Milk Camembert** and **Goat Brie,** the same sizes and shapes as their namesakes. (The Brie is a 2-pound, 8-inch round; the Camembert is an 8-ounce, 4-inch round.) The rinds are very white, the ivory interiors much paler than the original cheeses. A bit saltier, they have the sour goat taste. The Camembert is slightly more successful, oozing like the original cheese and having a better flavor than the Brie. Some are simply called **Goat Brie** or **Chèvre Brie.** Others, like **Bougon,** have brand names. They make interesting substitutes for the originals, particularly when served as part of a cheese course.

Layered

Among the less serious goat cheeses is **Chevrette Fines Herbes,** a 2-pound rectangle made of layers of very young herb-flavored goat cheese and garlic. The whole block is coated with the herb mixture. **Buches Nappées** combines herb-flavored layers of goat and cow's milk cheeses. Serve them with strips of raw green beans, red bell peppers, endives and zucchini and chilled wines or cocktails.

American Varieties

Sparked by the growing pride in our native ingredients, production of domestic goat cheeses has grown into a thriving cottage industry. Many restaurateurs, led by Alice Waters of Chez Panisse and including Wolfgang Puck of Spago, Jeremiah Towers of Stars, and Barry Wine of the Quilted Giraffe, regularly feature dishes made with goat cheese on their menus.

A leader in convincing Americans of the high quality of our own chèvres is Laura Chenel, owner of California Chèvre in Santa Rosa, California. Encouraged by the interest Alice Waters and others showed in her first cheeses, Ms. Chenel went to France to study their techniques and returned to make cheeses following the French methods, using their shapes and names.

Freshest of all is the **Fromage Blanc.** Very mild and fluffy, the plain is perfect spread on toast with raspberry jam or spooned over a bowl of bright blue and red berries for dessert. The herb and garlic makes a ready-made dip.

When a single, small cheese is all you need, consider **Chabis,** mild, but a bit firmer and zestier than Fromage Blanc. Formed into traditional 5-ounce cylinders, this versatile cheese is good for eating and cooking. **Banon,** 5-ounce flat rounds, is very mild and creamy. It comes flavored with dill, herbs, black pepper or paprika to have with wine before dinner or as an afternoon snack.

Slightly larger is the 8-ounce **Log,** also called **Ste. Maure.** It is creamy around the edges and chalky in the middle, an excellent replacement for Montrachet. The **Pyramide,** also 8 ounces, is younger and creamier than most French versions. It is made plain and coated with ash.

When we want fuller tasting chèvres to stand up to the tannin in many California Cabernets, we look to the large **Fourmes** aged for months rather than days. These 2½- to 3-pound rounds are stronger and drier than the others. They are very much like Chenel's superb *Taupière, a 10-ounce domed cheese, ashed and sprayed with mold, possibly the best American goat cheese on the market.

Dry and tasty are the round **Crottins,** 2½ to 3 ounces each, and the **Cabecou,** which California Chèvre sells in an olive oil and herb bath. Like their French counterparts, these can be breaded and browned in oil or crumbled into salads of endives and bitter greens.

There also are goat cheeses of very high quality made in many states, including New York, New Jersey, Oregon, Massachusetts and Iowa. Most are fresh, creamy cheeses, often flavored with herbs. Some have unusual shapes and sizes completely different than the French. The production is small and distribution is local (although some will take mail orders). We can't discuss all the farmers here, but urge you to try any locally made goat cheeses you find. Among the best are the cheeses of the Goat Works in New Jersey, where they make a firm aged **Tomme,** a full-flavored but slightly sweet cheese to use in an assortment.

Kendall in California makes unusually rich white-mold cheeses that are technically double creams. Called **Chevrefeuille** and **Camembert,** they are excellent with soft California Merlots. Their latest creation is a **Chèvre Bleu,** a young goat cheese with shots of blue in it. Both flavors come through and continue to develop with age. The 4½-pound rounds, shaped like midget Stiltons, are a fine addition to any cheese board. Toss some of this crumbly cheese with spinach pasta and fresh tomatoes or add it to a salad of dandelion and bibb. **Monterey Goat Cheese** from Massachusetts is young, fresh, and spreadable. Marie-Claude Chaleix, an expert who learned her craft in her native France, has started making her own cheeses in upstate New York under the Coach Farm label.

Decidedly unlike any French cheese are the **Goat's Milk Cheddars** from Iowa and California. They have the texture but not the full flavor of an aged Cheddar, nor do they taste much like goat cheese. Because of the high costs involved in production, they are much more expensive than cow's milk Cheddars. Buy them only if you want Cheddar and can't digest cow's milk. They are sold in 5- and 10-pound rindless blocks.

Italian Varieties

Goat cheeses do not rank among Italy's most superb because production is limited, almost entirely for home use. As interest in Italian food and native Italian products increases in the United States, however, creative cheesemakers are meeting our demands by making pleasant, usually young goat cheeses, often copies of French chèvres. Called *formaggio di capra* or *caprino,* most weigh 8 ounces or less.

The exception is *Leggerello Goat,** a fresh, thick cheese, much like sour cream in texture. Scooped from 4-pound tubs, it has more flavor than most Italian goat cheeses. Spread it on cranberry muffins in the morning. It also comes marinated in oil with black peppercorns. Toss it with hot pasta and chunks of tomatoes for a refreshing first course.

The mildest are the small, moist logs, **Toma Caprino** and **Caprini di Capra,** sometimes made with a portion of cow's milk. Fine mixed with spices for a spread or plain on banana-nut or other cakelike quick breads, each weighs 3 to 4 ounces.

Sant' Pier, also mild and fresh, comes in 10-ounce rounds, plain or flavored with pepper. Try it spread on bread with oily Italian olives.

Castagneto, a very creamy, rich cheese is ideal with berries or cut-up fruit. The name means chestnut explaining the brown paper leaf it is wrapped in. The 15-ounce forms are originally wrapped in real leaves but then replaced with the paper before being exported. The cheese is very perishable.

Also wrapped in the leaves are **Castagnola,** a 6-ounce fresh cheese from Piedmont, and **Castagnetta,** also fresh, but hand-shaped and smaller.

Aged a little more, **Caprella** is a white-mold cheese. These 8-ounce rounds are slightly sharper and saltier than young goat cheeses, quite good with fruity Italian red wines.

Similarly, there is an Italian goat's milk Camembert from the Piedmont region called **Cravet.** A mild cheese with a pleasant tang, it has a snowy white rind and ivory interior that oozes at room temperature. An excellent dessert with Bosc pears, it comes in 10-ounce plastic-wrapped rounds.

Dutch and Scandinavian Varieties

The Dutch, not wanting to be left out of the goat cheese market, now make a **Goat Gouda.** The pale, flaky cheese, in thick, 6-pound wheels, is among the best of its kind. Try it in place of Cheddar the next time you make macaroni and cheese.

The Norwegians make a goat cheese, **Gjetost,** that doesn't look or taste like any other in the world—it is very sweet, almost cloying. The milk, often including cow's milk, is boiled until it becomes thick and brown, then formed into 8-ounce, 1-pound or 9-pound rectangular bricks that look like bars of ordinary soap. Norwegians slice it thin to eat on bread for breakfast or thin crackers for a snack. Pure goat's milk Gjetost will say ekte (real) on the label. Made only in 1-pound bricks, it is a bit stronger but still sweet.

Sheep's milk cheeses, usually grouped with goat cheeses, are set apart by the distinctive taste of the milk, fuller in flavor and saltier than cow's milk, almost redolent of the sheep themselves. While goat and sheep's milk are sometimes substituted one for the other, the cheeses traditionally made with each milk are different. Most sheep's milk cheeses are made in small amounts for local eating. Those sold here are usually either young, firm white cheeses, often packed in brine, or aged cheeses, many hard enough to grate. An exception is blue-veined Roquefort, the world's most famous sheep's milk cheese. Although in many ways a typical sheep's milk cheese, Roquefort is so strongly a blue, we discuss it in that section. For similar reasons, Pecorino Romano, southern Italy's grating cheese, is discussed in the Hard and Grating section.

Sheep's milk is creamy and rich, almost buttery—so thick it needs to be mixed with water to be drinkable. Sheep give even less milk than goats, a mere two quarts a day, so sheep's milk cheeses are scarcer. As rocky mountains, previously suitable for little more than grazing sheep, have been turned into profitable ski resorts and farms, the number of sheep raised for milk (different from those raised for wool) has dwindled. There are no American sheep's milk cheeses to speak of because our native sheep are raised for their wool and give even less milk. Nor is it probable that a grass roots movement will rise to bring in different varieties of sheep. Because of certain diseases they are prone to, it is virtually impossible to get sheep through United States Customs. There are, fortunately, no quotas on sheep's milk cheeses.

Some cheeses originally made exclusively with sheep's milk are now made with

Sheep's Milk Cheeses

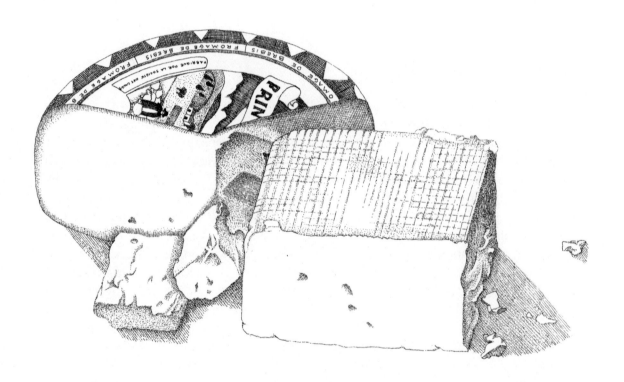

part or all cow or goat's milk. Cheesemakers try, with mixed success, to duplicate the flavor of the sheep's milk by adding more salt. Although technically not sheep's milk cheeses, they share a common history so we are discussing them here.

Buying and Storing

It is especially important to taste sheep's milk cheeses before buying since many have generic names that tell nothing about who made them and may be vague about where. The Greek Feta from the same shop may vary from month to month. How strong a cheese you want depends on personal taste, of course, and how you plan to use it. One that is perfect in a salad of dandelions and Bibb lettuce may be too mild for a casserole of zucchini and mushrooms. The young cheeses may be creamy or firm. They should be almost pristine white. The older, drier cheeses are slightly yellow but still whiter than aged cow's milk cheeses.

Some sheep's milk cheeses come packed in brine, usually a mixture of milk and salt water. The longer they remain in the liquid, the firmer and saltier they get. To slow the aging, drain and discard the brine. Bring equal parts of milk and water to a boil, cool to room temperature, and pour over the cheese in a glass jar. The liquid must completely cover the cheese. Cover the jar and refrigerate. If you want the cheese to get stronger, add coarse salt to the brine. If it is too salty, let it soak in cold water for two to three hours before adding the new brine. Keep other cheeses in the refrigerator wrapped in foil or plastic. Before serving, leave them at room temperature for four to six hours.

Serve sheep's milk cheeses with Greek olives, pita bread and chilled Pinot Grigio. Use them in omelets with roasted peppers; crumble them into salads with tuna, red onions and artichokes flavored with thyme.

Feta

A beautifully versatile cheese, firm cubes of white, salty **Feta** are essential for Greek salads made with oily black olives and ripe red tomatoes, all redolent of the Mediterranean sun. Feta is blended with spinach to add zest to filo-wrapped spanakopitta or used alone in tiropitta. Chunks are generally firm enough to hold their shape when sautéed in olive oil with shrimp but soft enough to crumble on bread or over pasta. Snowy white, young Feta, kept in brine, is creamy, though firm enough to crumble. It should be pleasantly salty, not puckery. The aged, having less moisture in it, is saltier, drier and much more crumbly. Most Americans prefer the milder cheese. When used in cooked dishes, however, it is so mild it can get lost.

Called a "pickled cheese" because much of it is kept in brine, Feta is made in all the Mediterranean countries and some of their neighbors from either sheep or goat's milk. Those imported to the United States, all made from sheep's milk, come from Greece, Italy, Corsica, Hungary and Rumania. **American** and **Danish Fetas,** always made from cow's milk with salt added, are not as interesting as sheep's milk Feta, but they are less expensive.

Balkan and Hungarian Varieties

For hundreds of years, travel among Balkan States and neighboring Hungary was common, allowing them to exchange ideas and customs. Today, many of their favorite dishes and cheeses are so much alike, only natives can tell them apart. It is virtually impossible to know where any of them was first made. Sometimes the names are the same, with variations on the spelling; other times, the names are quite different.

It is a rare home in the region that does not always have a spread on hand made from **Brynza,** a moist and creamy sheep's milk cheese, usually mixed with butter, cream cheese and herbs, then stuffed into bell peppers. Rumanians use Brynza to season mamaliga, corn meal porridge like Italian polenta, almost a national dish. Snowy white with only a trace of saltiness, the Brynza sold here comes from Rumania and Hungary in 10-pound pails and 8-ounce plastic containers. Unfortunately, because of its high moisture content, it molds easily.

When you want firmer cheeses to take on picnics and eat in sandwiches, there is **Kasseri** from Greece, Hungary and Bulgaria. Left to age enough to get firm, this white cheese, shaped into 18-pound wheels, is fairly mild. When aged longer, it gets sharper and saltier. Serve fried slices with Greek ouzo.

Kaskaval, from Rumania, Greece and Italy, is made much like Mozzarella and has a pliable texture and salty flavor, often redolent of the herbs from the hillside where the sheep graze. Use it to top a Mediterranean pizza with olives and onions sprinkled over thick tomato sauce.

Greek **Kefalotyri** is a hard, yellowish grating cheese much like Romano. Quite salty, it is best grated and added to rice and lamb casseroles.

Italian Varieties

Historically, Italy is divided between the rich northern land, home to herds of cows, and the poorer South where sheep roam. It is southern Italy, therefore, that gives us *pecorini,* the flavorful sheep's milk cheeses that range from fresh, moist Ricotta, actually made from the whey, to firm Romano, the South's answer to Parmesan. Ricotta is discussed in the Fresh Cheeses section; Romano, with other grating cheeses.

There is a pleasant tang to **Lacheso,** a firm cheese from Lombardy. Try it by itself with firm bread and a soft red wine. The thick, 8-pound wheels have an orange rind. The texture is supple, not crumbly. Buy a lot; it's the kind of cheese you'll keep returning to.

When it comes to a fine pecorino for eating in chunks with juicy, ripe peaches or grapes, **Formaggio Dolce Siena** is a wonderful choice. The firm, crumbly, rounded 3-pound loaves have the full tart flavor of the sheep's milk, no bitterness, and not much salt.

Ricotta Romano, made near Rome during the days of the Roman Empire, is now made in Sardinia, where sheep are still abundant. It starts like fresh Ricotta but is pressed and salted until it becomes a very smooth white cheese similar in texture to Feta but milder in taste. It slices easily and is not too salty. Eat it with bread and fruit and a California Zinfandel or in place of Feta in a Greek salad. It comes in 5-pound rindless wheels. Some let it age until it is hard enough to grate.

Sardinian **Fiore Sardi** is a fine cheese similar to Ricotta Romano. Unfortunately, most sold here is poorly made in Argentina with salted cow's milk.

Toscanello, another grainy cheese, has a pleasing sharp flavor, a fine addition to pasta or scrambled eggs. Made in Sardinia and Tuscany and aged 6 months, the wheels weigh 6 to 8 pounds.

Baked Ricotta, made with sheep's milk, is Italy's answer to Baked Farmer Cheese. Slightly salty and tangy, it is a firm, white 1-pound loaf, oven-browned on the top and sides. Try a slice on toast or a bagel for breakfast with chunky apricot preserves.

French Varieties

A superb cheese to serve with Lillet or other apéritifs, *** Brin d'Amour,** a twig of love, is a firm, oval, 1½-pound loaf coated with rosemary, savory, coriander and juniper berries. Fairly mild, it is a good introduction for those who think sheep's milk cheeses have to be salty and coarse.

The French Pyrénées, known for fine cheeses, are most readily associated with the sheep's milk cheese that bears their name, **Fromage des Pyrénées.** In the confusion of cheese nomenclature, some cow's milk cheeses have the same name. The original Fromage des Pyrénées is aged enough to be firm but still mild enough to be a superior eating cheese. It reminds us of the taste and texture of a young Parmesan and is also firm enough to grate. Include it in an assortment of cow's milk cheeses to show the sheep's milk flavor to advantage. It is too expensive for everyday cooking. Many are sold by brand names, like **Prince de Claverolle,** in 8- to 9-pound yellow wheels, coated in thin, inedible orange layers. Not as dry in texture, although still aged, is delicately flavored **Brebignal.** The 10-pound forms are easy to slice.

Fromage du Larzac, a mild but tangy cheese from the Roquefort region that is mixed with butter and packed into 7-ounce crocks, is relatively new to the market. Serve it at room temperature or gently warmed as a quick spread for crackers or crisp radishes and red pepper spears.

Spanish Varieties

Few Spanish cheeses are brought into the United States. Occasionally, some **Manchego,** a dry sheep's milk cheese, arrives in 5- to 6-pound wheels either aged or young. The young is only mildly salty and slices easily. Serve it with a glass of sherry for a quick tapa. The aged gets dry enough to grate. It adds interest to Spanish tortillas filled with sautéed mushrooms and tomatoes.

Cheddar Family

Each fall when nature paints the leaves gorgeous reds, rusts and golds, we head for New England to spend lazy days driving down quiet country roads through covered bridges, marveling at the beauty around us. Although the air is crisp, it is not too cold to picnic on corncob smoked hams and whole grain breads with chunks of aged Vermont Cheddar cheese that we break with knives to eat out of hand, letting it almost melt in the mouth, or add to our uneven sandwiches, washed down with newly milled cider.

Cheddars are equally good with thick beef and barley soups in winter, grated in salads with the first spring onions, and sliced alongside summer's beefsteak tomatoes. They're delicious in rye bread sandwiches with spicy salamis or in elegant egg-coated croque monsieurs. They make a satisfying dessert with a slice of warm cinnamon-apple pie. Should you have a wheel of aged Cheddar, serve it whole, its black wax still glistening, with a wooden bowl piled high with walnuts and almonds still in their shells in place of a sweet dessert.

Cheddars and their relatives run the gamut from young and moist to crumbly, firm, aged cheeses, sharp in taste. For eating, our preference is for wheels at least six months old, almost nutty tasting, sometimes even zesty, usually pale in color, wrapped in cheesecloth and wax. Since it's impossible to cut even slices, we don't try, giving our guests stubby knives so they can chisel out chunks to eat with firm breads: crusty baguettes, chewy whole grain loaves, nut-studded rolls. In sandwiches, we pair them with ripe avocados and Vidalia onions, oil-cured olives and roasted red peppers.

For cooking, we look to those cheeses a mere two months old, relatively easy to slice, often bright orange. These softer wheels may be broken with a fork, melted with beer and poured over buttered toast for nourishing Welsh rarebit (or rabbit) suppers like those they've been serving in England and New England for centuries. They can flavor dainty cheese straws flecked with cayenne pepper and flaky ham and cheese biscuits, bread-and-butter puddings and creamy spinach soufflés. We grate or crumble any leftover bits to top beef and potato casseroles, flavor soups, omelets or rice. Mixed with butter and hot peppers, they make tasty spreads.

The British are due the accolades for developing the cheesemaking technique known as cheddaring. They cut the soft curd into slabs, stack them in molds, and press to eliminate the liquid. The variations depend on the size of the curd, amount of aging and richness and flavor of the milk. The qualities of the milk, in turn, depend upon what the cows eat and where they do their grazing. Made from pasteurized or raw milk, cheeses in the Cheddar family do not develop rinds. Farmhouse and better commercial cheeses are wrapped in cheesecloth and then dipped in paraffin, wax or a combination. This lets them breathe and age. Others are sealed in plastic, retarding the aging process. Most Cheddars are aged at least two months; those made from raw milk must be.

Orange and White

Years ago, dairymen noticed that those cheeses made from May to September, when cows fed on lush grazing lands and gave the richest milk, developed a golden hue as they aged. To impart a similar color to cheeses made with ordinary milk or not aged as long, some cheesemakers added strands of saffron, one of the world's costliest spices, to the curd. They soon turned to less expensive marigolds for the color, later using annatto, a virtually tasteless spice from the West Indies, or other natural colorings. In some regions, enough coloring was added to make the cheese bright orange, called red by the British.

The practice of making orange Cheddars was brought to the American colonies, where it was very popular. For a time, almost all our Cheddars were bright orange. In the 1960s, the "natural" foods movement began when many people became justifiably concerned about unnecessary additives put into foods to preserve them and make them more attractive. Orange Cheddar, usually just as natural as the white, got caught up in the backlash. Today, most farmhouse and some commercial Cheddars are white. Cooks continue to buy orange wheels for macaroni and cheese, Welsh rarebit, cheese sauces and other dishes where the color adds to the visual appeal of the dish.

Sizes

Cheddar not only names a specific cheese and a cheesemaking method, but also describes the traditional shape of the cheese—a flat wheel, about 14 inches wide and 24 inches high, weighing 70 to 78 pounds. Daisies, only about 4 inches thick, weigh

21 to 23 pounds. Flats or Twins weigh 37 to 40 pounds and are 14½ inches wide and 12 inches high. Distinctive Longhorns, only 6 inches wide, are about 13 inches high and weigh 12 to 13 pounds. There are also convenient 1-pound loaves and 3- and 5-pound rounds called Midgets.

Buying and Storing

We keep a chunk or small wheel of Cheddar in the house at all times, ready for a quick snack or nourishing sandwich, to add to salads, pastas or soups. It lasts for weeks if wrapped tightly in foil in the refrigerator. Let it warm to room temperature before serving; the flavor is much better. Since most Cheddars are sold in wedges cut from large rounds, you can often taste before buying to see if the flavor suits your needs. Remember that the moister cheeses will melt into smoother, richer sauces to pour over fish fillets or blanched beans. To taste an unopened wheel, insert a long narrow cheese tester in the middle of the side. Twist it and pull out the sample. Break off and taste the pointed end. Push the rest of the piece, including the wax coating, back into the hole. This will reseal the cheese so it can continue to age.

Cheesemakers all agree that their aged cheeses, like vintage wines, are prizes to bring out for honored guests or special holidays. Just as most winemakers sell their bottles before they are at their prime, few cheesemakers can afford to tie up their money for years waiting until the cheeses are at their peak to sell them. Fortunately, it is easy to continue the aging at home. Leave a small, unopened wax-coated wheel out in a cool room, turning it over every three days. After three or four weeks, it will be firmer and more flavorful. If you have the patience, defer gratification and leave it for a few months. The cheeses will also age, but more slowly, in the refrigerator.

English Varieties

If you are in England, look for an old-fashioned working-class pub where the regulars play darts. Pass by hearty servings of bubble and squeak or bangers and mash and ask for the ploughman's lunch: a wedge of aged Cheddar, freshly baked bread, pickled onions and a pint of dark ale. If you are lucky, you will get a cheese made by hand on a small farm: full flavored and crumbly with age.

Time was that every region of England, sometimes every town, had its own distinctive Cheddar-style cheese. No connoisseur would ever confuse a tangy Cheshire with a sharp Gloucester, mild Lancashire or sour Wensleydale. The differences are still apparent among the farmhouse cheeses, but plentiful commercially made forms, made from the same blended milk, tend to an unfortunate sameness. Among the regional Cheddars that still exist are Cheshire, Gloucester, Caerphilly, Wensleydale, Leicester, Derby. As a general rule, farmhouse cheeses are wrapped in cheesecloth and wax and aged longer than the plastic-wrapped commercial cheeses.

Of all the farmhouse cheeses, **Cheddar,** still made in Somerset, is best known. These pale, slightly crumbly cheeses have a grainy feel. They are made from raw cow's milk and aged at least a year to give them a distinctive, not overpowering, slightly sharp flavor. Serve one alongside a fine Brie, a firm chèvre, a creamy Saga, with a full-bodied Bordeaux or Cabernet Sauvignon. Whole cheeses come in 10-pound blocks and 60-pound rounds. For the holidays, there are also 2- and 4-pound midgets, a thoughtful gift, especially when accompanied by a fine Claret.

Commercially made Cheddars, more reasonably priced, can be excellent values. Often coated with red wax, they are milder and younger than the farmhouse cheeses, excellent over hamburgers or grilled in sandwiches with Black Forest ham. Read the label carefully. Some manufacturers, bent on confusing the consumer, use words like "farm*stead*" on their labels.

It is said that **Cheshire** was originally molded in the shape of the mythical Cheshire cat. We doubt anyone would have chosen such an illusionary form for a very real cheese. Some speak of it as *the* English cheese after Stilton because cows there graze in some of England's finest pastures, near the salt-mining town of Northwich. There is little doubt that the saltiness of the surrounding meadows contributes to its tangy flavor. A creamy orange or white cheese, younger than Cheddar, Cheshire is firm and slightly crumbly, a fine toasting cheese to have with light red wines. The farmhouse wheels weigh 22 pounds; commercial rounds are 9 pounds.

Double Gloucester, made from rich summer milk, got its name by being much thicker than Single Gloucester, rarely seen these days even in England. Pale yellow and somewhat granular, Double Gloucester has a slightly sharp taste well complemented by tart apples and thick-skinned red grapes. After dinner, serve it with tawny port. There are 6-pound farmhouse wheels. The commercial versions, young enough to slice easily for sandwiches, come in 9- and 28-pound wheels. Some Double Gloucester is now flavored with mustard pickles; others have layers of walnuts.

Cotswold, known also as **Sturminster, Bellshire** and **Ilchester,** is a commercial Double Gloucester flavored with chives or scallions, leaving green specks in the cheese. More suitable for nibbling with drinks than for serious eating, it comes in 12-pound rounds.

Caerphilly, originally the cheese Welsh miners took for lunch, is now made in England. The miners knew they could eat this relatively mild white cheese without any worries about indigestion in the cramped caves. Firm and crumbly like Cheshire, Caerphilly has a slight salty and sour aftertaste something like buttermilk. The English like it on slabs of thickly buttered brown bread. A good melting cheese, it makes creamy soufflés.

Also mild and white, **Lancashire** is soft enough to spread on toast for breakfast, good in a freshly baked potato still hot in its skin. There are 9-pound wheels and blocks.

Wensleydale, called "the best of all English cheese" by André Simon, is flaky and white with a slightly sour taste like that of yogurt or sour cream. Serve it on a warm day with fresh radishes and a chilled Chenin Blanc. It is made in Yorkshire in 9-pound rounds.

Leicester, also called **Red Leicester,** is a favorite with cooks for its bright orange color. Semifirm but crumbly with a mild flavor, it is frequently used for tomato rarebits and pasta casseroles. Both farmhouse and commercial versions come in 6- and 23-pound rounds.

Less dense than others in the Cheddar family, **Derby** flakes when cut. The tall 4-pound rounds are either plain, port flavored or generously mixed with crushed sage leaves to give them a beautiful green color, particularly festive at Christmas. Serve the plain cheese with Anjou pears and wafer crackers, ale or hearty red wines. Add some to chicken and seafood salads.

In eighteenth-century England, creative cheesemakers would take two Derbys—one plain, one sage—and cut the same figure from the center of each using special templates. The figures were then exchanged so the green cheese had a plain center and the plain cheese a green one, a secret known only to the cheesemaker. Even more complex were those checkerboards of yellow marigold and green sage cheeses. Modern combinations are more straightforward. *Huntsman, also called **Stilchester,** is made of layers of blue-veined Stilton and pale Cheshire. **Cromwell** has layers of Derby contrasting with bright Red Leicester.

Canadian Varieties

It is logical that the finest Cheddars made outside England are found in lands settled under her flag—Canada, the United States and New Zealand. Canada's sharpest and tastiest Cheddars are made in Ontario. Crumbly and white, they are excellent with port for dessert, breaded and toasted with a spicy tomato sauce or grated into a chive and dill omelet. The best known are the **Black Diamond** Cheddars so named because they were considered of diamond quality and coated in black wax. Aged one to three years, they are on a par with the extraordinary generic Cheddars from the same region and considerably more expensive. We'll take the generic cheese every time, with no sacrifice to quality and at a much lower price, unless we want a small wheel as a gift.

Canadian Cheddar comes in 40-pound blocks, usually aged 2½ to 3 years. The Black Diamond comes in 5-pound waxed wheels and blocks, or 2½-, 3½- and 40-pound forms in plastic.

American Varieties

Cheddar making in the United States started on small farms in New York and New England. By the 1850s, the first commercial factory had been established in upstate New York. As settlers moved west, they took their cheesemaking abilities with them. Consequently, fine Cheddars are made today from coast to coast. Cheddar has become so ubiquitous, in fact, it is commonly called "store cheese," reminding people of the days when there was a Cheddar in every general or grocery store in every town, large or small. Rather less flattering, it is also called "rat cheese" because chunks are good bait on rat traps. As in England, regional differences affect the final product, ranging from mild orange Wisconsin Colbys to aged, crumbling Vermont Cheddars. The best are those made on small farms and factories where they are wrapped in cheesecloth and coated in wax to allow aging to continue.

Today some of the finest Cheddars come from Vermont and New York, although excellent cheeses are made in Wisconsin and other states. **New York State Cheddars** are especially good if aged from nine to eighteen months—the longer, the better. Those only four to six months old are bland. Because New York Cheddars are aged in very dry curing rooms, they are crumblier than other cheeses, good for grating into cheese biscuits and straws. Both orange and white cheeses come in 40-pound flat wheels and blocks.

Cooper, an orange New York Cheddar, is young, ideal for slicing on a machine to make neat sandwich squares to grill with freshly cooked bacon. Of far better quality than those packaged slices sold in supermarkets, Cooper comes in 5-pound blocks.

In Vermont, as in New York, aged Cheddars have the most taste. **Vermont Cheddars** are more mellow and moist than those as old from New York and Canada. Excellent after dinner or for a snack with crisp fall apples and fresh cider, they can be the base for velvety soups and soufflés, golden sandwich breads and tomato rarebits, called rinktum ditties. To serve with drinks, grate some, mix it with butter and spices, shape into balls or logs and roll in chopped walnuts to coat. Vermont Cheddars come in 3- to 5-pound flats and blocks, and forms close to 40 pounds. During the holidays, most cheesemakers sell green sage Cheddars, a Vermont specialty. They add interesting flavor and color to omelets. Smoked Cheddars are excellent in sandwiches with leftover holiday turkey.

One of the finest Vermont Cheddars is **Shelburne Farmhouse Cheese,** made in a picture-book stone and brick farm off the shores of Lake Champlain. They've been making their fine Cheddar since 1886 from the milk of their own Brown Swiss cows. Aged at least a year before sale, the 40-pound blocks are firm and grainy with a pleasant nuttiness. Once aged, they are cut into smaller blocks, waxed and shipped out. Serve it with full-bodied Cabernet Sauvignons or hard sparkling cider, with crisp Vermont apples or crusty country breads.

Almost all the rest of Vermont's sharp Cheddars come from the **Cabot** Farmers' Co-operative Creamery in the northeast. Although the cheesemaking is mechanized in many ways, the flipping and stacking of the curds is done by hand. The 3-pound wheels, made from raw milk, are aged from two months to two years. The finest are the Private Stock, carefully selected blocks of aged cheese, worthy of a glass of vintage Calvados or Cognac. The younger cheeses make lush grilled sandwiches and custardy bread puddings.

The **Crowley** family has been making **Colby** cheese in Healdville, Vermont, since 1824. In 1968, the last Crowley in the business died. Randolph Smith, a retired school director from New York City, took over and has maintained the high standards set by the Crowleys. Made much like Cheddar, the curds for Crowley are washed with spring water to eliminate all the whey from the raw milk cheese, which makes it creamier. Having much more character than Wisconsin Colbys, the 2½- and 5-pound wheels are aged two to three months for mild, four to five for medium and at least six months for sharp. Grate some into zucchini and carrot fritters, or sprinkle it on top of croutons in vegetable soup.

Ask Wisconsin cheesemakers if their cheese is white or orange and they'll tell you it depends who they're making it for. Locals like it "colored" and Easterners like it white. As a rule, **Wisconsin Cheddars,** including **Colby** or **Longhorn,** are meant to be eaten young and mild. They are used for snacks and sandwiches, to top bowls of meaty chili, make thick soups, melt in omelets, over hamburgers and tuna sandwiches. Colby, often sold a few days old, rarely more than three months, is most popular in its native state and throughout the Midwest. The Longhorn, shaped in a tall cylinder that leans slightly, is ubiquitous in the Southwest for Tex-Mex dishes. It is shredded and sprinkled on tacos, meaty chilies and refried beans; cubed and stuffed into peppers for chiles rellenos; melted with jalapeños for chile con queso; served with tortilla chips. The best Wisconsin Cheddars come in 20-pound Daisies and 3-pound Gems. There are some raw milk Daisies, but most are made from pasteurized milk.

Although most Wisconsin Cheddars are commercially made, small cheesemakers continue to produce cheeses worth seeking out. Among them is Hook's Cheese Company, a small dairy cooperative that makes firm, flavorful Colby and mild Cheddar. Both are excellent for sandwiches with kielbasa and chilled beer, and they make creamy Welsh rarebits, macaroni and cheese, and stuffings for enchiladas and tomatoes.

Isaar Cheese makes yellow Colby for easy eating and firmer Cheddar for cooking. Farmers bring the cheesemaker their milk daily and some stay to eat the fresh, unpressed curds. Most of the cheese is sold a bit older, however. The medium is up to six weeks old; the aged, up to a year. Colby, softer with more holes, tends to sour if left to age but the medium is very pleasant on its own or grilled in a sandwich with smoked turkey.

Tillamook is a medium-sharp raw milk Cheddar from Oregon. Most are aged three months, some as long as seven. The older the cheese, the more flavor. Try it with black-skinned Hass avocados and tomatoes, artichokes and other West Coast foods. Since production is small, Tillamook is sold mostly on the West Coast. It comes in 40-pound yellow blocks and 2-pound salt-free forms.

Among other Cheddars are those of Kentucky, much like Wisconsin commercial cheeses. The Amish in Pennsylvania and Monterey Farms in California make 5-pound blocks of white **Raw-Milk Cheddars,** which tend to be sharp and dry.

There are also Cheddar types of cheeses made with goat's milk for those who cannot digest cow's milk products. These are discussed in the Goat Cheese section. Made like Cheddars but eaten so much younger they are still soft are the Monterey Jacks, discussed in the Semisoft section.

French Varieties

Given the rich variety of cheeses made in France, those in the Cheddar family are sometimes overlooked. Firm **Cantal,** one of France's oldest cheeses, gets crumbly as it ages. The flavor is nutty-sweet. Use it for sandwiches or snacks with country hams and whole-grained breads. Pale white with a natural grayish rind, 20-pound forms are shaped like top hats about 15 inches high.

Mimolette, another French Cheddar, is identical to a spherical-shaped Dutch cheese with the same name. Similar to Wisconsin Cheddar, these 6-pound orange balls have a nutty flavor and firm texture.

New Zealand Varieties

Surprisingly, most of the Cheddar we import is from **New Zealand.** Usually quite good, sharp and aged, it comes in large orange or white blocks and rounds. Almost all of it is used in processed cheeses by commercial manufacturers.

Swiss-Style Cheeses

High among the fortuitous culinary accidents must surely rank the creation of those large holes in Swiss Emmentaler, probably the world's best-known cheese. Somehow the gases in the cheese expand to form those pockets of air called "eyes" while giving the cheese its rich nutty taste. Try as they might to duplicate it—and thousands of cheesemakers the world over have tried mightily—true Swiss cheese can be made only in Switzerland. These golden rounds can be sliced for sandwiches with smoked turkey and horseradish mayonnaise or grilled with Canadian bacon and green peppercorn mustard. Julienne strips add distinction to chef's salads with roast beef and artichokes or with radicchio, arugula and sun-dried tomatoes. Grate it over potato and beef casseroles to make a golden crust. Melt cubes into fondues laced with kirschwasser.

The golden wheels are firm enough to hold their shape, still soft enough to slice easily. The flavor may be mild or nutty. While true Swiss is made in Switzerland in 200-pound wheels, copies come from just about every cheese-producing nation. Some are fine; none is quite like the original. The eyes may be quite small. Most are made with partly skimmed milk, adding minimal salt. Some cheeses in this family come in 20-pound wheels and rectangular blocks, designed for sandwich slices.

Very good eating on their own with robust red wines or delicate Gewürztraminers, hard cider or cold beer, Swiss cheeses are the key to many of the world's greatest cheese dishes—thick, rich fondues and soufflés, all kinds of quiches, crusty cheese puffs, batter-fried croque monsieurs. Well-made Swiss is also a wonderful sandwich cheese with smoked ham, ripe tomatoes and spicy mustards on firm whole wheat breads and French rolls. Serve it on the buffet table with cold meats.

Buying and Storing

Choosing the Swiss-style cheese to buy depends on how you want to use it, your taste preference and how much you want to spend. For making a special fondue, select a flavorful, aged cheese that will melt well and lend the dish its distinctive flavor. For a chef's salad with julienned ham, tongue and roast beef, a lesser cheese will be fine. In a Swiss salad with a mustardy vinaigrette, an aged cheese is superb.

The cheese should be semisoft to firm and moist, not dry or cracked. The taste may be mild or sharp. Sliced packaged Swiss cheese is convenient for sandwiches, but the best is sold in chunks. If neat slices are important, have it sliced to order in the shop. Buy only what you will use that day. The cheese will dry out. Refrigerate it wrapped in foil or plastic, and leave it at room temperature for a few hours before serving.

Emmentaler

Switzerland Swiss, a full, nutty-flavored cheese with a milky aftertaste, is called **Emmentaler** in its native land. Cut wheels reveal golden cheese, firm and slightly oily, randomly but completely covered with holes (the famous eyes) from nickel to half-dollar size. It is these eyes, of course, that make Swiss cheese identifiable to every child, perfect for pushing stubby fingers through. To show off its nutty sweetness, julienne it as the Swiss do and mix it in a summer salad with tender scallions. Melt it for a luxurious fondue or shred it over hot, beefy onion soup and run it under the broiler to make a thick, chewy crust. It can flavor onion tarts, as well as quiches made with spinach, broccoli and shrimp. It makes crisp, oozing fritters, delicate pastries. On its own before or after dinner, it goes well with a fine Beaujolais, a full-bodied Côtes du Rhône.

Although 200-pound Emmentalers are among the largest cheeses in the world, they are not mass produced. Fifteen hundred small dairies each make only about three wheels a day from milk delivered within twenty-four hours. Cheesemakers care for each cheese, carefully salting and turning it daily and thumping it knowingly to find the exact moment the wheel should be moved from the warm drying cellar to the cooler aging room. The total aging is usually ten to twelve months. All the care makes Switzerland Swiss more expensive than most others, but worth it. Since all except our domestic Swiss cheese is imported, the unwary customer asking for imported Swiss may be sold an imported cheese that is not Emmentaler. The smooth rind is stamped SWITZERLAND in large red letters as an assurance of authenticity. On even a thin slice, some of those red letters are visible.

Copies of Switzerland Swiss

It is surprising that the exacting Swiss didn't foresee the popularity of their cheese and protect its name. "Swiss" cheese is made all over the world. Aside from the holes, many of these copies have little in common with Switzerland Swiss. Emmentaler is usually firmer, drier and more flavorful. Even the best copies, fine in their way, are not the same.

One of the first Swiss copies to come to the United States was Danish **Samsoe,** a firm cheese resembling Gruyère. Now that there are so many similar cheeses on the market, it has lost some of its popularity. It remains an enjoyable, inexpensive everyday cheese available in 30-pound wheels.

Among the other copies of Switzerland Swiss are **Finnish** and **Dutch Swiss, French Emmental, Austrian** and **American Swiss, Danish Emmentaler** and **Bavarian** from West Germany. All are made in large wheels like Switzerland Swiss and have eyes. They are shipped here in sections. Usually not aged as long, they are moister, less flavorful and less expensive than Switzerland Swiss. Use for sandwiches and snacks; add to casseroles.

The mildest Swiss-style cheeses are the mini-wheels. Usually mere 20-pound wheels, they are fine substitutes if priced well. Most popular among Americans is Norwegian **Jarlsberg.** Introduced here to appeal to the customer who found our domestic Swiss cheese too bland and Switzerland Swiss too strong, Jarlsberg was a very good value. Now it often costs as much as Emmentaler. Aged less, it is much softer. It has become a safe cheese that many Americans keep buying because they know what they are getting amid a sea of unfamiliar cheeses. A perfectly fine choice for everyday eating, it does not compare to Switzerland Swiss. Like Jarlsberg are Holland's **Westland, Bergumer** and **Leerdammer; Israeli Swiss;** Australia's **St. Claire,** and Norway's **Fjordland.**

Gruyère

Switzerland is also famous for **Gruyère,** an essential ingredient in Swiss fondue. Made since the twelfth century, it is named for the town of Gruyères. Wheels were often used to pay taxes so the collectors became known as *agents gruyers.* Related to Switzerland Swiss, Gruyère is also firm, naturally ripened and aged. It is washed and stored in a more humid environment, making its rind brown and wrinkled like an almond's. Gruyère has a decidedly more pronounced, nuttier flavor. Its holes are small, sometimes nonexistent. A well-aged, saltier Gruyère will have small cracks in it.

Once considered only a cooking cheese because it melts so well, Gruyère is also an excellent eating cheese, as Americans are now discovering. Include it in an assortment with Valençay, Coulommiers and Port-Salut served with a Cabernet Sauvignon.

Use it in a salad with rare beef fillet and mottled radicchio or to make puffy rings of browned gougères and custardy quiches. Eighty-pound wheels are aged longer than Switzerland Swiss. They are marked SWITZERLAND GRUYÈRE clearly around the top of the cheese in dark blue letters.

The first Swiss to make Gruyère were French-speaking. By the thirteenth century, the cheesemaking skills had spread to their relatives in France. Today, the French make excellent Gruyères. **Comté,** from small communities in the Jura Mountains, is a firm, drier cheese with a fruity flavor and larger holes. Like Swiss Gruyère, it will add grace to quiches and make beautiful grilled sandwiches with thick slices of bacon. Comté comes in 85-pound wheels and may be even more expensive than its Swiss cousin.

Beaufort is a French Gruyère resembling Fontina. It has few holes, if any, but may have some cracks. Not aged as long, it is softer in texture and milder in taste. It comes in the same 85-pound wheels and is more difficult to find in the United States than other members of the Gruyère family, perhaps because it is quite expensive. It is good for cooking and eating. Serve it with a zesty Zinfandel or cider and fall apples.

Appenzeller has been made since the eleventh century by the monks of St. Gall in the Swiss Canton of Appenzell. While most Swiss-style cheeses are rubbed with salt or brine, Appenzeller is brushed with white wine and spices. This gives it a delicate but pronounced flavor, often used to spice up quiet fondues. It has a wrinkled brown rind like Gruyère but is moister. The eyes are pea sized. Wheels weigh between 15 and 18 pounds and are aged six to eight months.

Vacherin Fribourgeois

One of the most interesting Swiss cheeses is ***Vacherin Fribourgeois,** little known here but becoming more popular. It is the essential ingredient in Fondue au Vacherin, much stronger than the traditional fondue and a special way to end a hard day's skiing. Vacherin Fribourgeois has a semifirm texture with few holes. The flavor and aroma are pronounced. At its best during fondue season—late November through March—it is excellent to flavor casseroles of sausage and potato. Supple, room-temperature chunks are a fine ending to a meal with a robust Cabernet Sauvignon. It is definitely worth the splurge.

Raclette

Raclette, Switzerland's other national cheese dish, is gaining steady popularity on our shores. Unlike fondue, the cheese is softened, not melted. Half or quarter wheels are

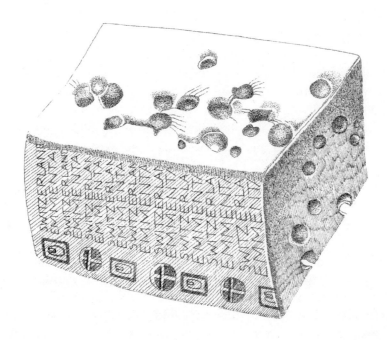

warmed in front of a fire, scraped away in long strips, and served with boiled potatoes, bündnerfleisch and cornichons. The cheese is called ***Bagnes** when made in the original valley and ***Raclette** when made in other parts of Switzerland. Richer than other Swiss-style cheeses, it has a semisoft texture and few small holes. It is mild when cold, getting more interesting when it warms. Although usually bought for raclette, it is excellent on its own with bread and red wine. Wheels are 12 to 18 pounds.

Le Brouère

The makers of **Le Brouère** are so pleased with their cheese, they carefully decorate the border with intaglio birds and trees. They're right to be proud of their creation. These firm 25-pound wheels, somewhere between Gruyère and Aged Gouda in taste, are often used in Alsatian fondues. Use some in a chef's salad with hard salami and olives or in a pumpernickel sandwich with ripe tomatoes, smoked ham and grainy mustard.

Blue Cheeses

Mold is unpredictable. It ruins most perfectly good food but can transform ordinary grapes and cheeses into fare for the gods. The effect of mold on cheese was discovered hundreds of years ago, probably when some white cheese was left in a cave with a piece of bread. The bread became moldy and imparted the mold to the cheese. The new cheese turned out far more interesting than the original so cheesemakers set about to repeat the accident in controlled circumstances. They began in damp caves and went on to inject the mold directly into the cheese. They haven't always succeeded, but the process has worked often enough to create a large family of mottled blue cheeses.

Threaded with veins of bluish-green mold, the cheeses may be creamy or firm, relatively mild or decidedly strong. It is the special flavor the mold imparts that unites these otherwise divergent cheeses. We often serve blues at the end of a meal with salad or bread or for dessert with pears or grapes and nuts. Many prefer to let blues star on their own. They can work well, however, in assortments of all but the strongest and most delicate cheeses. In the kitchen, a little blue can add zip to otherwise bland foods. Use some instead of Swiss in chef's salads with ham, tongue and turkey or with creamy avocados and beefsteak tomatoes. Mix some with cream and spread on daikon slices or stuff into cherry tomatoes. Crumble some into scrambled eggs and chives.

Finding wines that can stand up to blues can be very difficult. Full-bodied reds—Bordeaux and Cabernet Sauvignons—and light, fruity Beaujolais are often excellent. Some of the sharper blues do amazingly well with great sweet wines—Sauternes, Late-Harvest Rieslings, Trockenbeerenauslese. Stilton is best with vintage port.

Exactly where and when the first blues were made will never be known for sure. Roquefort, from southwest France, has the strongest claim for the longest history, said to be over two thousand years. The only well-known blue made exclusively from sheep's milk, Roquefort today ranks with Italian Gorgonzola and English Stilton as the finest blue cheeses in the world. Excellent blues, usually inspired by one of these three, are now made in almost all cheese-producing regions.

Most blues are aged in damp caves or in cavelike rooms for at least three months to allow the mold to develop. Many are pierced to help the mold spread. As the veins develop, they often resemble sprigs of curly parsley, a condition described as *persillé,* "parsleyed." Often more parsley green than blue, the mold develops from the center of the cheese to the outside edges. The molds used are *Penicillium glaucum* and *Penicillium roqueforti.* While related to the antibiotic penicillin, these have different properties. Those allergic to penicillin can often eat blue mold cheeses without getting allergic reactions. The surface of the cheeses, usually rubbed with salt, does not often develop a rind, but the edges become firmer than the center. Some are sprayed on the outside with another related, but different, mold that forms a white crust.

Because the mold creates paths in the interior, blue cheeses are never as smooth as semisoft and soft-ripened, more likely to crumble than slice neatly. The butterfat content is usually between 45 and 50 percent. Most forms are rounds, either flat wheels or tall cylinders, weighing 5 to 18 pounds.

With some exceptions, the quantity of blue cheese that may be brought into the country each year by an individual importer is dictated by United States government quotas. Importers bring in the most popular cheeses first, filling in with lesser-known varieties at the end of the year if they have space. November and December are the months to look for unusual blues. But if the popularity of blues continues unabated and the quota system is not revised, fewer and fewer importers will have space for the rarer cheeses.

Buying and Storing

If possible, taste any blue before you buy it. The cheese should be flavorful but never harsh on your throat. In peak condition, it will be creamy or firm, not dry and cracked. The aroma may be strong but not nasty. The amount and color of mold will vary; it should be spread relatively evenly through the cheese from center to edge.

Blues will keep a long time in the refrigerator wrapped tightly in foil. Since they have definite aromas, keep them away from delicate foods that might pick up their flavor. The texture won't change much at room temperature, but the flavor will be truer, more balanced. Use a thin sharp knife or a cheese wire to cut them.

If you have a whole, firm blue, cut off the top about ½ inch down to use as a lid.

Cut rounds as you need them and replace the original top. You can also cut wedges about three inches deep. Continue to cut wedges until the top is even again, repeating until the cheese is finished.

English Varieties

If Englishmen had to choose only one cheese to eat every day, most would select *Stilton without hesitation. The undisputed king of English cheeses, it is milder than Roquefort and Gorgonzola. Stilton has a delicate aroma and taste, ideal to serve with bread or toast and a vintage claret or port, too special for the kitchen. It is firm enough to cut into fairly even slices. The creamy white interior becomes yellow toward the edges. The veins, clear and blue-green, spread evenly through the cheese. The brownish outer rind is smooth. If it has cracks, it is either very old or was exposed to extreme cold.

Credit for Stilton's creation in the early eighteenth century is often given to Mrs. Paulet of Wymondham. Another story says that rather than make the first, or in fact any, Stilton, she helped popularize the cheeses made by her sister. Both versions agree that the cheese was sold to travelers who stopped at the Bell Inn in Stilton. Its fame soon spread to London and beyond.

Until World War I, Stilton was made in farmhouses, mostly in Leicestershire. Today most is made in commercial creameries in Leicestershire, Nottinghamshire and Derbyshire. The cheeses, still treated individually, are aged for at least three months. Farmhouse varieties, which are the finest, can be identified by the black labels that tell where they were made.

While all Stiltons are cylinders that sit on their short ends, they vary in size. The traditional 18-pound form is 8 inches high. The 5-pounders are popular holiday gifts. Ideally, they should be stored in a damp, cool cellar. For those of us without that luxury, the warmest part of the refrigerator works well. Either way, keep the cheese wrapped in foil. Should it get dry around the edges, wrap it in a cloth dipped in salt water.

The proper way to serve whole Stiltons has been debated for years. In the past, when Stilton was served in private clubs, restaurants and grand homes, diners dug into the center with a scoop. The resulting cavity was then often filled with port. Cheesemakers no longer recommend that method. Scooping increases the exposed cheese surface, much of which dries out. It is better to cut Stilton, like other firm round cheeses, into wedges and rounds. The saying is, "Cut high, cut low, cut level." Pouring port on the cheese enhances neither cheese nor port. A holiday meal, however, could have no grander ending than farmhouse Stilton served with vintage port and freshly cracked walnuts.

Seeming to have a mind of its own, ***Blue Cheshire** is one of the most unpredictable blue cheeses. It is the rare cheesemaker who can turn ordinary Cheshire into Blue Cheshire with anything close to regular success. None can do it every time. It retains the creamy texture of Cheshire, but the addition of the blue mold makes the flavor quite sharp. The blue veins stand out clearly against the orange-yellow ground and brown edges. Lacking the grace of Stilton, Blue Cheshire is an acquired taste, definitely not for the timid eater. Try it on crusty bread with a full-bodied Zinfandel or Burgundy. Whole wheels are cylinders shaped like Stilton.

French Varieties

Roquefort successfully combines the salty flavor of sheep's milk with the tang of blue molds to make one of the world's most memorable foods, undoubtedly the most famous ewe's milk cheese in the world. Firm and white, with a smooth, unblemished rind, it reveals a network of greenish-blue veins when cut. It will be salty in peak condition, but never nasty. Of all the cheese regulations, none are as strict as those for making Roquefort. According to a decree dating to Charles VI in 1411, the cheese must be made and aged for at least two months in the limestone caves of Cambalou in

south central France. Only sheep's milk from a designated area may be used. Most of France's sheep's milk goes to making Roquefort. Some Roquefort may be made in Corsica from Corsican sheep, but the cheeses must be aged in the Cambalou caves.

Since Roquefort is expensive, we use it at the table rather than in the kitchen. In France, it precedes dessert with bread and perhaps butter. The wine is often a full red from Burgundy or Bordeaux. Some serve it only with a golden Sauternes, believing its soul mate to be Château d'Yquem, an experience worth the splurge.

Whole forms, weighing 6 pounds, are 4 inches high. Some wheels are split into 2-inch high forms. Every wheel has a foil wrapping with a border of red sheep. Each manufacturer's sheep look a little different, but all are red and go completely around the edge of the cheese. The finest brand is **Le Papillon.** Nowadays, foil-wrapped wheels of Roquefort are sealed in cryovac for shipping overseas. Since this stops the cheese from breathing, the mold, while spreading through the cheese, does not always appear. It is not unusual to find a Roquefort that tastes like a blue but still looks white. To bring out the blue, leave the cheese completely unwrapped at room temperature for a few hours. After even an hour, the color should start to appear. It will also come out if the cheese is wrapped in foil and refrigerated. When fully ripened, the cheese will be greenish. Kept foil-wrapped in the refrigerator, Roquefort will be fine for many weeks. It will continue to get sharper and saltier.

Always seeking to please customers, French cheesemakers decided in 1950 to make whole blue cheeses weighing less than a pound. The light, supple cheese they created is **Bleu de Bresse,** made in the style of Gorgonzola. Creamy with light blue veins, it has a mild aroma and distinct but not sharp flavor. Whole 4- or 8-ounce cylinders are ideal for small groups at the end of a meal with a fruity Beaujolais or with pears poached in red wine and pepper. The small forms are fragile, however. Buy them only in December when turnover is high. When they are old, they get strong, smelly and brown. The larger forms, which go up to 4½ pounds, are usually better.

In the same family is **Pipo Crem',** a pale blue cheese lightly molded throughout. As creamy as Gorgonzola, it has a distinctive, but not overwhelming blue flavor. Serve it at the end of the meal with a light Côtes du Rhône. It is also a fine choice for cooking. Add some to creamy pasta sauces, sprinkle over potato casseroles, melt over hamburgers, crumble into chicken salads. Made in the French region of Bresse, Pipo Crem' comes in 6-pound cylinders. They are sometimes split into squat halves.

An oversized doughnut, **Belle Bressane** is a soft-ripened white-mold cheese injected with blue mold. Lovely and creamy, it has a mild blue flavor and gets spreadably soft. A 4-pound round, most often available toward the end of the year, is a good choice for a holiday buffet placed next to a bowl of walnuts or almonds. Serve it with a fruity Zinfandel. If overripe, it will be brown and smell of ammonia.

France's copy of Stilton, **Bleu de Gex** is made by small dairies near the Swiss border. These 14-pound wheels are excellent with lively Burgundies or vintage ports.

Bleu d'Auvergne is Roquefort made with cow's milk. Less salty, it is a firm, slightly oily cheese with a strong aroma and sharp taste. The blue veins are well distributed through the 5-pound wheels. Use it in creamy salad dressings and dips with celery and tomatoes.

Bleu des Causses is a pleasant, inexpensive blue that looks like Bleu d'Auvergne. Add it to salads or creamy pasta sauces.

Sharpest of all the French blues, **Fourme d'Ambert** is a firm cheese with a grayish rind. Serve it by itself after dinner with nuts and port. It comes in tall 3-pound cylinders.

Italian Varieties

Gorgonzola, Italy's oldest blue cheese, has been made in the Po Valley since at least the ninth century. Soft and creamy, it has decidedly green mold visible throughout the white cheese. There is a thin, brownish, edible rind. Stronger than Stilton, a young Gorgonzola is beautifully balanced, appealing to those who find Roquefort a little difficult to appreciate. It is a superb cheese to serve with juicy pears and cracked nuts in place of dessert. It shows fine Italian Barolos to advantage. Use it to flavor extraordinary dishes from fresh fettuccine to grainy polenta. Mixed with cream or Mascarpone, it can be spread on toast or celery, used as a filling for thin crêpes. Mixed with butter and shaped into rounds, it melts over hot steak or fish as a simple sauce.

As the cheese ages, the flavor of the mold becomes more pronounced. Try some before you buy to be sure it is to your liking. If it is too mild, leave it wrapped in foil in the refrigerator or at room temperature until it gets strong enough. It will ripen faster at room temperature. A full wheel of Gorgonzola is 13 pounds, wrapped in foil and parchment, then boxed. There are also half and quarter wheels. One of the best brands is *Colombo.

Dolcelatte, also called **Sweet Gorgonzola,** is meant to be eaten young and mild. Made exactly like Gorgonzola, Dolcelatte is aged only very slightly so it has less blue mold. The packaging is the same. If you were to let it ripen, Dolcelatte would get as strong as regular Gorgonzola. The beauty of the younger cheese, however, is in its delicate, sweet flavor. Serve it with crisp green beans and red peppers and a cool Beaujolais; stuff it into ripe pears or use it to make creamy soufflés. It can replace regular Gorgonzola in any recipe. The result will be more subtle.

American Varieties

American blues, while not as well-known as their European counterparts, are often excellent. One we particularly like is *Maytag Blue, a smooth white cheese from Iowa

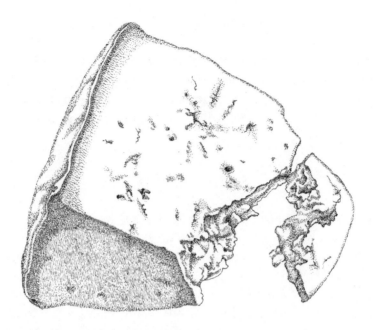

with a heavy lacing of mold and a distinctive, pleasant blue flavor. Aged in caves to develop the mold, it is well-balanced enough to include in an assortment with a creamy Brillat-Savarin and smooth Saint Paulin. Serve it by itself with a salad of Boston lettuce, watercress and arugula. One of our best native cheeses, Maytag Blue is an ideal selection for Thanksgiving with a well-made California Cabernet Sauvignon or Zinfandel. The 4-pound wheels are occasionally sold in retail stores, but are primarily available through the mail in whole forms or split crosswise into 2-pound cheeses. There are also 1-, 4- and 8-ounce wedges, but the wheels are better.

Made in the French style, Wisconsin's **Bresse Bleu** is creamy and mellow, much like Bleu de Bresse and Pipo Crem'. Add some to pasta sauces with Monterey Jack. The tall cylinders are about 3 pounds each.

The oldest commercially made American blue cheese is that of **Treasure Cave** in Minnesota. It is made with raw milk and aged in caves for three to four months. The cheese is mostly white with a lacing of blue veins, saltier than Maytag Blue. It is fine for salad dressings and dips made with cream or butter, seasoned with cayenne pepper. Treasure Cave comes in 5- to 6-pound foil-wrapped wheels as well as 4-ounce squares and wedges. The squares, dipped in wax, are wrapped in foil. The wedges, cut from a wheel, are wrapped in plastic. Most Treasure Cave is sold in supermarkets.

Oregon Blue is a creamy yellow cheese with a tart flavor, sharper than most in this family. It is made with buttermilk. Although less mold is evident than in many blues, the flavor is there. Most is sold on the West Coast. If you find some, try it melted over hamburgers, on sourdough bread and tomato sandwiches, chunked into chicken salads and blended into vegetable spreads. Wheels are 4 pounds.

Sallie Kendall in California has created a goat cheese laced with blue that is discussed in the Goat Cheese section.

Scandinavian Varieties

Danish Blue (also called **Danablu**), similar to its relatives **Finnish Blue** and **Swedish Blue,** is the generic blue cheese. White with a heavy lacing of blue veins, the cheeses are firm and crumbly. They lack the finesse of the great blues, but are reasonably priced cheeses that are excellent in salads, omelets, cheeseburgers and other dishes that call for a distinct blue flavor. Usually sold by the pound, they sometimes come in 4- to 8-ounce packages.

The Danes make several creamy blues in the style of Gorgonzola. Technically double creams, **Cremo, Mycella** and **Portella** have 60 percent butterfat. Like traditional blues, however, they are aged in caves to enhance the blue flavor. Creamy and spreadable, they have greenish-blue veins evenly spread throughout. They are excellent with bread at a cocktail party or at the end of the meal with a full-bodied Côtes-du-Rhône. Wheels are 4 to 7 pounds.

Saga, a Danish invention, is even richer than the double creams. Triple creams laced with blue mold, Saga and its many clones are not aged so the creamy texture is more distinctive than the blue flavor. They are discussed in the Double and Triple Cream section.

Hard and Grating Cheeses

Freshly grated aged cheeses from Italian Parmesan and aged Dutch Gouda to American Dry Jack have an intense, salty, often nutty flavor that can transform plates of simply buttered pasta, creamy risotto, chunky minestrone from the ordinary to the sublime, thickening and seasoning at the same time. Firm and crumbly, these hard cheeses blend into sauces, never getting stringy like some softer varieties. They are wonderful sprinkled on top of casseroles and run under the broiler to brown, stirred into soups, folded into omelets, tossed into tomato salads. Mixed with bread crumbs they make excellent coatings for chicken or fish.

Few Americans realize that many aged cheeses are even more extraordinary eaten out of hand in chunks or on a slice of bread brushed with olive oil. A squat, rounded knife is perfect for chipping pieces from a wheel. If the cheese is soft enough, use a plane to make paper-thin slices. Serve a large piece alone or as part of an assortment with Selles-Sur-Cher, Coulommiers and Oka. Aged cheeses make fine endings to meals served with bowls of grapes or olives and a robust red wine from the Piedmont.

Made like semisoft cheeses, the hard cheeses don't develop their full flavor until they have aged a year or more. At the same time they become firmer and drier, usually crumbling when sliced. A few are good in both their soft and hard states, but they usually are not interesting when young. Because most of the moisture evaporates during the aging, the flavor is more intense, like that of reduced stocks and sauces. The decreased liquid makes the cheeses hardy enough to last for years. Some go on for decades, developing more character with time. Just a little grated cheese can make the difference in a dish, bringing together diverse flavors in meaty tomato sauces, potato-sausage casseroles, beefy stews.

Most are made from cow's milk, but there are excellent dry sheep's milk cheeses as well as some goat's milk. The butterfat content ranges from 30 to 40 percent.

Buying and Storing

As with other cheeses, what you buy depends on what you want to use it for. Like aged beef, fine aged cheese can be very expensive. A little, however, goes a long way so the extra cost may be slight. If using the cheese only for cooking, a medium-priced cheese is probably more appropriate than the very best. Always taste it before using and adjust the amount needed according to its strength. If you serve the cheese as part of an assortment, get the best.

Since forms tend to be very large, the cheeses are sold in ragged chunks. The texture should be even, firm and crumbly, never rock hard. You should be able to break off pieces with a firm knife. The color ranges from white to golden. The cheese may be salty, but it should never be bitter.

Even if you use hard cheeses for cooking, try to buy chunks rather than grated packages. The flavor fades quickly once it is cut up. It is also impossible to be sure of what you are getting. Shops sometimes mix two or more cheeses together. It is easy to grate cheese at home in a food processor or with a hand grater. If serving the cheese at the table, it is nice to give your guests a large chunk and a hand grater. They can add as much as they want and you won't have leftover grated cheese.

If the cheese is very dry and your kitchen is cool, leave it at room temperature wrapped in foil. If the air is dry, wrap it in a wet cloth to replace some of the moisture. Bury softer cheeses, wrapped in foil, in the vegetable compartment of the refrigerator. They will be protected there from the extreme cold. These aged cheeses will last for months, aging and getting stronger. Should they mold, scrape away the moldy part and use the rest. Although the texture won't really change, the flavor will be truer at room temperature.

Italian Varieties

Parmigiano-Reggiano

If you've never tasted ***Parmigiano-Reggiano,** true Italian Parmesan, you've missed one of the great cheeses in the world. Cut a thin slice and eat it slowly, savoring its slightly sweet, nutty taste. Feel the grainy texture as it dissolves in your mouth. As Americans, we're just starting to learn what Italians have known for hundreds of years: Parmigiano-Reggiano, the king of Parma, is as extraordinary as the finest Brie, a rival to farmhouse Stilton. Even the chauvinistic French use it often in cooking, having never succeeded in making anything quite like it.

Among the most expensive cheeses, it has an even pale to deep yellow interior that flakes when cut. Each wheel is made under strict controls dictating the origin of the milk and the production of the cheese. The seventeen hundred member dairies each make only four to six cheeses a day and only from April 1 to November 11 when the cows can feed on fresh grass. All the wheels are identifiable by thin brownish rind evenly stamped all around in red with the words PARMIGIANO-REGGIANO.

Grating it only for memorable dishes, Italians prefer to make salads of thin Parmesan slices and crunchy celery or to serve it with ripe pears and sweet grapes. Of course, homemade tender tortellini may be filled with spinach and freshly grated Parmesan, and pasta primavera made with the first tiny vegetables of spring is always given a delicate sprinkling.

The wheels, flat on top and convex on the sides, usually weigh between 80 and 85 pounds. After they are aged a year, they are marked with an oval stamp of authenticity and the date of production. Those cheeses aged from eighteen months to two years are called *vecchio,* aged. Those from two to three years are called *stravecchio.* Rarely does a form arrive here that hasn't been aged at least two years.

Other Granas

Although Parmigiano-Reggiano stands by itself, the Italians make other fine grating cheeses. Called **Granas** because they have grainy textures, they are straw-colored and savory. **Grana Padano,** made in the Po Valley, is the best. Most Granas are aged for a year and are usually moister than Parmesan. The unmarked wheels are slightly smaller than those of Parmigiano-Reggiano. Discerning palates prefer the spring cheese, Maggengo, over the winter Vernengo. While Granas may be served after dinner with fruit or as part of an antipasto with bread, most are used in the kitchen. Soak it in cream, strain, and use the liquid to make custardy, nutty-sweet ice cream. Sprinkle it over baked zucchini, caramelized onion soup, turkey tetrazzini, ravioli stuffed with prosciutto and olives.

An exciting new Grana to come on the market is **Reggenello Parmesan.** Made by a manufacturer of Parmigiano-Reggiano and with the same care, these 25-pound "midget" wheels are aged only twelve to fifteen months. At about half the price of Parmigiano-Reggiano, this is a superb substitute in cooking.

Romano and Other Sheep's Milk Cheeses

What Parmesan is to northern Italian cooking, **Romano** is to the South, where sheep are more abundant than cows and many cheeses are *pecorino* (sheep's milk). Young Romano is salty and white, eaten alone or with fruit. The aged cheese, grated, is added to hearty tomato-macaroni casseroles, mixed with potatoes to make crisp dumplings and with mushrooms to stuff chicken. Robust sauces may benefit more from the saltiness of Romano than the subtlety of Parmesan. Because of its sharp taste,

Romano is often blended with Grana. Most aged Romano, called **Grating Romano,** **Grating Pecorino** and **Pecorino Romano,** is sold in the United States. Few southern Italians can afford it, and northerners prefer Grana. Their loss is our gain. Romano is a marvelous cheese.

Should the word *genuino* be on the cheese or its tag, it means the cheese comes from Rome, once home to herds of sheep. Today most Romano comes from Sardinia. It is produced there from May until August when sheep's milk is most plentiful. Aged for eight to twelve months, whole wheels weigh 40 to 60 pounds. The thin brown covering may be waxy or natural. **Locatelli,** the best imported brand, is a little more expensive, but worth it.

Ricotta Salata, bearing little resemblance to the better-known fresh Ricotta, is a flavorful, crumbly sheep's milk round from southern Italy. As the name indicates, the 5-pound, snowy rounds are quite salty. Serve the young cheese in chunks with cut-up peaches and plums. Grate the aged to sprinkle over blanched broccoli heads, into white bean and lamb stew. Ricotta Romano, a similar cheese, is discussed in the Sheep's Milk section.

Unique in this group, **Pepato** is a pale yellow cheese flavored with black pepper-corns. The spicy flavor works well with the saltiness of the sheep's milk. Grate some over shirred eggs on a bed of creamed mushrooms for a bit of zip. It is made in Sicily and southern Italy and comes in 35-pound foil-wrapped rounds.

Other Hard Italian Cheeses

Montasio is a cow's milk cheese that gets sharp, dry and crumbly when aged from twelve to fifteen months. When aged six to nine months, it is still a young, smooth cheese to serve at the table.

Asiago, originally a sheep's milk cheese, is now made from cow's milk. Called a poor man's Parmesan, this straw-colored cheese is solid with small, uneven holes throughout. Use it to flavor pastas and salads. Although some imported Asiago does reach our shores, most of what we see is **American Asiago,** made in Wisconsin. Not as well made as the Italian, the aged is a satisfactory, inexpensive substitute for Grana. Younger cheeses are often bitter. Young, imported Asiago can be a pleasant cheese, slightly salty and granular. American Asiago comes in 12-pound half wheels coated in black wax. Imported wheels run from 20 to 22 pounds.

American Varieties

During World War II, when trade with Italy was cut off, cheesemakers in California aged some Monterey Jack as a substitute for Parmesan. The resulting **Dry Monterey Jack,** also called **Dry Jack,** was a finer cheese than they'd expected, an interesting substitute for Parmigiano-Reggiano. It has a similar sweet, nutty flavor. Add it to hominy grits for a side dish with roast chicken. Stir it into some Texas pecan-flavored rice made with chicken stock. Use it over tender pasta tossed with California artichokes. Aged for about nine months, the 8-pound wheels are coated with cocoa, ground pepper and vegetable oil to seal and keep them from molding.

Other domestic grating cheeses are not in the same league. Aged up to ten months, **Domestic Parmesan** is pale in color and taste. To make matters worse, it is most often sold grated in jars and cardboard containers, dissipating what little flavor had been there. **Fontinella,** somewhat like a dry Fontina, is a whitish cheese with a crumbly texture and mild taste.

Swiss Varieties

When a child is born in the Swiss canton of Berne, a 40- to 60-pound **Saanen** is made and dedicated. A piece is served at each birthday and special day; the wheel is finished after the funeral. Saanen has a rich, nutty flavor like a sharp Gruyère. Usually aged up to a year, it adds extra flavor to fondues. Cut it into very thin slices.

Somewhere betweeen Parmesan and Aged Gouda in flavor, **Alpkäse,** also called **Mountain Cheese,** is pale yellow with a dry texture. It is cured up to a year in the Swiss Alps. Grate some over boiled potatoes and bündnerfleisch.

Tête de Moine, literally "monk's head," is an aromatic cheese with a strong taste. It in no way resembles anyone's head; each cheese is shaped like a tall cylinder, 5 inches high, 4 inches across. Made of cow's milk, it is best in the fall and spring. Serve it after dinner with a spicy Zinfandel.

In the Swiss Alps, outside Emmental, they make **Hoberfeld,** a nutty cheese somewhere between Aged Gouda and Parmigiano in taste. We first had it in Switzerland served in paper-thin slices on peasant bread with a local wine and were delighted with the flavor. Grate some over spinach pasta with fresh shiitake, add it to zucchini and pasta laced with heavy cream. Whole 70-pound wheels, aged two to three years, are sold here in 8-pound pieces. The brown rind, resembling that of Gruyère, is drier.

While most hard cheeses can be eaten sliced, **Sap Sago** must be shredded or grated to be in any way palatable. Having no fat in it at all, it is a dieter's dream. Sprinkle it on soups or pastas, add it to salads. It is best mixed with some butter or cream, of course, but that defeats the purpose. Flavored with herbs or cloves, each 3-ounce cone-shaped piece is wrapped in foil.

Argentine Varieties

Argentina makes two grating cheeses: **Argentine Regginato** and **Sardo.** Both are inexpensive and salty, strictly grating cheeses. A few crafty merchants sell it as "imported Parmesan," leading customers to think they are getting Italian cheese at a low price. Don't be fooled. It is inexpensive, but it's no bargain.

Some Other Kinds of Cheeses

Low-Fat, Low-Salt Cheeses

As a nation, we have become obsessed with worrying about the fat in our foods. As a result, many people swear off all but Cottage Cheese believing all cheese is incredibly fattening. They get particularly confused when they read labels that speak of butterfat contents, or *matières grasses*. The butterfat content is a scientific calculation that tells us what percentage of the cheese solids are fat. The moisture, which has virtually no fat, is not included. Say a cheese has a moisture content of 40 percent and a fat content of 50 percent. The solids amount to 60 percent of the cheese and the fat is 50 percent of that, or 30 percent of the whole cheese. The older and drier the cheese, the less moisture. Therefore, those cheeses will have more fat per ounce. Few people can eat much of these cheeses, however, precisely because they are so rich.

Dieters are always looking for low-fat cheeses and one of the most popular is **St. Otho** from Switzerland with only about 4 percent fat. It is pale white and comes in 4-pound rounds about 8 inches wide and 2 inches high. It doesn't last as long as most cheeses, and when old it gets bitter.

New Holland is known more for its low-salt and low-fat content than for its taste, which is so mild as to be virtually nonexistent. The manufacturers realized this so they flavored it with jalapeño peppers, herbs and garlic, and caraway. It comes in 5-pound rectangular loaves 8 inches long and 4 inches high. They maintain an ounce has only 90 calories and less than 1 percent salt. The white cheese is coated in yellow wax and cellophane.

Gold-N-Lite cheeses are made like Monterey Jack but with reduced salt and fat. These 12-pound wheels come flavored with hot jalapeño peppers and with garlic and chives.

Premonde is another cheese reduced in both fat and salt. Resembling Monterey Jack when young and Cheddar when aged, Premonde comes plain, smoked, and flavored with dill or basil.

Finnish **Lappi,** similar to Monterey Jack and Mozzarella, is another bland cheese, low in salt and fat. It comes in 6-pound loaves wrapped in cryovac.

Also low in fat, salt and cholesterol is **Garden Vegetable,** made in Illinois, sort of a Monterey Jack with vegetables (carrots, tomatoes, onions, cabbage, etc.) mixed in. It comes in cryovac-wrapped loaves and has little to recommend it except its dietetic appeal.

Swiss Light claims to have 25 percent fewer calories per ounce than true Swiss cheese. It has only a fraction of the flavor, of course, but it does have the familiar eye formation and will appeal to those more concerned with calories than taste.

Since there is sodium in milk, all cheese must have some sodium. Certain cheeses, however, are now made without any additional salt, among them Mozzarella and Farmer Cheese, Dutch Gouda, American Munster and Cheddar. These no-salt-added cheeses are always marked on the label. Among the aged cheeses, the sodium level will always be higher because it gets more concentrated as the cheese loses moisture.

Among the low-sodium cheeses are American **Swiss Criss, Swiss Lorraine** and **Baby Swiss,** expensive cheeses made in the Swiss style, with eyes. Swiss Criss is the best of the bunch. These rindless cheeses come in cryovac-wrapped blocks.

Kosher Cheeses

Most cheeses are made with rennet, which comes from the lining of a cow's stomach. Since Jewish dietary laws prohibit the mixing of milk and meat, many Jews consider all cheeses made with rennet to be nonkosher. For similar reasons, certain vegetarians have eschewed these cheeses. For years, they limited their cheese consumption to fresh cheeses made without rennet. Now there are cheeses made with synthetic enzymes that are kosher and strictly vegetarian. Besides those made in Israel, like Israeli Swiss, there are a number of cheeses from California that are made under strict rabbinical supervision. These include a Monterey Jack and Pepper Jack. The California Chèvre line is made with synthetic enzymes but not under rabbinical supervision. There also are kosher Swiss, Munster, Edam and Goudas. Many manufacturers make kosher Cottage Cheese, Farmer Cheese, Pot Cheese, Cream Cheese, etc.

Entertaining With Cheese

We approach any occasion with an admitted bias, serving cheese whenever we have friends over, whether for a casual drink in the afternoon or a formal dinner. We have it at picnics and midnight suppers, winter brunches and summer barbecues. Sometimes it is the focus; more often it is a quiet but essential part of the occasion. Exactly what we serve depends on the size of the crowd, the time of day, and what other food we're having.

As to amounts and varieties, there are no hard and fast rules but there are guidelines. The rule of thumb is to figure three to four ounces of cheese a person if you presume your guests will be hungry, as they will be at five or six in the evening. This assumes that you are serving only cheese, fruit and bread or crackers. If you are serving platters of hors d'oeuvre, pâtés, salads and other food, plan on only two ounces of cheese a person. If your party is in the early afternoon or late in the evening, when your guests have probably had a meal, two ounces will be plenty. At a dinner party, the two-ounce rule holds as well. If you aren't sure how many people there will be, estimate as best you can and have extra bread and crackers (much cheaper than cheese) so no one need go hungry.

When choosing the specific cheeses, vary them in terms of taste, texture and appearance. You might, for example, select a soft-ripened cheese, a double or triple cream, a semisoft, a Swiss, a Cheddar or other aged cheese and a blue. If the group is large, you might want two cheeses from one or more categories, providing they are not too similar. One herb-flavored cheese would be fine but two would be repetitious. A goat cheese is excellent with many groups, especially Pyramides or others with interesting shapes, although we recommend them only if your guests are drinking wine, not hard liquor.

Cheese for a Hundred

Following these guidelines, for a crowd of one hundred you will need twenty-five pounds of cheese without food, twelve or thirteen pounds with. Divide it among five to seven cheeses for the larger amount, four or five for the smaller, usually whole or half wheels or large quarters. Pieces of cheese that weigh only a pound get lost for a crowd. For the twenty-five pounds, you might include a large soft-ripened Brie, either plain or flavored with herbs; one or two double and triple creams (whole St. André, Saga or Bonchampi); a semisoft Port-Salut or a three-pound wedge of Fontina. For a firmer cheese, you could have an aged Gouda or Canadian Cheddar. In the Swiss family, serve a large wedge of Gruyère or a quarter Holland Swiss. Among the chèvres, a Bucheron would be an excellent choice.

For twelve to thirteen pounds, look for pieces from two to three pounds such as a one-kilo Brie, a wheel of Crèma Dania, a half of Huntsman with its orange and blue layers, and a half of Doux de Montagne or another Fromage des Pyrénées.

Cheese for Twenty-five, Twelve or Six

Should your entertaining be a little more intimate, consider a group of twenty-five for drinks with food or at a sit-down dinner where the cheese is served as a course by itself or as dessert. Three pounds of cheese will be plenty, preferably in three one-pound pieces. A whole Explorateur would be an excellent choice along with half a Domen and part of washed Wynendale or Vacherin Mont d'Or. If it is a sit-down dinner, divide each cheese into equal pieces so there is one for each table. For a buffet, leave them whole.

At a dinner for twelve, serve two or three cheeses to weigh a total of a pound and a half to two pounds. Look for interesting choices, perhaps a Gratte Paille along with an oval Brin d'Amour and a piece of Stilton or Maytag Blue or a chunk of Parmigiano-Reggiano. For six, choose two half-pound cheeses or one weighing a pound, perhaps Reblochon, Caprice des Dieux or Montrachet.

At an informal supper, you might serve the cheese along with the main course to complement a hearty soup, salad or an omelet. In the winter, serve a flavorful Pont l'Evêque, Swiss Emmentaler or Parmigiano-Reggiano to eat in chunks or grate over the soup.

If you prefer, forgo a main dish entirely and serve an assortment of breads and cheeses as a meal in itself with or without fruit. Include a soft-ripened Camembert, a buttery Morbier and an English Cheshire. Have plenty of robust red wine or beer on hand.

Cheese with Salad

With a salad of mixed greens and a light vinaigrette, serve one or two cheeses with bread. Among the soft-ripened, Coulommiers or Chaource are excellent. Any of the big blues—Gorgonzola, Stilton or Roquefort—are good as are the rich double and triple creams—Brillat-Savarin and Boursault. Bucheron or a Brie chèvre complement the salad as does Taleggio.

Picnics

Picnics can range from sandwiches and beer on the beach to elaborate affairs with chilled Champagne and smoked turkey. The cheeses you choose will obviously reflect the setting. If everyone will be making impromptu sandwiches with assorted hams, pâtés and salamis, have semisoft and firm cheeses, ready to slice. Among the mild cheeses to serve are Monterey Jack, Bel Paese, Fropain de Mages. Include at least one more flavorful cheese: Swiss Gruyère, Bagnes, Appenzeller, Aged Gouda, Vermont Cheddar. With roasted peppers and tapenade, have some Crottins, chunks of Feta and a freshly made Mozzarella. Figure two to three ounces a person.

Cheese Tastings

Cheese tastings can be entertaining and informative. When you want to taste and compare the cheeses seriously, serve plain bread or crackers along with some apples, grapes or other fruit. Have pitchers of water as well as a good, but not great wine. If the cheeses are washed, you might serve cold beer. Five or six cheeses are enough to give variety without being confusing, although you can certainly serve more. Because everyone will want to taste everything at least once, estimate an ounce of each cheese for each guest.

The cheeses can be compared in different ways. Consider first tasting a variety of goat cheeses from young chèvre to an aged Dolmen. Have a Pyramide and log to see if the shape affects the taste. Include one rubbed with ash. Avoid the herb-flavored cheeses because they hide the goat flavor. Have an Italian caprini and one of Laura

Chenel's Chabis. When the tasting is done and cheese is left, bring out a platter of lush red tomatoes and fresh basil to make a salad dressed in olive oil.

For an indulgent group, serve triple creams, including buttery Mascarpone, Saga blue, mushroom-flecked Bonchampi, Explorateur and Corolle. Serve a young Cabernet Sauvignon or Beaujolais along with bread and berries or other juicy fruit in season. Since these cheeses are so rich, plan on some other food if it is to be a long evening.

The variation among blues is quickly apparent when you serve Roquefort, Stilton and Gorgonzola at the same time. Compare them with each other and with Maytag Blue, Bleu de Bresse and Blue Cheshire. You might also include a triple cream blue like Lymeswold. Have some apples or pears ready. If you want to carry the experimenting further, have different wines: a full-bodied Bordeaux, a Sauternes, a Chablis, as well as some aged port. The subtleties of flavor among the cheeses will change with the drink.

Washed cheeses are another fascinating group. The range of flavors will be quickly apparent at a tasting that includes Pont l'Evêque, Epoisses, Chaumes, Liederkranz and St. Nectaire. Serve a rustic, grainy loaf and full red wines, perhaps some beer as well.

For a more varied evening, serve pairs of cheeses that seem similar but are actually quite different, such as Swiss Emmentaler and Jarlsberg, Italian and Danish Fontinas, French and Danish Port-Saluts, New York, Canadian and English Cheddars, California and French chèvre.

Another possibility is to serve an assortment of unusual cheeses that most people have probably never tasted. If they are available, include Vacherin Mont d'Or, l'Ami Chambertin, Blue Cheshire, Gratte Paille, Vacherin Fribourgeois, Belle Bressane. Try to find any local cheeses you can. Organize them roughly from the milder to stronger, beginning with Gratte Paille or a fresh chèvre and ending with Blue Cheshire.

Presentation

The most important rule in serving cheese, the one we can't overemphasize, is to have the cheeses at room temperature; cold cheese is never as good. Place the cheeses on separate boards or plates that your guests can easily reach. Have a separate knife or other cutter for each cheese. Do not cut the cheese ahead of time; all those little pieces will just get dried out. If you have a whole wheel of Brie or St. André, however, and are concerned that no one will make the first cut, do cut out a small piece. In the same way, cut into a round of Cheddar or Stilton. Depending on the arrangement of the room and people, you might want to halve each cheese and have the same varieties in two places. Where possible, wheels and rounds of cheese should be cut into wedges for eating. Semisoft wedges can then be sliced with a knife or plane. Crumbly Cheddars and hard Parmesans won't work neatly that way but can be divided into large wedges fairly evenly. Soft chèvres and other fresh cheeses are meant to be spread, but firmer logs can be cut into crosswise rounds. In the same way, a square Livarot should be cut into strips.

Although some cheeses can be eaten in chunks out of the hand, most people like their cheese on bread or crackers. Either way, serve relatively bland bread and crackers that will not interfere with the taste of the cheese. Fruits and nuts are excellent companions to many cheeses. Serve them near the bread.

Cheese Tools

Most cheese is fine served with an ordinary knife, but there are tools especially designed for cheese and there are times when they are useful. Most common are probably the cheese planes, usually made of stainless steel with wood or porcelain handles. The plane is used on semisoft or firmer cheeses to give thin, even slices. In the kitchen, it is handy when making sandwiches. Most guests are more comfortable with it than with a sharp knife and you can use it with a good plate without worrying about knife marks.

The wire cutter, sometimes adjustable so you can make slices of varying thickness, can be used in the same way, although maneuvering it is a little more tricky. Professional wires are at least a foot long with wooden handles, meant to be held taut when cutting through a whole wheel of Swiss-style or other firm cheese.

There are various graters on the market from the four-sided tool that stands in the bowl to the hand-held rotary, fine for small quantities of Parmesan or other hard cheese. The four-sided grater will shred Mozzarella for topping pizza rather quickly but other jobs can be tedious. You also have to watch out for skinned knuckles as you get toward the end of the chunk. Drum graters catch everything neatly in their storing containers. They have fine holes designed for Granas and other aged cheeses. A food processor is our favorite grater for large quantities. We put chunks of cheese in the work bowl and process them with the metal blade. The result is technically chopped rather than grated, but it is fine for soufflés, dips and toppings.

There are small, triangular knives designed to remove chunks from aged wheels and double-handled knives to split wheels of Cheddar.

Storing Cheese

Many customers worry that cheese is fragile and will go bad quickly. In fact, cheese is a fairly hardy food. It was invented in Biblical times as a way to preserve milk, and if it managed to survive without refrigeration, it seems only logical that it will keep well in our modern kitchens.

Wrap the cheeses in foil or plastic to keep them from drying out. Refrigerate until several hours before you want to serve them. If you are cooking with the cheese, just keep it refrigerated. Soft cheeses have more moisture in them than hard cheeses and are, therefore, more readily subject to mold. The molds on natural cheeses, while not appealing, are not harmful. Since it takes a long time for the mold to penetrate the whole cheese, especially hard cheeses, usually only a small portion is affected. Cut off the moldy part and eat the rest. Mold usually forms from moisture around the cheese. Therefore, a cheese wrapped in foil is less likely to mold than one wrapped in plastic, since the foil allows the moisture to escape and lets the cheese breathe. If you do wrap the cheese in plastic, change the wrapping every day or so. Very moist, fresh cheeses may spoil quickly so buy only enough for a day or two at a time.

Whole cheeses coated in wax are protected from the air and will continue to breathe and age. They do not need any additional coating. As these cheeses, either whole or cut, age, they lose moisture, getting firmer in texture and usually stronger in flavor. In the shop, we often age cheeses for weeks or months before we sell them. Whole Goudas or Cheddars, among others, can be wonderfully transformed with age.

Since firm Cheddars and hard cheeses are fine if refrigerated for weeks, there is no reason to freeze them. There are, however, occasions when you have a large portion of a soft-ripened cheese that you know you won't use quickly. In that case, cut the fully ripened cheese into pieces convenient for one serving and wrap each well in foil. Freezing keeps the cheese from aging further, so if it is not ripe when you freeze it, it will never get there. A full day or two before you want to serve the cheese, remove it to the refrigerator to defrost, bringing it to room temperature early in the day. Do not refreeze leftovers.

The Recipes

Cooking with Cheese

Cooks have been using cheese for centuries, seasoning soups and pastas with it, stuffing pastries and vegetables, mixing it into salads, stirring it into sauces, tossing it into omelets. The recipes that follow show ways you can use cheese. In some recipes, one or more cheeses are the major flavoring; in others, the cheese adds to the overall taste, balancing with other ingredients.

In general, using cheese in the kitchen is not difficult. Remember, however, that it reacts fairly quickly to heat. Therefore, it is best to use relatively low heat for slow cooking. High heat usually works fine with very short exposure. When you want the cheese to melt completely, chop, grate or shred it first. For spreads or dips, it may need to be puréed.

There are various ways to prepare cheese for cooking. A knife and cutting board generally allow the most control. When you want a firm cheese chopped very fine, or even grated, a food processor works well. Rather than use the grating and shredding disks, roughly chop it and place in the work bowl fitted with the metal blade. Unless you want a true purée, run the machine with pulses, scraping down the sides from time to time. To keep semisoft cheeses firm enough to chop neatly, keep refrigerated until you need them.

If you want to shred soft cheeses like Mozzarella, and not risk puréeing them, use moderate pressure on a hand grater with fairly large holes. To finely grate a hard cheese, such as Parmesan, use the processor for large quantities, a rotary hand grater for small amounts. If the cheese is being grated to top a dish at the table, consider bringing the small grater in with the dish and letting guests grate their own.

As a rule of thumb, 1 ounce of grated or chopped semisoft or firm cheese is about ¼ cup. Therefore, ¼ pound cheese measures about 1 cup and a pound of cheese is about 4 cups. Fresh cheeses with a lot of moisture, such as Cottage Cheese or Ricotta, are closer to ½ pound a cup.

When you want to spread cheese into a bread or other batter, add the cubes or grated cheese in batches so it doesn't clump together.

The recipes that follow give you an idea of how versatile cheese can be. Some are for dishes as classic as Welsh rarebit or macaroni and cheese. Others are newer, especially those using goat cheese, which was virtually unheard of a few decades ago. Now we use chèvres in pastas and pizzas, pancakes and salad dressings. Some of the dishes mentioned in the cheese section are given here in detail. Others are offered as suggestions to inspire you to try your hand at new ways to use cheese.

We divided the recipes into general categories, grouping the basic recipes, like doughs and sauces, at the end. You will probably notice that most of the dishes in the book are vegetarian. Like an increasing number of Americans, we find that when cheese provides the protein, meat or seafood is not necessary. We often, however, have meat as part of the same meal.

Beginnings

Cheese lends itself well to an array of simple dips and spreads, as well as to more complex baked and fried dishes. The recipes in this section might be served with wine or cocktails as a snack or before a meal. Some are true first courses, meant to be eaten at the table. Others are finger food, delicious for nibbling.

We find that cheese makes such interesting and satisfying beginnings that the rest of the meal may be simpler: poached fish with an herb sauce, roasted lemon chicken, lots of quickly cooked vegetables. We may serve another very different cheese too with the salad or for dessert.

Chile con Queso

Chilies with Cheese

This Tex-Mex dip has its origins in authentic Mexican cooking, where it is often made with Queso Fresco, fresh white cheese. North of the border, however, most people use Cheddar. Leftover dip can be cooled and used to fill enchiladas or spread on flat tortillas and reheated.

1 tablespoon vegetable oil
2 garlic cloves, minced
1 medium onion, cut into ¼-inch dice
¼ pound fresh tomato, cut into ¼-inch dice
1 can (3 ounces) roasted chilies, cut into ¼-inch squares
½ pound mild Cheddar, cubed
Red pepper sauce to taste
Tortilla chips

Heat the oil in a saucepan and add the garlic and onion. Cook, stirring often, until they are soft but not brown. Add the tomato and chilies and stir to mix, then add the cheese. Turn the heat low and cook, stirring constantly, until the cheese has completely melted. Add pepper sauce to taste. Serve hot with tortilla chips.

Makes about 1½ cups.

Shelburne Farms Cheddar Cheese Spread

The people at Shelburne Farms created this excellent spread. Serve it on crackers or apples with the wine you use in it, or with hard cider. It also makes a thoughtful house gift.

1½ pounds Cheddar, chopped
¼ pound unsalted butter, at room temperature
⅔ cup sour cream
½ teaspoon Dijon mustard
½ teaspoon ground mace
½ cup dry white wine
Salt
Freshly ground pepper

Place the cheese in the work bowl of a food processor and run until smooth. Add the butter, sour cream, mustard and mace. Run until smooth. With the machine running, gradually pour in the wine. Add salt and pepper to taste and blend well.

Serve immediately while spreadable or refrigerate for later use. Let soften each time. If you want to keep it for more than a few days or give it as gifts, spoon into crocks and seal the tops with a layer of clarified butter.

Makes 4½ cups.

Sesame-Cheddar Rounds

These are easy and delicious, good with drinks. You can make up a batch, shape it into rolls and keep it in the refrigerator for weeks.

¼ **pound sharp Cheddar (use orange for the color), broken into small pieces**
4 **tablespoons unsalted butter, at room temperature, cut into pieces**
½ **cup all-purpose flour**
¼ **teaspoon kosher salt**
¹⁄₁₆ **teaspoon cayenne pepper**
½ **cup sesame seeds**

Place the cheese in the work bowl of a food processor and process until chopped well. Add the butter and process until well mixed and smooth. Add the flour, salt and cayenne and process just until blended. The dough will be soft.

Lightly flour your hands and remove the dough to the work surface. Divide it in half and roll each half into a smooth cylinder about 1 inch in diameter and 5 inches long. Wrap it in wax paper and chill for several hours or freeze.

Heat the oven to 400°F.

Place the sesame seeds in a flat bowl or plate. With a sharp knife, cut each cylinder into even rounds ³⁄₁₆ inch thick. Dip one side into the sesame seeds to coat, then place on an ungreased baking sheet, sesame side up, leaving about ½ inch space between the rounds.

Bake for 8 to 10 minutes in the preheated oven. The rounds should be just beginning to brown at the edges. Let cool on a rack until firm. If not using immediately, store in a sealed container.

Makes about 60 rounds.

Blue Cheese Dip

This is delicious with spears of celery and zucchini, carrots and fennel. If you have any left, spread it on a hamburger.

⅓ cup crumbled **Danish Blue**
6 ounces **Cream Cheese**
2 tablespoons minced onion
2 rounded tablespoons mayonnaise
¼ cup sour cream
½ teaspoon prepared horseradish
1 tablespoon chopped parsley
Dash Worcestershire sauce
Dash cayenne pepper

Mix everything together until smooth. Refrigerate for an hour or two before serving.

Makes a generous cup.

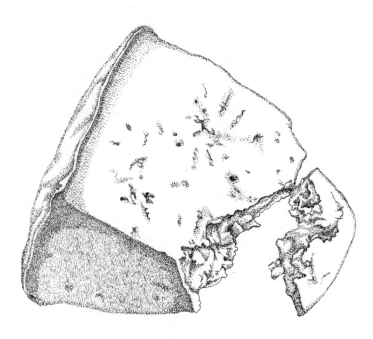

Jacques Pépin's Fromage Blanc à la Crème

Fresh Cheese with Cream

In France, diners are often offered servings of creamy white *fromage blanc* topped with the yellowy, slightly tart *crème fraîche* as part of the cheese course. We sprinkle on some sugar and eat it slowly, relishing every bite. No other dessert is necessary, although a few fresh berries in season are lovely.

Unfortunately, finding true fromage blanc and crème fraîche in the United States can be difficult and expensive, so Jacques Pépin, teacher and chef *extraordinaire,* has come up with a wonderful substitute, inexpensive and easy to make. He serves it with a savory seasoning of herbs and garlic, which is excellent before dinner or as a snack. At the end of the meal, try it with sugar instead of the herbs.

½ pound Cottage Cheese
3 ounces Cream Cheese
Salt
1¼ cups heavy cream
½ cup sour cream
Small bunch chives or 2 scallions, minced
2 garlic cloves, minced
1 bunch parsley, minced
Freshly ground white pepper

Have ready a 16-inch square of cheesecloth. If it has a fairly tight weave, use a single thickness. If it is loosely woven, double it. If in doubt, use a single thickness or the cheese may not drain.

Put the Cottage Cheese, Cream Cheese and ½ teaspoon salt in the work bowl of a food processor and run for 45 to 60 seconds, until smooth. Remove to a mixing bowl. If you don't have a food processor, push the cheeses through a fine sieve and stir in the salt.

In a separate bowl, whip ¾ cup of the heavy cream until it holds firm peaks. With a wire whisk, beat the cream into the cheese mixture just until smooth.

Spoon the mixture onto the cheesecloth. Bring the corners together and tie them with a string to make a bag. Tie the string around a wooden spoon or chopstick and suspend the bag over a bowl so the bag does not touch the bottom. Refrigerate overnight to let the mixture drain. It will get firmer.

When you are ready to serve, untie the bag and turn the cheese onto a serving plate. Discard the cheesecloth.

Mix together the remaining ½ cup heavy cream and the sour cream. In a separate bowl, mix together the chives, garlic and parsley. Pour the cream mixture over the cheese and sprinkle the herbs and salt and pepper on top.

Serves about 4.

Aphrodite Lianides's Bourekia

Cheese and Herb Pastries

Aphrodite Lianides, whose husband owns New York's famed Coach House restaurant, is an excellent cook, especially when it comes to her native Greek dishes. Bourekia, the Turkish name for these pastries, are served with drinks. Assemble them early in the day and refrigerate, or make them weeks before and freeze, then bake just before the company arrives.

½ pound Feta, crumbled
3 ounces Cream Cheese, at room temperature
2 ounces (⅓ cup) grated Romano
8 to 10 parsley sprigs, minced
1 tablespoon minced fresh dill
Good pinch freshly grated nutmeg
1 large egg yolk
½ pound filo dough
6 tablespoons unsalted butter, melted

Place the Feta, Cream Cheese, Romano, parsley, dill, nutmeg and egg yolk in the work bowl of a food processor and process until smooth. You can also mix the ingredients with an electric mixer or by hand.

Cut the filo into 8 x 3-inch strips. Keep them covered with plastic wrap or a cloth as you work to prevent them from drying out.

To make each triangle, take one strip of filo and lay it flat on your work surface. Brush it lightly with melted butter. A feather brush works particularly well. Place a rounded teaspoon of the cheese mixture on one corner of the strip. Fold the corner over to make a triangle. Continue folding the filo over in triangles down the length of the strip, like folding a flag. Place the finished triangle, seam side down, on a baking sheet. Continue making triangles in this way until the filling and filo are all used. Leave a little space between the triangles on the baking sheets. If the filo should tear as you work, don't worry. If the hole is small, the other layers will cover it. If it is large, either discard the strip or use a second one. If exposed holes are left, the filling will leak.

Once all the triangles are finished, refrigerate for an hour or freeze. To freeze, place the baking sheets in the freezer for a few hours until the triangles are firm. Then remove the pastries from the sheets and place in plastic bags or containers. Seal well.

About 30 minutes before you want to serve the bourekia, heat the oven to 350°F. Brush the top of each triangle lightly with melted butter. Bake in the preheated oven for about 15 minutes if refrigerated, 20 minutes if frozen. They should be light brown and fluffy. Serve warm.

Makes about 60 triangles.

Curried Cream Cheese with Chutney

This spicy spread is particularly good with refreshing summer daiquiris or chilled beer.

½ pound Cream Cheese
1 tablespoon curry powder
⅛ teaspoon cayenne powder
¼ cup mango chutney
⅓ cup toasted sliced almonds

Place the Cream Cheese, curry powder and cayenne in a food processor and run until the curry and cayenne are completely blended into the cheese. Scoop the cheese onto a serving plate and shape it into a smooth dome about 5 inches wide.

Chop any large pieces of chutney and spread it over the cheese in an even layer. Sprinkle the almonds on top. Place in the refrigerator to set for at least half an hour.

Serve with crackers.

Makes about 2 cups.

Blue Cheese Rounds with Horseradish Cream

Similar to the Cheddar-Sesame Rounds, these are filled with a Cream Cheese and horseradish mixture to complement the blue cheese flavor.

¼ pound crumbled **Danish Blue**
4 tablespoons **unsalted butter**, at room temperature, cut into pieces
⅔ cup **all-purpose flour**
¹⁄₁₆ teaspoon **cayenne pepper**
6 ounces **Cream Cheese**, at room temperature
¼ cup **heavy cream**
1 tablespoon **white prepared horseradish**

Purée the blue cheese in the work bowl of a food processor with the butter. When they are well blended, add the flour and cayenne. Process until all the flour is absorbed. The dough will be soft.

Shape the dough into a flat round disk and wrap it in wax paper. Refrigerate or freeze until firm, at least several hours.

Heat the oven to 400°F.

Roll the dough out on a floured work surface until it is a scant ¼ inch thick. Using a 1-inch round floured biscuit cutter, cut out rounds of dough and place them on an ungreased baking sheet ½ to 1 inch apart. Bake for 7 to 8 minutes, until the rounds are lightly brown. Remove to a rack to cool. Take the scraps and form them into a ball to chill and roll again.

While the rounds are cooling, soften the Cream Cheese in a food processor or in a bowl with a fork. Beat in the cream and horseradish. The mixture should be spreadable but not runny.

When the cheese rounds have cooled and crisped a bit, turn half over and spread with a thin layer of the horseradish cream. Top each with a second round, flat side down. If not serving immediately, keep refrigerated.

Makes about 30 rounds.

Goat Cheese and Basil Tart with Sun-Dried Tomatoes

These rich pastries are excellent to begin a meal or as a luncheon snack. The intense flavor of the sun-dried tomatoes heightens the subtlety of the chèvre.

1 recipe Pastry Dough (see page 240)
¼ pound goat cheese (Montrachet, Ste. Maure, other logs or pyramides)
½ cup heavy cream
1 large egg
2 drops red pepper sauce
Salt
½ cup julienned basil
4 whole sun-dried tomatoes packed in oil

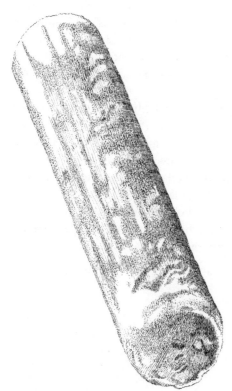

Heat the oven to 400°F.

Roll the dough out into an oval less than ⅛ inch thick. Using a 5-inch round pastry cutter or plate, cut out as many circles as you can. Fit the circles into 4-inch-wide, ¾-inch-deep metal tart pans. Reroll the scraps so you are able to make eight circles.

Place the pans in the freezer for 15 minutes to chill the dough. Line each pan with aluminum foil and rice, beans or aluminum scrap weights. Place on a baking sheet in the preheated oven for 8 minutes. Remove the foil and beans and prick the bottom of each tart shell with a fork.

Return to the oven and bake for 5 to 7 minutes longer. The pastries should be light brown. Carefully remove each pastry shell from its pan, placing the shells on the baking sheet. Lower the oven to 375°F.

In a food processor, mix together the cheese, cream and egg. Add red pepper sauce and salt, if needed. Pour into a bowl and stir in the basil strips. Carefully ladle some of the mixture into each of the prepared pastry shells.

Pat the tomatoes dry and separate them into their halves. Place a half, skin side up, in the center of each tart.

Put the filled shells in the oven and bake for about 15 minutes. The tops should be set but not brown.

Makes 8 individual tarts.

Stuffed Grape Leaves

Pile these on a platter surrounded with lemon wedges.

1 pound grape leaves, packed in brine
½ cup plus 2 tablespoons olive oil
1 large (¼ pound) onion, chopped
½ pound ground lamb
¾ cup rice
¼ pound crumbled Feta
¼ cup minced fresh dill
2 tablespoons minced fresh mint, or 2
    teaspoons dried
¼ cup toasted pine nuts (pignoli)
Salt
Freshly ground pepper
2 garlic cloves, halved
Juice of ½ lemon

Remove the grape leaves from the brine and place them in a mixing bowl. Add boiling water to cover and let soak for 20 minutes. Drain and rinse with cold water. Drain again.

Heat 2 tablespoons oil in a skillet. Add the onion and cook for a minute or two until soft but not brown. Add the lamb and cook, stirring, until it has lost all its raw, red color. Stir in the rice and 1½ cups water. Cover and cook for 20 minutes. Leaving any excess fat and liquid in the pan, remove the lamb and rice to a bowl. Add the Feta, dill, mint and pine nuts. Add salt and pepper to taste.

Work with one grape leaf at a time. Place it, vein side up, on your work surface so the stem end is at the bottom. Place a generous teaspoon of filling in the center of the leaf about ¾ inch up from the bottom. Fold the bottom over and then the sides. Roll up and set aside. Continue in this way until you have used all the filling. Some leaves will be bigger than others and can hold more filling. If some are torn, patch them with a piece of another torn leaf or set aside.

When all the rolls are made, line a 3-quart saucepan with some of the torn leaves. Place the rolls over the leaves, seam sides down, making as many layers as necessary. Add the halved garlic cloves and the lemon juice. Mix the remaining ½ cup olive oil with ½ cup water and pour over. Place another layer of leaves on top.

Bring the liquid to a boil, cover the pot and lower the heat. Simmer for about 2 hours, until the leaves are tender. Let cool to room temperature.

Makes about 40 stuffed grape leaves.

Parmesan and Bacon Potato Skins

Potato skins, popular now with drinks, can be flavored many ways. This version is simple and satisfying.

Four ½-pound baking potatoes
8 slices bacon
2 tablespoons unsalted butter, at room temperature
½ cup grated Parmesan

Heat the oven to 400°F. Bake the potatoes on the rack of the oven until done, about 45 minutes.

While the potatoes bake, cook the bacon until brown and crisp but not dry. Drain and crumble. Set aside.

Cut each potato in half lengthwise and scoop out all but a thin shell of the potato. Use the potato to make German Potato Salad with Port-Salut (see page 191) or for another recipe. Brush each shell with some of the butter, then sprinkle with cheese. Top with crumbled bacon.

Place the filled shells on a baking sheet and return to the oven. Bake until brown and crisp, about 10 minutes. Serve hot.

Makes 8 potato skins.

Suppli

Rice and Cheese Fritters

These delicate rice fritters reveal strands of melted Mozzarella when cut open. Serve them hot with drinks. If it is more convenient, make them early in the day and reheat in the oven.

2 cups leftover Risotto (see page 192)
1 large egg, beaten
¼ pound Mozzarella, cut into ½-inch
cubes
½ cup bread crumbs
Vegetable oil

Beat the rice and egg together until smooth. Take a ball of rice in your hand and shape it around a cube of cheese. Roll in your hand until smooth and set aside. Continue in this way until you have used all the rice and cheese.

Roll each ball in bread crumbs to completely coat. Refrigerate for at least an hour.

When ready to cook, heat a ½ inch of oil in a 10-inch skillet until hot. Add the rice balls, keeping them from touching each other, and cook until well browned on the bottom. Turn and cook until brown all over. Remove with a slotted spoon, drain on absorbent paper and serve at once or keep warm in the oven.

Makes about 24 rice fritters.

Gougères

Cheese Puffs

This traditional dish from Burgundy takes the basic cream puff recipe and adds cheese, usually Gruyère, at the end. The dough can be shaped into an attractive crown or individual balls and may be served hot or cold. The recipe is not difficult, but it does take a strong arm to mix the dough.

¾ cup water
¼ pound unsalted butter
1 cup all-purpose flour
1 teaspoon kosher salt
4 large eggs, at room temperature
5 ounces (1¼ cups) minced Gruyère
1 teaspoon Dijon mustard
¹⁄₁₆ teaspoon cayenne pepper
Milk

Heat the oven to 400°F. Grease a baking sheet at least 12 inches wide and set aside.

Heat the water and butter in a 2-quart saucepan. When the butter has melted, raise the heat so the liquid boils. Add the flour and salt all at once. Stir vigorously, still on the heat, until the mixture comes together into a smooth ball that clears the side of the pan.

Remove the pan from the heat and add 1 of the eggs. Stir vigorously until it is completely absorbed and the mixture is smooth again. Continue in the same way to add the remaining 3 eggs. The dough will be fairly stiff until the last egg is absorbed. At that point it will be a little softer, though not at all runny. Stir in all but about 2 tablespoons cheese, the mustard and cayenne pepper.

Using a soup spoon, drop balls of dough onto the baking sheet so they form a ring about 12 inches in diameter. You should have about sixteen balls that almost touch. If you prefer, you can leave the balls completely separate. Brush each ball with some milk and sprinkle on some of the remaining cheese.

Place in the preheated oven and bake for 10 minutes. Without opening the oven door, lower the heat to 375°F. Cook about 30 minutes longer, until the ring is well browned and firm. Turn off the oven and prick each ball toward the bottom to let some of the steam escape. Prop open the oven door a bit and leave the Gougères in the turned-off oven for about 10 minutes before serving.

Serves about 8.

Cheese Beignets

Cheese Fritters

These are made with the same dough as the Gougères, but they are deep fried. This is a good way to use leftover soft-ripened, semisoft, semifirm and hard cheeses, alone or in combinations of two or more. Serve the beignets plain with drinks or partnered with a spicy tomato sauce as a first course.

6 tablespoons water
4 tablespoons unsalted butter
½ teaspoon kosher salt
½ cup all-purpose flour
2 large eggs
½ teaspoon Dijon mustard
2 ounces (½ cup) minced cheese:
    Gruyère, Brie, Cheddar, Swiss,
    Alsatian Muenster, etc.
Cayenne pepper
Vegetable oil for deep frying

Follow the procedure for making the dough as described in the Gougères recipe, adding all the cheese to the batter.

Heat oil to a depth of at least 2 inches to 360°F. If you don't have a deep fat thermometer, check the temperature by dropping a tiny bit of batter into the oil. It should fall to the bottom and pop up to the top. If it stays on the bottom a while, the oil is not hot enough. If it doesn't go down, the oil is too hot.

When the oil is at the proper temperature, drop about ½ tablespoon dough into the hot oil. The oil will sputter a bit. Cook several fritters at a time but do not crowd them in the pan or they won't cook through properly. It should take about 2 minutes to get them perfectly golden on the outside and cooked through on the inside. Sometimes they will turn over when they are halfway cooked. If not, use a spoon to help them. Remove with a slotted spoon to a plate lined with paper. Keep warm until ready to serve. Continue cooking until all the dough is used. Check the temperature of the oil between batches since it will change as you cook.

Makes about 48 small fritters.

Deep-Fried Won Tons with Cheese

The crisp won ton skins encase melted cubes of cheese. Just about any semisoft, Cheddar or Swiss-style cheese works fine in this recipe. Serve plain with drinks or at the table with a tomato sauce.

¼ **pound cheese**
1 pound (about 50) won ton skins (see note)
Vegetable oil for deep frying

Cut the cheese into about 50 equal pieces. Place a won ton skin on your work surface, cornstarch side down. Place a piece of cheese just off center on the skin. Brush the rim with water and fold over to make a triangle. Press tight all around to seal. Rub a little water on one of the bottom tips of the triangle. Bring the other bottom tip around to meet it and press to seal. Set aside. Continue filling won ton skins in this way.

Heat at least 4 inches of oil in a pot. It is hot enough when a piece of dough falls to the bottom and comes right up to the top. If it sits on the bottom, the oil needs to be hotter. If it stays on the top, the oil is too hot. When the oil is the right temperature, add the won tons, a few at a time. Cook until brown on both sides, 2 to 3 minutes. They will puff up so that some won't turn over. In that case, spoon hot oil over the top side until it turns brown.

With a slotted spoon, remove the browned won tons to a plate lined with absorbent paper. Keep warm as you continue cooking the rest or serve immediately.

Makes about 50 won tons.

NOTE: Won ton skins are available refrigerated or frozen in oriental groceries and some gourmet shops.

Craig Claiborne's Gruyère Toast

Craig Claiborne, well-known food editor of the *New York Times,* says eating these is like having fondue without having to work at it. You can make the mixture ahead and spread it on the toast just before your guests arrive. They'll be baked by the time the drinks are mixed.

2 teaspoons unsalted butter
1 tablespoon all-purpose flour
½ cup milk
1 large egg yolk
½ pound Gruyère, grated
¼ teaspoon freshly grated nutmeg
Dash cayenne pepper
1 tablespoon dry white wine
1 garlic clove, minced
Freshly ground black pepper
Salt
10 to 12 ½-inch-thick slices French bread, toasted

Melt the butter in a small saucepan. Stir in the flour and cook over medium heat to get rid of the raw taste, 2 to 3 minutes. Pour in the milk and cook, stirring with a whisk, until the sauce thickens. Remove the pan from the heat and stir in the egg yolk. Transfer the sauce to a mixing bowl and cool.

Heat the oven to 400°F.

Stir the cheese, nutmeg, cayenne, wine and garlic into the sauce. Season to taste with pepper. Add salt, if necessary. Stir until the mixture is well blended. It will be very thick. Spread a generous tablespoon on each piece of toast, mounding it slightly higher in the center than at the edges. Place on a baking sheet and bake in the preheated oven for 10 minutes, or until the topping is melted and bubbly. Serve hot.

Makes 10 to 12 slices.

Roquefort Pithiviers

1 pound Puff Pastry (see page 239)
¼ pound Roquefort
3 ounces Cream Cheese
¼ teaspoon cayenne pepper
1 large egg
Egg glaze (1 egg beaten with 1 teaspoon
    water)

The town of Pithiviers in France is famous for a fabulous dessert of puffed pastry filled with almond paste. We substituted a Roquefort filling to make an elegant and impressive first course.

Roll out the pastry into a rectangle about 9 x 17 inches. Using an 8-inch plate as a guide, cut out two 8-inch rounds of dough. Use a small, sharp wet knife and cut straight down. (Sloppy cutting keeps the layers from rising properly later.) Place the rounds on baking sheet. Refrigerate.

Put the Roquefort, Cream Cheese, cayenne and egg in the work bowl of a food processor and process until well blended. Chill for at least an hour.

When the pastry and filling are both chilled, remove them from the refrigerator. Place one pastry round on a lightly floured work surface and roll it quickly in all directions so it is a little larger, 8½ to 9 inches in diameter.

Shape the cheese mixture into a 4-inch round and place it in the center of the smaller round of pastry. Brush the wide border with water. Center the larger pastry round over the cheese. Press the top of the dough so it adheres to the bottom round. Press well. You want to be sure the two sides bake together and the filling doesn't leak. Be careful not to touch the edges, or they won't puff properly. The pastry will look like a wide-brimmed hat. Cover it with a cloth and chill for at least an hour.

About an hour before you want to serve the pithiviers, heat the oven to 450°F. When it is ready, make a ⅛-inch hole in the center of the pastry going through to the filling. Place a buttered metal pastry tip, narrow side down, in the hole. If you don't have one, make a small tube with aluminum foil, butter it, and insert it in the hole. Brush the egg glaze over the top. For a traditional, attractive design, make swirling cuts into the pastry with a small knife starting at the center hole and going to the edge. When it bakes, these will show up lighter than the glazed pastry.

Place in the preheated oven and bake for 20 minutes. Lower the heat to 400°F. and bake for another 20 minutes, or until well browned. Serve hot.

Serves 6 as a first course, about 3 for lunch with a salad.

Fonduta

This is a very simple, very rich dish made with Italian Fontina, butter and eggs, poured over golden polenta (cornmeal mush). Traditionally, it is topped with thin slices of fresh white truffle still redolent of its woodsy home. Since most of us can't find—or afford—the truffles, we tested the fonduta without them and still had a dish fit for royalty, the thick, smooth sauce a perfect complement for the bland, slightly coarse polenta. It's worth the effort to find true Val d'Aosta Fontina for this recipe.

¾ pound Fontina, cut into ½-inch cubes
1 cup milk
9 cups water
Salt
3 cups cornmeal
4 tablespoons unsalted butter
4 large egg yolks
Freshly ground white pepper
White truffle slices (optional)

Place the cheese in a bowl with the milk. Let soak in the refrigerator for at least 4 hours, stirring occasionally to be sure all the cheese stays moist.

Before you are ready to serve, make the polenta. (You might find it easier to work with someone else in the kitchen so one can concentrate on the polenta while the other makes the sauce.) In a deep pot, bring the water to a boil. Add salt and lower the heat so the water is at a slow boil. Start stirring the water with a spoon in one hand as you dribble in the cornmeal with the other hand. If you don't keep stirring, there will be lumps. When all the cornmeal has been added, let the mixture cook for another 5 minutes or so, until it is quite thick. Keep it warm.

Place the cheese and milk in the top of a double boiler over simmering water. Add the butter and egg yolks. Stir until everything is melted and you have a smooth, thick sauce. It will take 15 to 20 minutes. Season to taste with freshly ground white pepper.

Put the polenta on a serving platter. Pour the sauce over and garnish with the truffle.

Serves 8.

NOTE: The sauce is also delicious over freshly cooked rice.

If the polenta does get lumpy, press it through a sieve before serving to remove the lumps.

Deep-Fried Goat Cheese with Tomato Mushroom Sauce

We make this dish with a firm goat cheese like Gail Le-Compte's Saanen. Gail recommends marinating it in equal parts walnut oil and white wine with a bit of garlic and some chopped herbs. It keeps for weeks that way.

Other firm cheeses, like Gruyère, Hoberfeld and Emmentaler, can be cooked in the same way. Softer cheeses tend to ooze into the oil.

¾ pound Saanen, Dolmen or other sliceable goat cheese, drained and patted dry if marinated in oil
3 large eggs
1½ cups bread crumbs
Vegetable oil for deep frying
½ recipe Tomato Mushroom Sauce (see page 231)
1 bunch parsley

Cut the cheese into relatively even pieces about 1 x 1 x 1½ inches. Put the eggs in a bowl and beat until the yolks and whites are completely blended. Put the bread crumbs in a separate bowl.

Put one piece of cheese in the egg to coat. Shake off any excess, dripping egg. Put the cheese next in the bread crumbs and pat the crumbs gently but firmly all over the cheese. Repeat with the egg and bread coatings. Put the coated cheese on a plate. Continue in the same way with each piece of cheese. Do not crowd the plate. When you have a full layer of cheese, start a second plate. Put the prepared cheese in the refrigerator for at least 2 hours.

Before you are ready to serve, heat the oil in a pot to a depth of at least 4 inches. Use a bit of the breading to test the heat. It is ready when the breading falls to the bottom of the pot, then rises to the top almost immediately. If it sits at the bottom, the oil is not hot enough. If it doesn't go to the bottom, it is too hot.

Once the oil is at the right temperature, drop three or four cheese pieces in the oil. Cook until golden brown, about 3 minutes. With a slotted spoon, remove each finished piece to a plate lined with paper towels. Keep in a warm oven until all the cheese is done. It may be necessary to adjust the heat as you work to keep the temperature of the oil constant. Continue cooking the cheese in the same way until it is all done. Never crowd the pot.

While the cheese is cooking, heat the sauce. Drop the parsley in the hot oil for 30 seconds. Drain. Spoon some sauce onto each of six salad plates. Arrange some fried cheese on top and garnish with some of the fried parsley.

Serves 6.

Layered Tortillas with Cheese

This is a delicious and attractive snack to serve with beer or margaritas.

2 scallions, green and white parts, minced
¼ pound Monterey Jack, minced
¼ pound sharp orange Cheddar cheese (for color contrast), minced
2 plum tomatoes, seeded and cut into ¼-inch cubes
¼ cup minced fresh coriander
6 corn tortillas, 8 inches in diameter
Melted butter
Green Salsa (see page 234)

Heat the oven to 350°F.

In a mixing bowl, combine the scallions, cheeses, tomatoes and coriander.

Place a tortilla on a baking sheet and brush it with some melted butter. Spread about ½ cup cheese mixture in an even layer on the tortilla. Top with two more tortilla and cheese layers. Make another tortilla "cake" with the remaining tortillas, cheese and melted butter.

Place in the preheated oven and bake for about 7 minutes, just to melt the cheeses. Cut each into half or thirds and serve hot with Green Salsa.

Serves 4 to 6.

Pasta and Pizza

Pasta and cheese have a natural affinity for each other in dishes ranging from one as simple as fresh fettuccine tossed with butter or olive oil and sprinkled with freshly grated Parmigiano-Reggiano to more complicated cooked sauces and luscious filled raviolis and baked lasagnes. Certain pasta dishes are too rich to serve more than small, first course, portions. Others are too hearty to be anything but main courses. Most are as appropriate beginning a meal as being the main, possibly only, course. Of course the portion size will vary depending on what else you're serving.

Pizzas, once considered almost junk food, are now recognized as being as versatile as sandwiches. Just about any combination is possible. Some are now found at chic restaurants. The ones that follow are an assortment, including deep-dish, individual and a calzone (technically not pizza, but the dough is the same). They can be eaten as snacks with wine or beer or as meals in themselves. When we have pizza for lunch or dinner, we always serve a salad.

Sue Huffman's Macaroni and Cheese Pie

To raise macaroni and cheese from nursery food to adult fare, use an authentic, flavorful Cheddar. Sue Huffman, former food editor of *Ladies' Home Journal,* has made the dish even more interesting by baking it in a flaky Cheddar crust for a marvelous lunch or supper dish. If you don't have time to make the crust, the filling is delicious on its own.

CRUST

1 cup all-purpose flour
½ teaspoon salt
⅓ cup vegetable shortening
2 ounces (about ½ cup) grated Cheddar
¼ cup ice water

Heat the oven to 450°F.

Put the flour, salt, shortening and cheese in the work bowl of a food processor fitted with the metal blade. Process with pulses until the mixture resembles coarse meal. With the machine running, pour the water through the feed tube. Process just until the dough begins to come together. Turn the dough out onto a lightly floured work surface. Shape it into a ball, then roll it out into an 11-inch circle. If the dough is difficult to handle and sticks to the work surface, roll it between sheets of wax paper, lifting the paper from each side from time to time so the dough doesn't stick.

Fit the dough into a 9-inch pie plate. Press it to fit in neatly, then flute the edge. Line the dough with a sheet of aluminum foil, then weight with dry rice or beans, or use aluminum scrap pellets. Place in the preheated oven and bake for 15 minutes. Remove to a rack to cool. Lift out the foil and weights.

Lower the oven temperature to 350°F.

FILLING

1 cup elbow macaroni
2 tablespoons unsalted butter
¼ cup all-purpose flour
2 cups milk
½ teaspoon salt
⅛ teaspoon cayenne pepper
3 ounces Cream Cheese, cut into pieces
7 ounces (about 2 cups) shredded
    Cheddar
½ cup parsley sprigs, minced

Bring a large pot of salted water to a boil. Add the macaroni and cook for about 12 minutes, until barely done. Drain and rinse under cold running water. Set aside.

In a heavy saucepan, melt the butter. Stir in the flour to make a smooth paste. Cook over moderate heat for 3 or 4 minutes. The mixture should be frothy but not brown. Add the milk. Beat with a whisk until the mixture is completely smooth. Continue cooking, stirring constantly, until the mixture thickens considerably. Beat in the salt, cayenne pepper and Cream Cheese. When smooth, stir in

1½ cups of the Cheddar, then the parsley and macaroni.

Pour the mixture into the partly baked shell. Bake in the preheated oven for 20 minutes. Sprinkle the remaining Cheddar on top and bake 15 minutes longer. Let cool a few minutes before serving if you want neat slices.

Serves 6.

Spaghetti with Shrimp and Goat Cheese

The whole shrimp sit majestically on this refreshing summer pasta.

1½ pounds large shrimp, all but tail shells removed, butterflied and deveined
¼ cup minced garlic
½ cup fresh lemon juice
½ cup plus 2 tablespoons olive oil
2 dried hot red peppers, split
1 pound spaghetti
2 cups (about 8) scallions cut into 1-inch pieces, both white and green parts
2 cups cored, seeded and cubed tomatoes
½ pound Montrachet or other mild goat cheese, crumbled or cut into ¼-inch slices
½ cup fresh mint, julienned

Put the shrimp in a mixing bowl with the garlic, lemon juice, ½ cup olive oil and hot peppers. Stir to coat the shrimp. Let marinate for at least 3 hours, stirring from time to time.

Bring a large pot of salted water to the boil. Add the pasta and cook until barely done, about 10 minutes.

While the pasta is cooking, heat the remaining 2 tablespoons olive oil in a 10-inch skillet. When hot, add the scallions. Cook, stirring, for 1 minute. Add the tomatoes and cook for another minute.

Drain the shrimp, reserving the marinade, and add them to the pan. Cook, stirring, for about 2 minutes, then add the reserved marinade.

Cook for about 1 minute and add the cheese and mint. Stir until the cheese dissolves to make a sauce.

Drain the cooked pasta and toss with the shrimp and sauce.

Serves 4 for dinner, 6 to 8 for a first course.

Gael Greene's Linguine with Goat Cheese and Walnuts

Gael Greene is best known for her enticing critiques of restaurant meals, but when she does cook it is to make simple but wondrous dishes like this surprisingly rich pasta, an excellent first course when fresh basil is in season.

2 tablespoons unsalted butter
2 tablespoons olive oil
3 large garlic cloves, minced
1½ cups chopped walnuts
1 cup tightly packed fresh basil leaves
½ pound soft, flavorful goat cheese, such as Bucheron or Dolmen
1 cup light or heavy cream, depending on how rich you like the dish
¼ cup freshly grated Parmesan, plus cheese for the table
1 pound linguine, preferably fresh
Freshly ground black pepper
Salt

Heat the butter and oil in a heavy skillet over moderate heat. Add the garlic and cook until soft, about 1 minute. Add the walnuts and cook, stirring, until they are lightly brown and crisp. Set aside off the heat.

Make small piles of basil leaves; roll them up and cut into thin strips. When all the basil has been cut, add it to the slightly cooled walnut mixture.

Put the goat cheese in a bowl and mash it with a fork until fairly smooth. Add the cream and Parmesan and stir until smooth.

Bring a large pot of salted water to the boil. Add the pasta and cook until done but still firm to the bite, *al dente*. Drain well, reserving about 1 cup cooking liquid.

Put the pasta back in the pot with the cheese mixture and ½ cup cooking liquid. Stir to coat evenly, then add the nut and basil mixture. If the sauce seems too thick, thin it with a little more reserved liquid. Add pepper and salt, if necessary, to taste.

Serve immediately with freshly grated Parmesan cheese.

Serves 8 as a first course.

Alice Waters's Three-Cheese Pasta

Alice Waters, owner of Chez Panisse, the wonderfully innovative restaurant in Berkeley known for its use of fine local produce, created this easy, elegant pasta. Very rich, it is perfect as a first course followed by roasted meat or fish with a creamless sauce. The exact proportions of Gorgonzola and Fontina, she explains, vary with the strength of the Gorgonzola. Look for one that is soft, creamy and full flavored.

½ pound fresh linguine
¼ pound Gorgonzola, cut into cubes
2 ounces Fontina, cut into cubes
⅔ cup heavy cream
2 ounces freshly grated Parmesan
Freshly ground black pepper
¼ cup toasted nuts

Bring a large pot of lightly salted water to the boil. Add the linguine and cook until barely done (al dente), about 3 minutes if very fresh, longer if dry. Drain well.

In a large pot, heat the Gorgonzola and Fontina with the cream over moderate heat, stirring often until the mixture is smooth. Add the drained linguine and stir to coat. The sauce will be somewhat runny; it will thicken by itself as it cools down at the table.

Put the pasta in a wide bowl. Sprinkle the grated Parmesan, a healthy grinding of black pepper and the toasted nuts on top. Serve immediately.

Serves 4.

Meaty Lasagne

This very hearty dish can be assembled ahead and baked just before serving.

½ pound spinach lasagne noodles
1 pound Ricotta
2 large eggs
1½ cups grated Parmesan
2 tablespoons chopped parsley
½ teaspoon kosher salt
Freshly ground black pepper
1 recipe Bolognese Sauce (see page 232)
1 pound Mozzarella, shredded

Bring a large pot of salted water to a boil. Add the lasagne, one strip at a time so they don't stick to each other, and cook until barely done, 10 to 15 minutes, depending on brand. Drain well and set aside.

Heat the oven to 375°F.

Mix together until smooth the Ricotta, eggs, 1 cup of the Parmesan, parsley, salt and pepper.

Spoon a thin layer of sauce into a 14 x 9 x 2-inch lasagne dish. Top with a layer of the lasagne noodles, over-lapping them slightly and trimming them if necessary to make a fairly neat layer. Spoon a third of the sauce over the pasta. Top with a third of the Ricotta mixture, drop-ping it in spoonfuls, not an even layer. Sprinkle a fourth of the Mozzarella and remaining ½ cup Parmesan on top. Make two more layers of noodles, sauce and the cheeses. Top with another layer of pasta. Sprinkle the remaining Mozzarella and Parmesan on top.

Bake in the preheated oven for 45 minutes, or until heated through and bubbly.

Serves at least 8.

Vegetarian Lasagne

This meatless lasagne is as satisfying as any meaty version. Though it takes a little time to cook the various parts, the finished product can be assembled ahead and then baked, or reheated, when your guests arrive.

½ pound whole wheat lasagne
1 teaspoon olive oil
3 tablespoons unsalted butter
4 scallions, sliced
2 pounds zucchini, sliced into ¼-inch rounds
½ pound soft goat cheese log (Montrachet, Ste. Maure)
15 ounces Ricotta
1 teaspoon kosher salt
1/16 teaspoon cayenne pepper
1 recipe Tomato Mushroom Sauce (see page 231)
⅓ cup grated Asiago or Grana
6 ounces Mozzarella, cut into slices ⅛ inch thick

Bring a large pot of salted water to the boil and add the lasagne along with the olive oil. Cook until the lasagne is barely done, about 12 minutes. Drain, run under cold water and set aside.

Heat the oven to 350°F.

Heat the butter in a large clean skillet. Add the scallions and sauté for a minute. Then add the zucchini and sauté until it is barely soft, about 10 minutes.

Crumble the goat cheese into a bowl. Stir in the Ricotta, salt and cayenne.

Ladle a thin layer of sauce over the bottom of a 9 x 14-inch baking pan. Try not to get any mushrooms into the layer. Cover with a layer of cooked lasagne noodles, then a thicker layer of sauce. Over that, evenly layer half the zucchini, half the Ricotta mixture and half the Asiago. Top with another layer of lasagne, sauce, zucchini, cheeses, lasagne. Spoon over the remaining sauce and top with a layer of the Mozzarella.

Bake in the preheated oven for 45 minutes, or until bubbly hot. Serve with crusty bread to soak up any oozing sauce.

Serves 6 to 8.

Shrimp and Fennel Ravioli

Making ravioli from scratch can be an arduous process, one we avoided until we learned to substitute ready-made won ton skins for the pasta. Available refrigerated or frozen in oriental groceries and gourmet shops, won ton skins make it simple to create all kinds of exotic raviolis. The number of skins per pound varies from brand to brand depending on their thickness, so buy extra until you know for sure.

½ pound medium shrimp, peeled and deveined
1 tablespoon Pernod
1 small fennel bulb
1 tablespoon unsalted butter
½ pound Ricotta
¾ teaspoon kosher salt
Pinch cayenne pepper
72 won ton skins (about 1½ pounds)
1 recipe Basic Tomato Sauce (see page 230) or Creamy Tomato Sauce (see page 230), heated

Place the shrimp in the work bowl of a food processor and chop with about ten pulses, until the shrimp is in small pieces. Do not purée. Set aside in a mixing bowl and stir in the Pernod.

Take about ¼ pound fennel and mince it in the food processor. Add to the shrimp.

Heat the butter in a small skillet. Add the shrimp and fennel and cook over medium heat until the fennel is soft and the shrimp barely cooked. Let cool, then stir in the cheese, salt and cayenne pepper.

Cover a tray with a clean cloth so you can place the ravioli on it as they are finished. When working with the won ton skins, you will usually find that one side has been sprinkled with cornstarch. Keep that side on the outside, away from the filling.

Place a won ton skin on the work surface. Put a rounded teaspoon of the shrimp mixture in the center. Brush the dough around the filling with water. Top with a second won ton skin and press around the filling to seal the dough. Try to incorporate as little air as possible. Press a 2½-inch round cookie cutter, preferably fluted, over the dough to make a finished ravioli. Press around the edges to be sure the seal holds and place on the prepared tray. Discard the trimmings. Continue in this way until you have used all the dough and filling. Keep the ravioli separate from each other so they don't stick. Put a towel between the layers if necessary. If you make them ahead, cover with foil and refrigerate. If you wish to freeze them, place them directly on a baking sheet in single layers so they do not touch. Once frozen, remove them to a plastic bag.

When you are ready to serve the ravioli, bring a large pot of salted water to the boil. Add the ravioli and cook until barely done, about 2 minutes if fresh, 4 to 5 minutes if frozen. Drain.

Spoon some of the heated sauce on each of six individual plates. Top with six cooked ravioli and some more sauce. Garnish each plate with a sprig of fennel leaf.

Serves 6 as a first course.

Cheese Ravioli in Cream Sauce

We usually make this rich dish for a first course to be followed by a poached fish or roast. Serve it on black plates to emphasize the contrast of the green peas and red radishes against the white pasta and sauce.

½ pound (1 scant cup) Ricotta
1 large egg
1 tablespoon minced parsley
1 tablespoon minced basil
Pinch grated nutmeg
1 teaspoon salt
Freshly ground white pepper
1 pound (about 50) won ton skins (see
    NOTE, page 125)
1 cup heavy cream
Pinch cayenne pepper
1 cup cooked or frozen, defrosted peas
½ cup thinly sliced radish rounds
¼ cup grated Parmesan

Whisk the Ricotta and egg together in a bowl until smooth. Stir in the parsley, basil, nutmeg, ½ teaspoon salt and white pepper to taste.

Cover a tray with a clean cloth to put the ravioli on as they are finished. When working with the won ton skins, keep the cornstarch to the outside, away from the filling.

Place a won ton skin on the work surface. Put 2 scant teaspoons cheese mixture in the center. Brush the dough around the filling with water. Top with a won ton skin and press around the filling to seal well. Try to incorporate as little air as possible. Press a 4-inch square ravioli cutter over the dough. Discard the trimmings. Place the filled ravioli on the prepared tray. Continue in this way until you have used all the dough and filling. Keep the ravioli separate from each other so they don't stick. Put a towel between the layers if necessary. If you make them ahead, cover with foil and refrigerate. If you wish to freeze them, place them directly on a baking sheet in single layers so they do not touch. Once frozen, remove them to a plastic bag.

When you are ready to serve the ravioli, bring a large pot of salted water to a boil. At the same time, bring the cream to a boil. Add the remaining ½ teaspoon salt and some cayenne pepper. Let simmer for 5 minutes to thicken a bit. Add the peas and radishes and cook to heat through.

When the water is boiling, add the ravioli and cook until barely done, about 2 minutes if fresh, 4 to 5 minutes if frozen. Drain and toss with the hot cream sauce and the Parmesan. Serve with additional Parmesan on the side.

Serves 4.

Blue Cheese Ravioli

The distinct blue cheese flavor makes these ravioli special.

¼ pound **Danish Blue or other blue
  cheese**
¼ pound **Cream Cheese**
½ cup **heavy cream**
1 large **egg**
⅛ teaspoon **red pepper sauce**
1½ pounds **(about 76) won ton skins
  (see NOTE, page 125)**
1 recipe **Basic Tomato Sauce, heated
  (see page 230)**

Place the cheeses, cream and egg in a bowl and mash together with a fork until fairly smooth. Add the red pepper sauce.

Cover a tray with a clean cloth so you can place the ravioli on it as they are finished. When working with the won ton skins, you will usually find that one side has been sprinkled with cornstarch. Keep that side on the outside, away from the filling.

Place a won ton skin on the work surface. Put about 2 teaspoons of the cheese mixture in the center. Brush the dough around the filling with water. Top with a second won ton skin and press around the filling to seal the dough. Try to incorporate as little air as possible. Press a 4-inch-square ravioli cutter over the dough to make a finished square. Press around the edges to be sure the seal holds and place on the prepared tray. Discard the trimmings. Continue in this way until you have used all the dough and filling. Keep the ravioli separate from each other so they don't stick. Put a towel between the layers if necessary. If you make them ahead, cover with foil and refrigerate. If you wish to freeze them, place them directly on a baking sheet in single layers so they do not touch. Once frozen, remove them to a plastic bag.

When you are ready to serve the ravioli, bring a large pot of salted water to the boil. Add the ravioli and cook until barely done, about 2 minutes if fresh, 4 to 5 minutes if frozen. Drain.

Spoon some of the heated sauce on each of six individual plates. Top with six or seven cooked ravioli and some more sauce.

Serves 6 as a first course.

André Soltner's Tarte Flambée

Flamme Kueche

André Soltner, chef and owner of New York's famed Lutèce restaurant, makes this wonderful tart, almost a pizza, to serve hot with drinks or as a first course at the table. The onions and cheese combine to create a rich, custardy topping that is superb.

1 recipe Basic Bread/Pizza Dough (see page 240)
1 pound sliced bacon
1 large (about 12 ounces) Spanish onion, sliced very thin
½ pound (about 1 cup) Cottage Cheese
2 large eggs
½ cup crème fraîche
1 tablespoon peanut oil
Salt
Freshly ground white pepper
Freshly grated nutmeg

While the dough is rising, heat the oven to 450°F.

Cook the bacon until crisp. Drain on paper towels, leaving all the fat in the pan. Add the sliced onion to the fat and sauté until it is soft and golden. Do not let the onion brown.

Put the Cottage Cheese, eggs, crème fraîche and oil in a food processor and process until smooth. Add salt, pepper and nutmeg to taste.

Punch down the dough and roll it into a 9 x 14-inch rectangle. Place on an ungreased baking sheet. Pinch all around the perimeter to form a lip. Spread the cheese mixture over the dough. Spread the cooked onion over that. Crumble the bacon and sprinkle it over the onion.

Bake in the preheated oven for 20 to 25 minutes, until the dough is brown and the filling set. Serve very hot.

Serves 6 as a first course, more if cut into small pieces and served with drinks.

Pizzapiazza's White Pizza

One of our favorite pizzas is this deep-dish version served at Pizzapiazza in New York, where the pizzas are delicious and much more interesting than those of our childhood. This one has four cheeses and is flavored with sautéed onions.

CRUST

1 rounded teaspoon dry yeast
½ cup warm water
1 tablespoon olive oil
1½ cups all-purpose flour
½ cup whole wheat flour
1 tablespoon kosher salt

Sprinkle the yeast on the warm water and set aside to dissolve for a few minutes. Stir in the olive oil.

Put the two flours and the salt in the work bowl of a food processor. Run for a few seconds to mix. With the machine still running, pour in the dissolved yeast mixture. Let the machine run until the mixture comes together. If necessary, add up to 2 tablespoons more water or flour. Knead the dough until it is smooth, then wrap in plastic and refrigerate for at least 10 minutes.

FILLING

2 tablespoons olive oil
1 large (½ pound) onion, sliced
6 ounces Mozzarella, grated, at room temperature
3 ounces Gruyère, grated, at room temperature
3 ounces Romano, grated, at room temperature
¾ pound Ricotta, at room temperature
Salt
Freshly ground pepper

Heat the oil in a skillet. Add the onion and cook until translucent and soft, 5 to 10 minutes. Put the cooked onion in a bowl. Add the cheeses and mix well. Season to taste with salt and pepper. Keep at room temperature until ready to use. (If you make it far in advance, refrigerate but bring back to room temperature before using.)

ASSEMBLY

The crust
The filling

Heat the oven to 475°F. Grease a 9-inch round cake pan that is 1½ inches deep.

Remove the dough from the refrigerator and roll it into a 12-inch circle. Fit the dough into the prepared pan, trimming the edges to make them neat, if necessary. Spoon in the filling and bake in the preheated oven until done, about 25 minutes. Serve immediately.

Serves 4 to 6 as a main course, more as an appetizer.

Blue Cheese–Mozzarella Pizza

Serve this in thin wedges with a fruity, chilled Riesling.

½ recipe Basic Bread/Pizza Dough (see
    page 240)
Olive oil
2 ounces Mozzarella, cut into ¼-inch
    dice
2 ounces Danish Blue, crumbled

Heat the oven to 475°F.

After the dough has risen, punch it down and roll out into a 12-inch circle. Place on a baking sheet sprinkled with cornmeal. If the dough shrinks a little in the transfer, don't worry about it. If it shrinks a lot, roll it out some more.

Brush the dough with olive oil to coat. Sprinkle the cheeses evenly over the dough, leaving about ½ inch border. Place in the preheated oven and bake for 15 minutes. The dough should be brown, the cheese beginning to brown.

Cut into wedges and serve hot.

Makes one 12-inch pizza.

Individual Pizzas

Small pizzas for one are a good way to use up all kinds of leftovers—an ounce or two of cheese, half a tomato, some fresh herbs, a few olives, a piece of ham or salami, some roasted peppers. Here are two recipes to give you the idea, but anything goes as long as it can take the heat, doesn't need to actually cook (raw meat doesn't work) and has some liquid. The dough takes a few minutes to make and can be done the night before and refrigerated, or weeks ahead and frozen.

1 recipe Basic Bread/Pizza Dough (see
    page 240) that has risen for 1 hour

Divide the dough into four equal pieces. Roll each into a 7-inch circle and place on a baking sheet sprinkled with cornmeal. You will need two baking sheets.

GOAT CHEESE/TOMATO TOPPING

1 packed cup parsley leaves
2 cans (4 ounces each) green chilies
2 tablespoons olive oil
½ teaspoon kosher salt
Red pepper sauce
8 Greek olives, pitted
2 plum tomatoes (3 ounces each), cored,
    seeded and cut into ⅓-inch cubes
½ pound young goat cheese (Laura
    Chenel's Pyramide, Montrachet,
    etc.), sliced

Place the parsley in the work bowl of a food processor and process until minced. Drain the chilies and add them to the work bowl along with the olive oil, salt and red pepper sauce to taste. Process until the chilies are finely chopped and the mixture is fairly smooth.

Spread ¼ cup of the parsley mixture over each round of dough, leaving about a ¼-inch border all around. Roughly chop the olives and sprinkle them, along with the tomato, over the parsley mixture. Cover with a layer of the cheese. Set aside to rest for 15 to 30 minutes, while the oven heats to 400°F.

Bake for about 25 minutes, until the dough is lightly browned around the edges.

Makes 4 pizzas.

MOZZARELLA/GOAT CHEESE TOPPING

Olive oil
4 plum tomatoes, sliced
¼ pound Mozzarella
2 ounces young goat cheese (Laura
    Chenel's Pyramide, Montrachet,
    etc.)
Freshly ground black pepper

Brush some olive oil on each dough round. Arrange the tomato slices in an even layer on top, leaving about a ¼-inch rim.

Cut the Mozzarella into julienne strips about ⅛ inch wide and 3 inches long. Arrange them over the tomato like spokes in a wheel. Crumble the goat cheese and put it on top of the tomato still showing. Grind some black pepper on top.

Set aside to rest for 15 to 30 minutes, while the oven heats to 400°F.

Bake for about 25 minutes, until the dough is lightly browned around the edges.

Makes 4 pizzas.

Three-Cheese Calzone with Sausage

Calzone are sort of stuffed pizzas. The dough is the same, but the toppings become fillings. The possible choices are as varied as for regular pizzas. This is one we like a lot.

1 recipe Basic Bread/Pizza Dough (see page 240)
½ pound hot Italian sausage
2 ounces Mozzarella, cubed
2 ounces Bel Paese, cubed
2 ounces Gorgonzola, cubed
½ teaspoon chopped fresh marjoram, or ¼ teaspoon dried
½ teaspoon fresh thyme, or ¼ teaspoon dried

While the dough is rising, cook the sausages. Prick them all over, then put in a skillet with about ¼ inch water. Cook until the water evaporates and the sausages are browned in their own fat. Remove from the heat and cut into ⅛-inch rounds. Place the sausages in a bowl with the cheeses and herbs.

Punch the dough down and divide it in half. Roll each piece out into a 12-inch circle. This will take a few minutes because the dough will tend to recoil. Once the dough is ready, put half the cheese filling on half of each circle, leaving 1-inch borders. Brush the borders with water. Fold the other halves over and press down to seal the half-moons. Pinch the dough together and back toward the center, making thick, tightly sealed borders. Place on a baking sheet sprinkled with cornmeal.

Set the filled dough aside to rise while the oven heats to 475°F., about half an hour. When the oven is hot, bake the calzone for 25 minutes. They should be brown and crisp. Serve hot with a knife and fork.

Makes two 10-inch calzone.

Main Courses

These main courses are mostly created to be the focus of a lunch, brunch or late-night supper rather than a typical sit-down dinner—perhaps because many of them are vegetarian. Hearty eaters might even prefer to have dishes like stuffed eggplant or spanakopitta as a side dish with a roast. The souf-flés could all be first courses. You'll find the meatier dishes toward the end of the chapter. We usually serve a salad of the best mixed greens of the season: Bibb lettuce and watercress, arugula and radicchio, with rounds of red radishes and cucumbers, some crunchy celery.

We have omitted recipes for omelets and scrambled eggs, choosing not to add to the endless arguments about the best technique. However, do add cubes or skinny shreds of cheese to the raw eggs or the almost-cooked dish. Creamy cheeses will blend right in. Cheddars and Swisses stay firmer.

Fondue

One of Switzerland's native cheese dishes, fondue is a social meal, best made for groups of four or six, all sitting cozily around the bubbling pot placed conveniently in the center of the table. There are many variations on the dish, some made with only Emmentaler or Gruyère, others made with the heartier Vacherin Fribourgeois. This recipe comes from Seppi Renggli of The Four Seasons, who learned it as a boy in Switzerland. Although cubed bread is always dipped into the fondue, he recommends wrapping strips of ham around the cubes and securing them with toothpicks. Then when you dip, you get ham, cheese and bread in each bite. It's also pretty to look at that way.

Some American restaurants serve fondue all year, but it is really an ideal winter dish to enjoy after a day spent skiing or skating. Use the same wine in it that you plan to serve with the fondue.

1 garlic clove, halved
¼ pound Emmentaler, cut into ¼-inch cubes
½ pound Gruyère, cut into ¼-inch cubes
¾ cup white wine, preferably a Riesling
1 teaspoon cornstarch
1 tablespoon kirschwasser
Pinch baking soda
Pinch grated nutmeg
French bread, cut into ¾-inch cubes

If you are using a thin-bottomed fondue pot, place it over a low flame or Flame Tamer in the beginning so the cheese won't burn.

Rub the inside of the pot with the cut garlic and leave the garlic in the pot. Add the cheeses and wine. Place over low heat and cook, stirring often, until the cheeses melt and the mixture is smooth.

Dissolve the cornstarch in some of the kirschwasser and add it to the cheese mixture along with the remaining kirschwasser, baking soda and nutmeg. Stir vigorously until the mixture is thick and smooth. Remove it to the table and place over a tabletop heater to keep the fondue hot. Each guest should spear a cube of bread with a long-handled fork and dip it into the fondue pot, turning it to coat with the cheese mixture.

Serves about 4.

Raclette

Switzerland's other national cheese dish, not as well known as fondue, is raclette, made by heating a chunk of cheese until the top softens enough to be scraped off in long strips onto freshly boiled potatoes in their skins. Suited to large groups, raclette is traditionally made with a half-wheel of Raclette or Bagnes held in front of a blazing fire. Today there are efficient electric machines for melting the cheese, and smaller pieces, even a half pound, can be used to serve two. Figure on 4 to 8 ounces a person.

The meal is very rich and meant to be informal. Give each person a bowl with warm potatoes in it. Scrape a strip of cheese on top. Continue scraping until everyone has been served. By then, the first person will be ready for seconds. If the scraper gets ahead of the eaters, remove the cheese from the heat so the cheese doesn't really melt.

Serve tiny cornichons on the side as well as thin slices of bündnerfleisch. Have plenty of chilled white wine or beer.

Welsh Rarebit

Welsh rarebit, also called Welsh rabbit, is one of the oldest recorded dishes, and a very simple one, actually a rich cheese sauce poured over toast. It is perfect for a late-night snack or as a change from grilled cheese at lunch. For a heartier meal, called Golden Buck, top each serving with a poached egg.

4 tablespoons unsalted butter
1 pound Cheshire or Cheddar, broken
    into small pieces with a fork
½ cup ale or milk
4 teaspoons prepared mustard
Red pepper sauce
Worcestershire sauce
8 slices white bread toast, buttered

Heat the butter in a saucepan. Add the cheese and cook over low heat, stirring constantly until the cheese is smooth. Stir in the ale or milk, then the mustard. Add red pepper sauce and Worcestershire to taste.

Remove from the heat and immediately pour over the toast on individual plates.

Serves 8.

Tomato-Cheese Rarebit

This American version of Welsh Rarebit is known by many fanciful names including Rinktum Dittie, Dinah de Ditty and Woodchuck. Because it is not quite as rich as plain Welsh rarebit, guests can eat more of it.

Since its invention, canned tomato soup has been a basic ingredient in most recipes, but starting from scratch isn't difficult and is certainly worth the few extra minutes.

2 tablespoons unsalted butter
2 tablespoons all-purpose flour
1 cup milk
1 cup drained and crushed canned tomatoes, seeds removed for elegant groups
Pinch baking soda
2 cups Cheddar broken into small pieces
1 teaspoon kosher salt
½ teaspoon dry mustard
⅛ teaspoon cayenne pepper
2 large eggs, beaten
6 slices white bread toast, buttered, or 6 toasted English muffins, buttered

Heat the butter in a saucepan until foamy. Add the flour and cook, stirring, for about 2 minutes to eliminate the raw taste. Add the milk and stir until smooth and thick. Stir in the tomatoes and baking soda, then the cheese. When the cheese is melted and the sauce is fairly smooth (except for some lumps of tomato), season with the salt, mustard and cayenne. Stir in the eggs. When it is smooth again, taste and adjust seasonings if necessary. Pour the sauce over the toast.

Serves 6.

Spanakopitta

This is a traditional Greek spinach and Feta pie originally from the island of Samos. It makes a lovely lunch or supper dish with a salad or light soup. We also serve it as a side dish with grilled lamb.

This recipe calls for more Feta than many traditional recipes because we used the milder Feta found in most of this country. Should you buy your Feta in a Greek neighborhood, it will probably be much stronger and saltier. In that case, you might want to use less.

2 pounds fresh spinach
2 tablespoons unsalted butter
1 bunch (about 8 medium) scallions,
    both green and white parts, minced
1 bunch parsley, minced
1 bunch fresh dill, minced
¾ pound Feta, crumbled
¼ teaspoon freshly ground pepper
3 large eggs, beaten
¼ pound melted butter
8 sheets (13 x 17 inches, about 6
    ounces) filo dough

Heat the oven to 350°F.

Remove and discard the thick stems from the spinach. Wash the leaves well to remove all the sand. Dry them fairly well, then place in a large nonaluminum pot. Cook over medium heat, mixing often, until barely wilted, 4 to 5 minutes. Put the spinach in a strainer and press firmly with a spoon to eliminate as much liquid as possible. Roughly chop the leaves and place them in a large mixing bowl. Set aside.

Heat the 2 tablespoons butter in a small skillet. Add the scallions and cook over medium heat until soft but not brown, about 2 minutes. Add to the spinach along with the parsley, dill, Feta, pepper and eggs. Stir just to mix.

Brush a 12 x 8-inch baking dish (preferably a pretty one you can take to the table) with some of the melted butter.

While working with the filo, always keep the extra sheets covered with a cloth so they don't dry out from exposure to the air. The sheets will have to be folded in half. You can cut them, but it isn't necessary. Place a half sheet on the bottom of the dish, brush it with butter and fold the second half over. Brush that half with butter. As you work, do not trim the filo, but try to vary the positions so it hangs somewhat evenly over all the edges.

Place three more sheets of filo in the baking dish, spreading butter between the layers, so you now have eight layers of filo. Spread the spinach/Feta mixture over the filo. Top with the remaining filo in the same way, brushing butter between the layers. Push all the excess filo down in around the edges and brush the top heavily with the remaining butter.

Bake in the preheated oven for 45 minutes, or until golden brown and crisp. Serve hot or at room temperature.

Serves 4 to 6 as a main course, 8 to 10 as a side dish.

Spanakopites Samiotikes

These attractive spiral-shaped individual pies use the spanakopitta filling for a flakier result.

Spinach/Feta filling for Spanakopitta (see page 152)
20 sheets (13 x 17 inches, about 1 pound) filo dough
6 ounces melted butter

Heat the oven to 350°F.

Work with the filo one sheet at a time, keeping the rest covered with a cloth.

With the shorter (13-inch) end of the filo facing you, brush butter over half the sheet. Fold the other half over. Spread about ¼ cup filling along the long edge of the filo. Roll the filo around the filling so you have a long, thin roll. Holding one end, wrap the roll around itself in a tight, flat spiral. Brush the top with butter and place on a baking sheet.

Continue in this way until all the filling is used. You will need at least two baking sheets. Bake in the preheated oven for 30 minutes, or until nicely browned and crisp. Rotate the baking sheets so everything bakes evenly.

Makes 20 spanakopites.

Basic Cheese Soufflé

The classic soufflé is often made with Gruyère, although many cheeses, either semisoft, Swiss-style or Cheddar, will work as well. You can make the base ahead, but don't beat the whites until just before you are ready to bake.

1 ounce Parmesan, grated
3 tablespoons unsalted butter
3 tablespoons all-purpose flour
1 cup milk
4 large eggs, separated
¼ pound Gruyère, grated
Salt
Freshly ground pepper
1 egg white

Butter a 6-cup soufflé dish and sprinkle it generously with some of the grated Parmesan. Set aside. Heat the oven to 400°F.

Melt the butter in a 2-quart saucepan. Add the flour and stir so it is absorbed by the butter. Continue cooking for 2 minutes to eliminate the raw taste. Pour in the milk and stir until the mixture is smooth. Bring to a boil and cook for a few minutes. The sauce will be thick. Remove the pan from the heat and stir in the egg yolks, Gruyère and salt and pepper to taste.

In a clean bowl, beat the egg whites until stiff but not dry. Carefully fold them into the cheese base, mixing just until the whites are absorbed. Quickly pour the mixture into the prepared pan. Run a spatula around the edge of the top to help make a cap as it bakes. Sprinkle the remaining Parmesan cheese on top.

Bake in the preheated oven for about 30 minutes. The top will be puffed and brown, the center still soft.

Serves 3 or 4.

Goat Cheese and Red Pepper Soufflé

The red pepper purée turns this soufflé a pastel shade between pink and orange.

2 red bell peppers
Dry bread crumbs
6 ounces goat cheese (Montrachet, Ste. Maure, other Logs or Pyramides)
3 tablespoons unsalted butter
3 tablespoons all-purpose flour
1 cup milk
4 large eggs, separated
2 tablespoons chopped chives
1 egg white

Heat a grill or broiler until hot. Place the peppers close to the heat and roast them, turning as needed, until black on all sides. Remove the peppers to a plastic bag and close tight so the steam from the peppers loosens the skin. Let rest a few minutes, then peel away and discard the charred skin along with the cores and seeds.

Cut the flesh of half a pepper into ¼-inch squares. Set aside.

Butter a 6-cup soufflé dish and sprinkle it generously with dry bread crumbs. Set aside. Heat the oven to 400°F.

Roughly chop the rest of the peppers and put them in a food processor with the cheese. Run until well mixed.

Melt the butter in a 2-quart saucepan. Add the flour and stir so it is absorbed by the butter. Continue cooking for 2 minutes to eliminate the raw taste. Pour in the milk and stir until the mixture is smooth. Bring to a boil and cook for a few minutes. The sauce will be thick. Remove the pan from the heat and stir in the egg yolks and goat cheese and pepper mixture. When smooth, add the chives and pepper squares.

In a clean bowl, beat the egg white until stiff but not dry. Fold them into the cheese mixture until well mixed. Spoon it into the prepared pan and bake for about 35 minutes, until set.

Serves 2 to 3 for lunch.

Tex-Mex Soufflé

We like this for lunch with a salad of arugula and water-cress and baking soda biscuits.

Fine, dry bread crumbs
3 tablespoons unsalted butter
2 scallions, both green and white parts, sliced
3 tablespoons all-purpose flour
1 cup milk
2 plum tomatoes (about 3 ounces each), cored and seeded, cut into ⅓-inch cubes
1 teaspoon kosher salt
¼ teaspoon red pepper sauce
¼ pound Monterey Jack, cut into ¼-inch cubes
4 large eggs, separated
1 ounce canned roasted chili peppers, cut into ¼-inch squares

Grease a 1-quart soufflé mold and coat it with the bread crumbs. Shake out the excess and set aside.

Melt the butter in a saucepan. Add the scallions and cook for 2 minutes over medium-high heat. Add the flour and stir so it is absorbed by the butter. Continue cooking for 2 minutes to elminate the raw taste. Pour in the milk and stir until the mixture is smooth. Bring to a boil and cook for a few minutes. The sauce will be thick. Stir in the tomatoes, salt and red pepper sauce. Let cool a bit, then stir in the cheese and egg yolks. This can be done ahead.

Heat the oven to 400°F.

When the oven is hot, beat the egg whites in a clean bowl until they are stiff but not dry. Fold them into the tomato mixture along with the roasted chili pepper. Spoon the mixture into the prepared pan and place in the oven. Lower the temperature to 375°F. and bake for 35 to 45 minutes. It will be set and brown on the top but still runny in the middle. Serve immediately.

Serves 2 to 4.

Shrimp with Feta

This quick sauté evokes the romance of the Mediterranean. Serve it with orzo, a rice-shaped pasta.

2 tablespoons unsalted butter
2 tablespoons olive oil
2 garlic cloves, minced
¼ cup minced shallots
2 pounds tomatoes, cored and cut into
    1-inch cubes
2 pounds shrimp, peeled and deveined
⅔ cup pitted black olives
¾ pound Feta, cut into ½-inch cubes
2 tablespoons Pernod
Freshly ground black pepper to taste

Heat the butter and oil in a 10-inch skillet. Add the garlic and shallots and cook for 1 minute. Add the tomatoes and cook 2 minutes longer. Add the shrimp and toss until they turn pink on the outside. Add the olives and cook a minute longer, or until the shrimp are done. Add the Feta and cook a minute longer. The cheese should soften but not dissolve.

In a separate pan, heat the Pernod and ignite it. When the flames die down, pour the liquid into the shrimp mixture. Stir to blend and add pepper to taste.

Serves 6.

Jane Joseph's Cheese Roulade

This roulade, created by Jane Helsel Joseph, is actually a fallen soufflé wrapped around a cheese and shrimp filling.

5 tablespoons unsalted butter
¼ cup all-purpose flour
2¼ cups milk
2 teaspoons Dijon mustard
2¼ teaspoons salt
⅛ teaspoon cayenne pepper
¼ teaspoon freshly ground white pepper
¼ cup plus 3 tablespoons grated
    Parmesan
1 cup thinly sliced red bell pepper, cut
    into 1-inch lengths
2 tablespoons thinly sliced scallion
    whites
½ teaspoon minced garlic
1 tablespoon fresh lemon juice
½ pound small peeled shrimp, blanched
    in boiling salted water
1 pound fresh spinach, well washed and
    trimmed
¼ cup thinly sliced scallion greens
Freshly ground black pepper
10 large eggs, separated
1¼ cups (about 5 ounces) grated
    Fontina
1 recipe Bell Pepper Sauce (see page
    235)

Melt 4 tablespoons of the butter in a saucepan. Add the flour and stir so it is absorbed by the butter. Continue cooking for 2 minutes to eliminate the raw taste. Pour in the milk and stir until the mixture is smooth. Bring to a boil and cook for another minute, stirring constantly. Remove from the heat. Stir in the mustard, 1½ teaspoons of the salt, the cayenne and white peppers. Set aside.

Heat the oven to 425°F. Lightly butter an 11 x 17½-inch jelly roll pan. Line it with wax paper so it overhangs about 1 inch at either end. Butter the paper. Sprinkle on 1 tablespoon of the grated Parmesan. Set aside.

Melt the remaining tablespoon butter in a skillet. Add the red pepper, scallion whites and garlic. Sauté for a minute, then add the lemon juice. Continue cooking until all the liquid has been absorbed, about 30 seconds. Set aside in a bowl with the shrimp.

Bring a large pot of salted water to the boil. Add the spinach and cook for 1 minute. Drain well and squeeze dry. Roughly chop the spinach and add it to the shrimp along with the scallion greens and ½ cup reserved white sauce. Season to taste with ½ teaspoon salt and black pepper. Mix well and set aside.

In a large bowl, whisk together the egg yolks and remaining white sauce. In a separate bowl, beat the egg whites and remaining ¼ teaspoon salt until the whites are stiff but not dry. Stir a fourth of the whites into the egg yolk mixture. Carefully fold in the remaining whites along with ¼ cup of the Parmesan and the Fontina.

Spread the mixture evenly into the prepared pan, smoothing the top. Bake in the preheated oven until puffed and brown, 15 to 18 minutes. Let cool on a wire rack for 10 minutes. Sprinkle the remaining 2 tablespoons Parmesan on top.

Cover the roulade with buttered aluminum foil, buttered side down, leaving a 3-inch overhang at either end. (If necessary, use two sheets and overlap them by at least two inches.) Grasping the ends of the foil, carefully but quickly invert the pan onto a flat surface. Lift off the jelly roll pan. With your fingers or a small knife, carefully peel back and discard the wax paper. Let cool 10 minutes longer.

Spread the shrimp and spinach filling evenly over the roulade, leaving a ½ inch border all around. Starting at one long end, roll up the roulade like a jely roll. Use the foil to help you.

Once the roulade is done, cut the ends off on a diagonal. Slice the rest into ten 1-inch slices. Serve with the Bell Pepper Sauce.

Serves 8 to 10.

NOTE: If you make the roulade ahead, wrap it tight in foil and refrigerate. Reheat in a 350°F. oven for 30 minutes still wrapped in foil, 5 minutes longer unwrapped.

Chuck Williams's Baked Eggs and Cheese

Chuck Williams, best known as the creator of the Williams-Sonoma mail-order catalogues and shops, is also an excellent cook, as this recipe will attest. He recommends serving this dish with crusty bread and chutney as a first course, or with a fresh green salad for lunch, brunch or supper. You can easily adjust the recipe to make individual one- or two-egg portions. Watch the cooking times; the whites should be just set and the yolks still runny like a perfect fried egg.

2 strips (about 2 ounces) bacon
½ pound grated Gruyère
4 large eggs
1 teaspoon finely chopped chives or
    scallions
Freshly ground white pepper
3 to 4 tablespoons fine bread crumbs
    made from day-old firm white bread

Heat the oven to 300°F. and lightly butter a 1-quart soufflé dish.

Fry the bacon until crisp. Drain well, then crumble into small pieces.

Sprinkle half the cheese in the bottom of the soufflé dish. Carefully break the eggs over the cheese, spacing them evenly. Sprinkle the bacon and chives over the eggs and cover with the remaining cheese. Season with freshly ground pepper, then sprinkle on the bread crumbs.

Bake in the preheated oven for 15 minutes, or until the eggs are just set. You can gently lift the top layer of cheese with a fork to check.

Turn the broiler to high and run the dish underneath just to brown the top slightly. Serve immediately.

Serves 4 as an appetizer, 2 for lunch.

Cheese Blintzes

A staple Jewish dairy food, these are perfect for lunch topped with dollops of sour cream. In season, you might add some fresh berries either on top or to the filling. If you have extras, freeze them after they are shaped. Before serving, brown them in butter over low heat while they are still frozen.

BATTER

3 large eggs
1 cup all-purpose flour
1½ cups water
½ teaspoon kosher salt
1 teaspoon vegetable oil

Put all the ingredients in a food processor or blender and process until smooth. Cover the batter and refrigerate for at least 2 hours.

FILLING

1 pound Farmer Cheese
2 large eggs
1 teaspoon kosher salt
2 to 4 tablespoons sugar
4 tablespoons unsalted butter, melted

Break the Farmer Cheese into small pieces and place them in the work bowl of a food processor along with the eggs, salt and sugar to taste. Process until fairly smooth. With the machine running, pour in the melted butter. Continue processing until smooth. The filling can also be mixed by hand until smooth.

ASSEMBLY

Batter
Vegetable oil
Filling
Unsalted butter

Remove the batter from the refrigerator and stir to blend if the mixture has separated.

Heat a heavy 6-inch crêpe pan over high heat. Brush with a thin layer of oil. Pour just under 2 tablespoons batter into the pan and rotate until the batter evenly coats the bottom. If there is excess batter, pour it back into the uncooked batter. When the crêpe is nicely browned on the bottom, remove it to a plate. Add more oil if needed and continue cooking crêpes until all the batter has been used. You should have about twenty-four crêpes.

To make the blintzes, take one crêpe at a time, and place it, browned side up, on your work surface. Place about 2 tablespoons filling on the crêpe about a third of the way up from the bottom. Fold the bottom over the filling, then fold in the sides. Roll it over.

When all the blintzes are formed, heat some butter in a skillet and cook the blintzes slowly until they are browned on both sides.

Makes about 24 blintzes, enough for eight for lunch.

Stuffed Eggplant

Half an eggplant stuffed with cheese and seasonings makes a satisfying lunch or supper with a salad of tomatoes and red onions.

1 eggplant, about ¾ pound
2 tablespoons olive oil
1 garlic clove, minced
1 medium onion, chopped
1 red bell pepper, cored, seeded and cut
    into ½-inch squares
1 teaspoon kosher salt
Freshly ground black pepper
2 teaspoons chopped fresh marjoram, or
    ½ teaspoon dried
2 teaspoons chopped fresh basil, or ½
    teaspoon dried
3 ounces Doux de Montagne or other
    Fromage des Pyrénées, cubed
1 tablespoon dried bread crumbs
1 tablespoon grated Parmesan

Heat the oven to 375°F.

Remove and discard the leaves from the eggplant and cut it in half lengthwise. With a sharp paring knife, cut out the eggplant pulp, leaving the skin and a ¼-inch shell. Roughly cut the eggplant into ¼-inch cubes. Set aside.

Heat the oil in a 10-inch skillet. Add the garlic and onion and cook for 5 minutes, until the onion is soft but not brown. Add the cubed eggplant and cook for 2 minutes. Add the red pepper and cook a minute longer. Season to taste with salt and pepper. Remove from the heat and stir in the herbs and cheese. Spoon half the mixture into each eggplant shell, mounding it up in the center.

Mix the bread crumbs and Parmesan together and sprinkle over each shell. Place them in a baking dish and bake in the preheated oven for 25 minutes, or until the eggplant is hot and the top is lightly brown.

Serves 2.

Rolled Eggplant

The smoky taste of the grilled eggplant works well with the cheeses and pepper sauce. If you prefer, serve one or two rolls as a first course.

½ pound goat cheese (Montrachet or other young chèvre), at room temperature
2 cups Ricotta, at room temperature
2 scallions, minced
¹⁄₁₆ teaspoon cayenne pepper
2 eggplants, about 1¼ pounds each
Vegetable oil
½ recipe Bell Pepper Sauce (see page 235), heated

Heat a grill until hot.

Put the goat cheese and Ricotta in a food processor and process until smooth. Remove to a bowl and stir in the scallions and cayenne. Set aside.

Cut the stems from the eggplants, then slice lengthwise into long strips about ¼ inch wide. Discard the outer slices that are all skin. You should have about nine slices from each eggplant. Brush each slice on both sides with vegetable oil and place on the grill. Cook until seared and soft on the bottom. Turn and cook the other side.

When the eggplant slices are cooked, place them on your work surface. Place about 2 tablespoons cheese mixture about 2 inches from the bottom of each slice. Fold the eggplant over the filling and roll up.

Spoon some sauce on each of six dinner plates. Arrange three eggplant rolls on top of the sauce on each plate.

Serves 6.

Eggplant Parmesan

This dish brings a hint of Mediterranean summer to even the coldest winter days.

SAUCE

3 tablespoons olive oil
4 garlic cloves, minced
4 medium onions (about 1 pound), chopped
2 cans (28 ounces each) plum tomatoes
½ cup red wine
4 teaspoons fresh thyme, or 1 teaspoon dried
4 teaspoons kosher salt
Freshly ground black pepper

Heat the olive oil in a skillet. Add the garlic and onion and cook until soft but not brown, 3 to 4 minutes.

Roughly crush the tomatoes and add them to the pot with their liquid, the wine and thyme. Let simmer for 30 minutes, then season to taste with salt and pepper. Set aside.

EGGPLANT

2 eggplants, about 1¼ pounds each
Salt
Flour seasoned with salt and pepper
¾ cup olive oil, approximately

Cut the stems and very bottoms off the eggplants, then slice them crosswise into ½-inch-thick rounds. Sprinkle them with salt and pile up in a bowl. Place a plate and weight on top to force them to exude liquid. Let stand for about 1 hour. Pour off all the liquid that accumulates.

Press each slice between paper towels to eliminate as much liquid as possible, then dust them lightly with the seasoned flour.

Heat 2 or 3 tablespoons olive oil in a skillet. Add a few slices of eggplant and cook until brown on each side and soft in the middle. Remove to a plate and add more slices. Add more oil as needed. Continue until all the eggplant is cooked.

½ cup bread crumbs
¼ cup freshly grated Parmesan
2 teaspoons fresh thyme, or ½ teaspoon dried
Tomato sauce
Cooked eggplant
1 pound Fontina, cut into slices ⅛ inch thick

Heat the oven to 350°F.

In a small bowl, mix together the bread crumbs, Parmesan and thyme.

Spoon a thin layer of tomato sauce in the bottom of a 9 x 14-inch gratin dish. Top with a layer of eggplant, then Fontina and some of the bread crumb mixture. Continue in this way until everything has been used, making thicker layers of sauce. Spread the Fontina on top.

Bake in the preheated oven for 20 minutes, or until the cheese is browned and the casserole bubbly.

Serves 6 to 8.

Jean Hewitt's Rice and Cheese Casserole

Jean Hewitt, food editor of *Family Circle,* created this easy way to use leftover rice, making a very satisfying lunch.

3 cups cooked rice
8 to 10 finely chopped scallions, both green and white parts (about ½ cup)
1½ cups large curd Cottage Cheese
1 cup sour cream
¼ cup milk
6 to 8 sprigs parsley, minced
Red pepper sauce or cayenne pepper
Salt
2 ounces Parmesan, grated (about ½ cup)

Butter a 2-quart ovenproof casserole and set aside. Heat the oven to 350°F.

Put the rice and scallions in a bowl. In another bowl, mix together the Cottage Cheese, sour cream, milk and parsley. Season to taste with red pepper sauce and salt. Stir in the rice mixture. Spoon into the prepared casserole and top with the Parmesan.

Bake in the preheated oven for 25 minutes, or until piping hot.

Serves 6.

Martha Shulman's Mushroom and Wild Rice Strudel

Martha Rose Shulman is a vegetarian who has convinced many carnivores that meals without meat can be wonderful. This hearty mushroom-filled strudel is a perfect example.

1½ to 2 ounces dried wild mushrooms, such as cèpes, girolles or Chinese black
½ cup wild rice, washed
Salt
1 tablespoon unsalted butter
1 tablespoon olive oil plus more if necessary
3 garlic cloves, minced
4 shallots, minced
1 pound fresh mushrooms, sliced through the caps
3 tablespoons dry white wine
Soy sauce
¼ to ½ teaspoon dried thyme
¼ to ½ teaspoon chopped fresh or crumbled dried rosemary
Freshly ground pepper
¼ cup chopped parsley
2 large eggs
3 ounces Gruyère, grated
1 ounce Parmesan, grated
2 ounces crumbled goat cheese
½ pound (about 9 sheets) filo dough
¼ pound unsalted butter, melted

Place the dried mushrooms in a bowl and add boiling water to cover. Let sit for 30 minutes, then drain through a strainer lined with dampened cheesecloth. Reserve the soaking liquid. Rinse the mushrooms briefly to remove any remining grit, then pat dry. Slice if very large, otherwise leave whole.

Add enough water to the soaking liquid to measure 1½ cups. Bring the liquid to a boil. Add the wild rice and salt to taste. Reduce the heat to a simmer, cover and cook for 30 to 40 minutes, until the rice is tender.

Meanwhile, heat the butter and oil in a large, heavy-bottomed skillet. Add one third of the garlic and the shallots. Sauté for about 30 seconds, then add the fresh mushrooms with half the remaining garlic. Sauté over medium heat until the mushrooms begin to soften and release their liquid. Stir in the soaked dried mushrooms along with the wine and soy sauce to taste. Continue cooking, stirring, for about 3 minutes. Add the remaining garlic along with the thyme, rosemary and salt and pepper to taste. Cook for another 5 minutes, then adjust seasonings to taste. Transfer the mixture to a bowl.

When the rice is tender, drain off any excess water. Add the rice to the mushroom mixture. Stir in the parsley and adjust the seasonings, adding more soy sauce, herbs or pepper as needed. Beat the eggs and stir them in along with the cheeses.

Heat the oven to 400°F.

Take the filo sheets, one at a time, and brush each with melted butter, stacking them neatly on top of each other until you have a pile nine layers deep with the longer side stretching across your work surface.

Beginning about 3 inches down from the top, and leaving a 2½-inch margin on either side, spoon the filling across the top in a strip about 3 inches wide. Fold the sides in over the filling, then fold down the top and roll up. Place on a lightly greased baking sheet and brush the top with more melted butter.

Bake in the preheated oven for 30 to 40 minutes, or until golden brown and crisp. It can sit for a few minutes before serving, but is best when still hot.

Serves 6 generously.

Jack and Avocado Enchiladas

Californians are as influenced by Mexico in their cooking as are the Texans. This dish uses the best of both areas.

6 ounces Monterey Jack, cut into small
    cubes
2 scallions, minced
⅓ cup diced avocado
¼ cup minced parsley
Vegetable oil
1 recipe Red Chile Sauce (see page 236)
6 corn tortillas, 8 inches in diameter
1 ounce grated Cheddar or Monterey
    Jack

Heat the oven to 350°F.

Place the cubed Monterey Jack in a bowl with the scallions, avocado and parsley.

Heat 1 tablespoon oil in a skillet. Add the chile sauce and cook, stirring frequently, for about 3 minutes. Keep warm.

Pour vegetable oil into an 8- to 10-inch skillet to a depth of ¼ inch. Heat the oil to just smoking. Holding a tortilla with tongs, drop it into the hot oil for about 30 seconds, turn and let cook on the other side. The tortillas should be soft and flexible. If they are crisp, the oil is too hot. If they are very greasy, the oil isn't hot enough. Cook all the tortillas in this way, one at a time.

When all the tortillas are cooked, spread about 1 tablespoon chile sauce in a strip about 2 inches wide down the center of each tortilla. Top it with about ⅓ cup cheese mixture, then fold the sides in so you have a roll. Place in a 9 x 14-inch baking dish, open side down. Continue in this way until all the tortillas are filled. They should fill the dish in a single layer. Pour about ¾ cup sauce over the enchiladas and sprinkle the grated cheese on top. Bake in the preheated oven for about 10 minutes. The top should be bubbly and the filling melted.

Serve one or two hot enchiladas per person with more chile sauce on the side.

Serves 3 to 6.

Farmer Cheese Enchiladas

This is a summery enchilada filling. In Mexico, they usually use Queso Fresco for stuffings. Farmer Cheese is quite similar.

1 pound or 2 packages (7½ ounces each) Farmer Cheese
2 tablespoons milk
2 large radishes, cut into ¼-inch cubes
2 scallions, cut into ¼-inch pieces
⅓ cup pitted black olives cut into ¼-inch pieces
3 tablespoons minced fresh coriander (cilantro or Chinese parsley)
1 teaspoon kosher salt
Vegetable oil
1 recipe Red Chile Sauce (see page 236)
6 corn tortillas, 8 inches in diameter

Heat the oven to 350°F.

Set about ½ cup cheese aside. Place the rest in a small bowl and mix with the milk. Stir in the radishes, scallions, olives, 2 tablespoons of the coriander and the salt.

Heat 1 tablespoon oil in a skillet. Add the chile sauce and cook, stirring frequently, for about 3 minutes. Keep warm.

Pour vegetable oil into an 8- to 10-inch skillet to a depth of ¼ inch. Heat the oil to just smoking. Holding a tortilla with tongs, drop it into the hot oil for about 30 seconds, turn and let cook on the other side. The tortillas should be soft and flexible. If they are crisp, the oil is too hot. If they are very greasy, the oil isn't hot enough. Cook all the tortillas in this way, one at a time.

When all the tortillas are cooked, spread about 1 tablespoon chile sauce in a strip about 2 inches wide down the center of each tortilla. Top it with about ⅓ cup cheese mixture, then fold the sides in so you have a roll. Place in a 9 x 14-inch baking dish, open side down. Continue in this way until all the tortillas are filled. They should fill the dish in a single layer. Pour about ¾ cup sauce over the enchiladas and sprinkle the reserved ½ cup cheese on top, then the remaining tablespoon coriander. Bake in the preheated oven for about 10 minutes. The top should be bubbly and the filling melted.

Serve one or two hot enchiladas per person with more chile sauce on the side.

Serves 3 to 6.

Stuffed Poblano Chilies

Poblano chilies, a standard in Mexican cooking, have a more subtle flavor than that of bell peppers. If you cannot get fresh poblanos in your neighborhood, use the pale green Italian frying peppers or bell peppers. Serve these with rice or tortillas to absorb the sauce.

12 poblano chilies, about 1½ pounds
1 tablespoon olive oil
1 large garlic clove, minced
1 medium onion, diced
1 pound tomatoes, cored and roughly
    chopped
¼ cup red wine vinegar
1 teaspoon kosher salt
10 ounces Queso Fresco, Monterey Jack,
    or other mild semisoft cheese, cut
    into ¼-inch dice
10 ounces spicy chorizo sausages, casing
    removed, roughly chopped

Heat a grill or broiler until hot. Cook the poblano chilies close to the heat, turning them as necessary until they are blistery all over. Parts will be black. Set aside to cool slightly, then pull the skin off with your fingers. If they are cooked enough, the skin will slip right off. Carefully cut out the core and remove the seeds inside, trying to keep the chilies as whole as possible. If necessary, rinse them briefly in water, but do not soak. Set aside.

Heat the oven to 375°F.

Heat the oil in a skillet and add the garlic and onion. Cook until the onion is soft but not brown, about 4 minutes. Add the tomatoes followed by the vinegar and salt. Cover and cook over medium heat for 5 minutes. Spoon the sauce into the bottom of a 9 x 13-inch casserole.

Mix together the cheese and chorizo. Carefully stuff each chili with some of the cheese and sausage mixture. They should be quite full. Press any slit ends together. Arrange the chilies over the sauce in as close to a single layer as you can, putting any openings in the chilies on the top. Cover the dish with foil and bake until everything is heated through and the sauce is bubbly, about 25 minutes.

Serves 4 to 6.

Stuffed Chicken Breasts

This is a nice dish for company since most of the work is done ahead and just finished off in the kitchen. We used Gruyère, but other Swiss-style or semisoft cheeses will work equally well.

4 large chicken breasts, about 1 pound each, skinned and boned, giving eight pieces
2 pounds mushrooms
4 tablespoons olive oil
¼ cup minced shallots
1 tablespoon kosher salt
¼ teaspoon cayenne pepper
¾ cup bread crumbs
3 tablespoons grated Parmesan or Romano
1 large egg
½ pound Gruyère, cut into eight slices
2 tablespoons unsalted butter
½ cup dry white wine

Place each chicken breast half between two sheets of wax paper and pound until it is about ⅛ inch thick. Refrigerate the chicken while you make the filling so it will be easier to work with.

Pull the stems from the mushrooms. Add enough caps to the stems to make one pound. Chop them into a fine mince. This is easiest in a food processor, using pulses. Cut the remaining mushroom caps into ¼-inch slices.

Heat 2 tablespoons of the olive oil in a 10-inch skillet. Add the shallots and cook for 1 minute. Add the minced mushrooms along with half the salt and cayenne pepper and cook for 2 minutes, until soft. Raise the heat and cook 2 minutes longer. The mixture should be fairly dry.

Mix the bread crumbs and Parmesan together in a flat bowl. Beat the egg in another flat bowl.

Work with one breast piece at a time, placing it so the smooth flesh that was closest to the skin is on the bottom. Put one slice of cheese on the breast to one side of the center. Spread about ¼ cup cooked mushroom mixture on top. Fold the rest of the chicken over to cover the filling. Dip the package first in the egg, then in the bread crumb mixture. Place on a plate. Continue in this way until all the chicken packages are made, then refrigerate at least 30 minutes.

To cook the chicken all at one time, you will need two 10-inch frying pans. If you have only one, cook them in two batches. Before you start, turn the oven on low. Heat 1 tablespoon oil and 1 tablespoon butter in each frying pan. Add the chicken in a single layer and cook over medium heat until well browned, about 5 minutes. Turn and cook until well browned on the other side, another 5 minutes.

Remove the cooked chicken to a plate and keep warm in the oven. If using one pan, add fresh oil and butter and cook the remaining chicken. Add it to the first batch. When all the chicken is cooked, deglaze the pan(s) by pouring in the wine and scraping the bottom with a wooden spoon. If using two pans, divide the wine between them and pour all the liquid into one pan. Add the sliced mushrooms and remaining salt and cayenne pepper. Cook until the mushrooms are soft. Remove the chicken from the oven, pour the mushrooms on top, and serve.

Serves 6 to 8.

Potato and Sausage Stew

In this recipe, the sauce is thickened with gently melted cheese to give it a creamy texture and full flavor. If Vacherin Fribourgeois is not available, use another semisoft cheese.

1½ pounds potatoes
1½ pounds (about 9) hot Italian
    sausages
2 tablespoons olive oil
1 large (about ½ pound) onion, cut into
    ½-inch cubes
1 can (35 ounces) tomatoes
1 tablespoon red wine vinegar
½ teaspoon kosher salt
Freshly ground black pepper
6 ounces Vacherin Fribourgeois, cut
    into ½-inch cubes

Bring a large pot of salted water to a boil. Add the potatoes and cook just until soft through when pierced with a skewer. Let cool slightly, then peel and cut into ½-inch chunks.

Prick the sausages and put them into a skillet with about ¼ inch of water. Cook over medium heat until the water evaporates and the sausages begin to give off some of their fat. Continue cooking, turning from time to time, until lightly brown on both sides. Set aside to cool slightly, then cut into ½-inch slices.

Heat the oil in a 10-inch skillet. Add the onion and cook until soft but not brown, about 3 minutes. Add the tomatoes with their liquid and the vinegar and simmer for 10 minutes to thicken slightly. Season with salt and pepper to taste.

Add the potatoes and sausages and cook 5 minutes longer. Just before you are ready to serve, add the cheese cubes and stir for 1 to 2 minutes until they melt and make a smooth sauce. Taste the sauce and add more salt and pepper if needed.

Serves 4.

Craig Claiborne's Cheese-Stuffed Capon

Craig Claiborne created this unusual stuffing. Light and delicious, it goes well with baked rice and tomatoes.

15 ounces Ricotta
2 ounces Parmesan, freshly grated
2 large eggs
¾ cup fresh bread crumbs made from about two slices firm white bread
6 parsley sprigs, chopped
Salt
Freshly ground white pepper
1 capon, about 5 pounds
½ lemon
2 tablespoons unsalted butter, softened
2 medium onions, chopped
2 carrots, chopped
2 ribs celery, chopped
¼ pound unsalted butter, melted
2 cups chicken stock

Heat the oven to 350°F.

In a large bowl, mix together the cheeses, eggs, bread crumbs and parsley with your hands. Season to taste with salt and pepper. Pull any excess fat from the capon and rub the inside of the cavity with the lemon. Fill with the stuffing and sew the opening with string. Rub the skin of the bird with the softened butter and season with salt and pepper.

Place the chopped onions, carrots and celery in a roasting pan just slightly larger than the capon. If the pan is much larger, put crumpled aluminum foil at one end to shorten it or the vegetables will spread out too much and burn. Place the capon, breast side up, on a rack directly over the vegetables. Cut a double layer of cheesecloth large enough to cover the breast, legs and thighs of the bird and soak it in the melted butter. Drape the cheesecloth over the capon.

Roast for 1 hour 15 minutes, basting every 20 minutes. Remove the cheesecloth and roast 30 minutes longer to brown. Test to be sure the capon is done. When it is pierced in the thickest part of the leg, the juices should run clear. It should also register 175°F. on a meat thermometer. Place the capon on a heated platter and remove the string.

Meanwhile deglaze the roasting pan with the chicken stock, scraping the bottom to loosen any particles that stick. Bring to a boil and cook until reduced to about 1½ cups. Strain the sauce into a clean saucepan. Remove all the fat. Cook about 5 minutes longer, then adjust the seasonings with salt and pepper to taste. Pour into a heated sauce boat and serve with the capon.

Serves 4 to 6.

Filled Cheeseburgers

Cheeseburgers can be simple to prepare: just throw a piece of Cheddar cheese on top of a broiled hamburger, let it melt and call it a day. Made with Vermont Aged Cheddar, the result will be delicious (especially served on a toasted English muffin or bun with a slice of ripe red tomato). Semisoft cheeses make the best traditional cheeseburgers because they slice and melt evenly. Fontina, Port Salut, Switzerland Swiss, all are terrific. For bacon cheeseburgers, put the bacon under the cheese to hold it in place and keep it from burning.

Not all cheeses slice evenly, however, so we often like to put the filling in the center. We take the opportunity to add other ingredients, mixing Cheddar with chutney, Brie or Mozzarella with tomato cubes and onion, Roquefort or Gorgonzola with crumbled bacon. Any relatively solid filling will work well and you need at least 6 ounces meat per burger to make a neat package.

To make these cheeseburgers, start by making your filling, figuring up to ⅓ cup per burger for 6 ounces of meat, a little more for 8 ounces. Season the meat with salt and pepper to taste (a little dried mustard wouldn't be amiss). Press each portion of meat into ½-inch-thick rounds. Place the filling in the center and bring the sides up around it. Pinch to seal and pat the burger until you have a smooth, thick patty.

You can grill, broil or pan-fry them. If you are grilling, make sure the seal is tight. In a pan, a leak won't matter. Cook 3 to 4 minutes a side. Firmer cheeses, like Cheddars, will not melt completely while the softer ones will.

Among other foods that make excellent fillings are relishes, hot peppers, sautéed onions, corn, ratatouille. These are also delicious served with hot or cold tomato sauce.

Nøkkelost and Ham Quiche

This flavorful quiche is somewhat like a hot open-faced ham and cheese sandwich on rye with mustard. Nøkkelost, an often forgotten cheese, provides a perfect mate for the baked ham and melts beautifully.

1 recipe Pastry Dough (see page 240)
2 teaspoons Dijon mustard
5 ounces Nøkkelost, cut into ½-inch cubes (about 1 cup)
¼ pound baked ham, cut into ¼-inch cubes (about 1 cup)
2 large eggs
½ cup heavy cream
½ cup milk
½ teaspoon kosher salt
Freshly ground black pepper

Roll the dough out into a 11-inch circle and fit it into a 9½-inch quiche pan. Chill for 30 minutes while the oven heats to 400°F. Line the dough with aluminum foil and weights—dried beans, rice or aluminum scrap pellets—and bake for about 8 minutes, until the edges are set. Remove the foil and weights and prick the bottom of the crust. Bake 4 or 5 minutes longer, until the bottom just begins to turn golden.

Remove the pan from the oven, leaving it on, and brush the bottom of the pastry dough with the mustard, then sprinkle in the cheese and ham cubes. Mix the eggs, cream, milk, salt and pepper together and pour into the shell.

Place in the preheated oven and bake until set and golden, 30 to 35 minutes. Serve hot, warm, or at room temperature.

Serves 6 to 8.

Keshy Yena

Beef-Stuffed Cheese

Curaçao is a Dutch island off the coast of Venezuela where Edam is readily available. Its national dish is made by stuffing a stew into a whole, hollowed-out cheese and baking the result. This is a variation, using a casserole lined with cheese slices rather than the whole ball. Should you prefer a more authentic taste, leave out the pine nuts and add chopped pickles and hard-boiled eggs.

2 tablespoons olive or vegetable oil
2 large garlic cloves, minced
1 medium-large onion, diced
1½ pounds ground beef
1 red bell pepper, cored, seeded and cut into ¼-inch squares
2 fresh jalapeño peppers, cored, seeded and minced
½ pound tomatoes, cored, seeded and cut into ½-inch cubes
⅓ cup raisins
¼ cup (scant 1½ ounces) pine nuts, toasted in a dry skillet
1½ teaspoons kosher salt
⅛ teaspoon freshly ground black pepper
⅛ teaspoon red pepper sauce
1½ to 1¾ pounds Edam
Roasted red pepper strips for garnish

Heat the oven to 350°F.

Heat the oil in a 10-inch skillet. Add the garlic and cook for about 30 seconds. Add the onion and cook a few minutes, until soft. Add the beef and cook for 4 to 5 minutes, until barely done. Drain off the excess fat.

Add the red pepper and jalapeño peppers, then the tomatoes, raisins and pine nuts. Cook for about 5 minutes longer. The tomatoes should be soft. Add salt, pepper and red pepper sauce to taste, remembering that the cheese is slightly salty so it is better to undersalt the meat.

Peel all the wax off the cheese and cut it into ¼-inch slices. Arrange them as evenly as possible over the bottom and sides of a buttered 2½- to 3-quart tall casserole or soufflé dish. Cut the pieces as necessary to make them fit but be sure they cover all the spaces. Fill the casserole with the meat mixture, then cover the top with cheese slices, folding over the side pieces to completely and neatly cover the filling.

Cover the casserole with foil and place it in a baking dish. Add boiling water to the baking dish until it comes about 1 inch up the side of the casserole.

Place in the preheated oven and bake for about 45 minutes. Turn the molded stew out onto a round serving plate the same size as the casserole. Garnish with strips of roasted red pepper and cut into wedges. Serve hot.

Serves 6.

Salads

We often make big salads using odds and ends around the kitchen—half a zucchini, some olives, a piece of cooked chicken, leftover string beans, artichoke hearts. We always include some cheese: crumbly blue, cubes of Feta, julienned strips of Swiss, grated Fontina. In the salads that follow, however, cheese is a primary ingredient. All can be first courses; some will make satisfying lunches or suppers. Most are best with chunks of crusty bread—white, dark or sourdough.

Since the cheeses in these recipes are not cooked, they retain their identities more than in other dishes. Make sure your choices are in excellent condition; the results will show it.

Parmesan-Mushroom Salad

In Italy, where Parmigiano-Reggiano is appreciated as one of the finest eating cheeses in the world, they use the delicate, nutty Parmigiano in salads with fresh porcini or other wild mushrooms picked from neighboring woods. Wild mushrooms are not yet common here (although they are beginning to appear in a few gourmet shops), so we made this salad with cultivated mushrooms. It is delicious served as a first course alone or on the side with broiled chicken or meat. If you can get fresh wild mushrooms, use them in place of some of those in the recipe. Buy them only from reputable shops, however. You might be tempted to use a lesser cheese, but this is not the place to substitute another *grana;* the cheese is too important.

3 ounces Parmigiano-Reggiano
1 pound fresh mushrooms
1 cup thinly sliced celery
6 tablespoons fruity olive oil
2 tablespoons fresh lemon juice
1 teaspoon kosher salt
⅛ teaspoon freshly ground black pepper

Cut the Parmigiano into thin slices. Most will crumble, which is fine. Trim the mushrooms and cut them into thin slices. Put the cheese, mushrooms and celery in a serving bowl.

Mix together the oil and lemon juice. Season with salt and pepper. Pour over the ingredients in the bowl. Toss to mix. Serve immediately.

Serves 4 to 6.

Mozzarella and Roasted Pepper Salad

The flavor of the roasted peppers and anchovies blends well with that of the Mozzarella. If possible, use red or yellow peppers along with the green. Do not, however, buy the expensive blackish-purple peppers for this recipe. When they are roasted, they turn green and look just like ordinary peppers. Serve this with crusty bread.

6 bell peppers
1 pound Mozzarella, cut into thin
    1-inch-wide strips
1 can (2 ounces) anchovies, drained and
    minced
2 tablespoons dried thyme
Freshly ground pepper
½ to ¾ cup fruity olive oil

Heat a grill or broiler until hot. Place the peppers close to the heat and roast them, turning as needed, until black on all sides. Remove the peppers to a plastic bag and close tight so the steam from the peppers loosens the skin. Let rest a few minutes, then peel away and discard the charred skin along with the cores and seeds. Cut the flesh into strips about 1 inch wide.

Make a layer of pepper strips in a rectangular earthenware container. Top with a layer of Mozzarella. Put some anchovies on top along with a sprinkling of thyme and pepper. Continue making layers until everything is used, ending with an attractive layer of pepper. Pour in olive oil just to cover and let marinate at room temperature for at least 8 hours.

Serve on plates, making sure everyone gets peppers, cheese and anchovies. This is also delicious served on French bread as open-faced sandwiches.

Serves 6 to 8.

Tomato and Mozzarella Salad with Basil Vinaigrette

La Caprese is a popular Roman salad made of slices of fresh Mozzarella and tomato topped with a few fresh basil leaves and some very fine olive oil. It's incredibly simple, relying, of course, on the finest ingredients.

We've made a somewhat heartier version by combining the basil and oil with vinegar and mustard for a fragrant vinaigrette that gently coats the cheese and tomatoes. It is a hit with friends, pretty to look at, and easy to prepare. Be sure to give your guests crusty bread to sop up any extra sauce.

2 large ripe tomatoes, cored
½ pound Mozzarella, the freshest available (Mozzarella di Bufalo would be ideal)
½ cup packed fresh basil leaves
2 teaspoons grainy mustard
2 teaspoons red wine vinegar
¼ teaspoon kosher salt
⅛ teaspoon freshly ground pepper
3 tablespoons fruity virgin olive oil

Cut the tomatoes and Mozzarella into neat ¼-inch slices. Arrange them alternating and overlapping on a serving plate or four individual plates.

Place the basil in a food processor and chop into small pieces. Add the mustard, vinegar, salt and pepper. Process 15 seconds longer, then pour in the oil. Process another 30 seconds. Spoon the vinaigrette in a line across the tomatoes and cheese.

Serves 4 as a first course.

Barbara Kafka's Prosciutto, Smoked Mozzarella and Celery Root Salad

One of the finest cooks we know, Barbara Kafka created this as a winter version of the tomato, Mozzarella and basil salad. The crunch and spice of the celery root and mustard vinaigrette contrast well with the strong flavors of the ham and cheese.

12 thin slices (about 6 ounces) prosciutto, halved
24 thin slices (about ½ pound) Smoked Mozzarella
2 tablespoons Dijon mustard
3 tablespoons red wine vinegar
½ cup olive oil
Salt
Freshly ground pepper
⅔ cup julienned, peeled celery root

On each of six salad plates, arrange four slices of prosciutto overlapping and alternating with four slices of Mozzarella. If you're not ready to serve, set aside covered with plastic wrap so they don't dry out.

Place the mustard in a bowl and whisk in the vinegar. Gradually whisk in the oil so it is absorbed by the mustard. Season to taste with salt and pepper, then stir in the celery root.

Just before serving, stir the dressing to make sure it is smooth. Spoon some dressing and celery root in a line down the middle of each plate.

Serves 6.

Farmer's Chop Suey

This fresh, crunchy salad shows Cottage Cheese at its fragrant best. Since the cucumbers will exude liquid, do not add them until just before serving.

1 small cucumber, preferably Kirby
4 large radishes
3 or 4 scallions
1 pound (2 cups) Cottage Cheese
½ cup sour cream
⅓ cup chopped fresh dill
½ teaspoon kosher salt
Freshly ground black pepper

If the cucumber has a waxy peel, remove it. Otherwise, just wash it and trim the ends. Cut the cucumber into ½-inch chunks. Trim the radishes and cut them into ½-inch chunks. Trim the scallions and cut them into ½-inch pieces, using both the green and white parts.

Stir the Cottage Cheese and sour cream together in a large bowl. Add the vegetables and dill and mix well. Season to taste with salt and pepper and serve immediately.

Makes enough for 3 to 4.

Tabbouleh with Feta

Tabbouleh, made with bulgur wheat, is a refreshing summer salad, perfect to take on picnics.

2 cups (¾ pound) cracked bulgur wheat
½ cup minced radishes
2 tablespoons minced fresh mint
¼ cup olive oil
¼ cup wine vinegar
1 cup cubed tomatoes
½ cup sliced scallions
¼ pound Feta, cut into ¼-inch cubes
⅛ teaspoon freshly ground pepper
1 teaspoon kosher salt

Put the bulgur in a large bowl and add boiling water to cover generously. Set aside for 30 minutes. The bulgur will absorb the water and expand. It should be soft but not mushy. Drain off the excess water.

Add the remaining ingredients and stir until everything is well mixed. Taste and adjust the seasonings if necessary. Let stand for at least 1 hour to let the flavors meld.

Serve at room temperature or chill.

Serves at least 4.

Jeremiah Tower's Salad of Greens with Goat Cheese

Jeremiah Tower, one of San Francisco's very talented chefs, is responsible for the birth of several of that city's most interesting restaurants. He created this salad with goat cheese several years ago when few of us knew the special qualities of chèvre.

4 cups mixed salad greens, including bitter greens, endive, chicory, baby dandelion, watercress, arugula, celery leaves
½ cup walnut or hazelnut oil
2 tablespoons fresh lemon juice
Salt
Freshly ground pepper
8 slices French bread, about ½ inch thick
1 garlic clove
4 firm but not dry Crottins, preferably about 1 ounce (see Note)
½ cup extra virgin olive oil
¼ cup fresh white bread crumbs

Wash and trim the salad greens, then wrap in a towel and refrigerate until ready to use. Have greens at room temperature for serving.

Mix together the walnut oil and lemon juice for the dressing. Season to taste with salt and pepper. Toss with the salad greens just before serving. Arrange the greens on each of four warm salad plates.

Rub the bread with cut garlic on both sides to flavor it, then set aside, discarding the garlic. Dip the Crottins in olive oil to coat, then into bread crumbs to coat.

Heat the same oil in a skillet large enough to hold the rounds in a single layer. Add the coated rounds and cook over moderate heat until golden on the bottom. Carefully turn the cheese over to brown the other side.

Place one warm and browned cheese round in the center of each plate of greens. Put the bread in the still hot oil and quickly brown on both sides. Place two croutons on each salad.

Serves 4.

NOTE: If you can't get 1-ounce rounds, buy somewhat larger, firm rounds and slice them into smaller rounds. The cheese must be firm enough that it won't fall apart when sliced.

Swiss Cheese Salad

The Swiss, recognizing the excellence of their native Emmentaler, often julienne it for a delicious salad like this one. Almost any cheese firm enough to julienne could be substituted, but try it with authentic Switzerland Swiss at least once.

4 teaspoons Dijon mustard
3 tablespoons wine vinegar
½ teaspoon kosher salt
½ cup olive oil
Freshly ground black pepper
1 pound Swiss Emmentaler, cut into
    long matchstick strips
1 cup chopped scallions
4 small or 2 medium heads Bibb lettuce,
    well washed and dried

Make a mustard vinaigrette by mixing together the mustard, vinegar and salt until smooth. Slowly pour in the olive oil, allowing it to be absorbed, then season to taste with pepper.

Put the cheese and scallions in a bowl and toss with about half the dressing.

Arrange a wreath of Bibb lettuce on a serving platter or individual wreaths on salad plates. Drizzle the remaining dressing over the lettuce and place the cheese mixture in the center.

Serves 4.

Goat Cheese and Lentil Salad

The goat cheese makes a subtle flavoring for the still warm lentils, a delicious first course served on a lettuce leaf. Or serve it as a side dish at a picnic or with grilled chicken or fish.

Do not add the salt earlier than called for because the lentils will get tough before they have a chance to soften.

2 tablespoons olive oil
2 garlic cloves, minced
⅓ cup minced shallots
1½ tablespoons minced ginger
½ cup carrots cut into ¼-inch dice
½ cup celery cut into ¼-inch dice
1½ cups lentils, rinsed and picked over
3 cups water
½ cup dry white wine
1 tablespoon kosher salt
¼ teaspoon freshly ground pepper
½ cup seeded tomato cut into ¼-inch dice
¼ cup chopped fresh dill
6 ounces firm but young goat cheese, crumbled

Heat the oil in a 3-quart saucepan. Add the garlic and cook for 30 seconds. Add the shallots and ginger and sauté for 1 minute. Add the carrots and celery. Cook and stir for 2 minutes. Add the lentils and stir to coat with oil.

Add the water and wine and turn the heat to high. When the liquid begins to boil, cover the pot and lower the heat to a simmer. Cook for 15 minutes, then remove the cover and simmer 15 minutes longer. Add the salt and pepper and cook about 10 minutes longer, until the lentils are soft and almost all the liquid has been absorbed.

Put the lentils in a bowl, discarding any liquid in the pan. Stir in the tomato, dill and cheese. Serve warm or let cool to room temperature.

Makes about 6 cups, enough for 6 to 12.

Seppi Renggli's Boiled Beef and Gruyère Salad

Seppi Renggli, chef at The Four Seasons, makes his boiled beef salad with a particularly flavorful parsley vinaigrette coating the beef and cheese. He serves the salad on individual plates garnished with mushrooms and cherry tomatoes. A typical Swiss salad, it is often made with Emmentaler, but Chef Renggli prefers Gruyère.

You can cook the ribs the day ahead. They make a good dinner served hot. Make extra so there are leftovers for the salad.

BOILED BEEF

5 to 6 pounds short ribs
1 medium onion, quartered
2 ribs celery, cut into 2-inch pieces
2 carrots, trimmed and cut into 2-inch pieces
1 teaspoon kosher salt
½ teaspoon freshly ground pepper

Heat the broiler. Place the ribs on a broiler rack and broil, 2 to 3 inches from the heat, for about 5 minutes on a side, or until browned all over.

Place the ribs in a large pot and add water to barely cover, about 6 cups. Bring the water to a boil and skim all the fat and scum that rises to the top. Add more water if needed to keep the meat covered. Lower the heat so the liquid simmers and add the onion, celery and carrots. Cook, skimming from time to time, for 1 hour. Add the salt and pepper and cook 30 minutes longer, until the beef is tender enough to pull apart with a fork.

Remove the meat from the pot and set it aside to cool. Strain the liquid, discarding the solids. Reserve the liquid as beef stock for soups and sauces. If you don't plan to use within a day or two, let cool, then refrigerate until the fat congeals. Lift off and discard the fat, then freeze the stock.

Once the meat is cool enough to handle, cut away and discard all the fat. The bones should all fall off. Discard the fat and bones. Cut the beef into thin slices and set aside, covered.

PARSLEY VINAIGRETTE

2 cups parsley leaves, stems removed
¼ cup red wine vinegar
1 small garlic clove
½ cup olive oil
½ teaspoon kosher salt
Few dashes hot pepper sauce
1 tablespoon Dijon mustard

Put the parsley, vinegar, garlic, olive oil, salt and pepper sauce in a saucepan. Cook over medium heat, stirring from time to time, until the parsley is completely wilted and soft, about 10 minutes. Put the mixture in a blender or food processor to purée. Stir in the mustard and adjust seasoning with salt and pepper.

ASSEMBLY

5 ounces Gruyère
Sliced boiled beef
Parsley vinaigrette
Garnish: Boston lettuce, sliced
mushrooms, cherry tomatoes,
julienned Gruyère

Cut the Gruyère into slices ⅛-inch thick. If necessary, halve them so they are not more than 2 inches long. Place the cheese in a bowl with the beef. Add the vinaigrette and toss to mix well.

To serve, place some lettuce on each of six individual luncheon plates. Put a spoonful of the beef and cheese mixture over the lettuce. Arrange some mushroom slices and cherry tomatoes around the salad. Sprinkle some julienned Gruyère on top.

Serves 6.

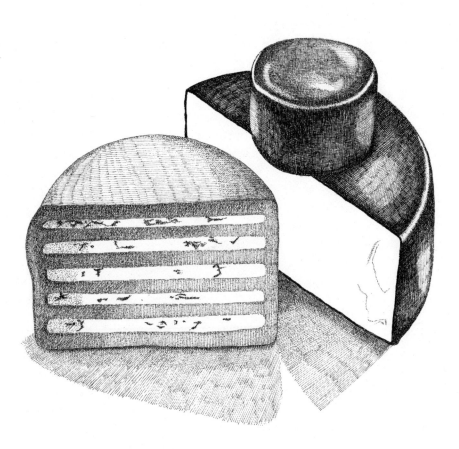

Side Dishes

These are but a few of the many side dishes flavored with cheese. We like most of them best with simple roasts of beef or chicken, grilled or poached fish served without a sauce.

We didn't include any recipes that just use a smidgen of cheese, but when we bake tomatoes or vegetable casseroles, we mix some grated cheese—usually Parmesan, Cheddar or Monterey Jack—with bread crumbs and sprinkle it on top to make a crisp, tasty crust.

Noodle Kugel

This rich noodle pudding is often served hot as part of a large meal, but we're also happy to eat the cold leftovers as a snack or dessert.

½ pound broad egg noodles
1½ cups milk
½ pound Cottage Cheese
1 cup sour cream
½ cup plus ½ teaspoon sugar
3 large eggs
½ teaspoon vanilla extract
4 tablespoons unsalted butter, melted
1 cup black raisins
3 tablespoons bread crumbs
1 tablespoon unsalted butter, softened

Heat the oven to 350°F. Butter an 11½ x 7 x 1½-inch baking dish. Set aside.

Bring 3 quarts of salted water to a boil. Add the noodles and cook for 8 minutes, or until they are barely done. Drain well and set aside.

In a large bowl, mix together the milk, Cottage Cheese, sour cream, ½ cup of the sugar, eggs and vanilla until well blended. Stir in the melted butter, raisins and cooked noodles. Pour into the prepared pan and smooth the top.

Mix the bread crumbs with the remaining ½ teaspoon sugar and sprinkle on top. Dot with the softened butter. Bake in the preheated oven for about 1 hour 20 minutes, until the top is light brown and the pudding is firm. If it browns too quickly, cover the top with aluminum foil.

Serve hot or at room temperature.

Serves 8 to 12.

German Potato Salad with Port-Salut

The soft cheese almost melts with the heat of the potatoes, making a delicate addition to the usual tepid potato salad.

2 baking potatoes, about ½ pound each
¼ pound bacon
3 ounces Port-Salut or Saint Paulin, cut
    into ¼-inch cubes
2 scallions, roughly chopped
1½ tablespoons red wine vinegar
Freshly ground black pepper

Heat the oven to 400°F. Place the potatoes on the oven rack and bake until done, about 45 minutes.

You can bake the potatoes ahead and let them cool or do the whole salad at once. Cut the potatoes in half lengthwise and scoop out the potato flesh in large pieces. Save the skins either to make the Parmesan and Bacon Potato Skins (see page 121) or to put the potato salad into.

Cook the bacon until crisp. Drain on absorbent paper, leaving the fat in the pan. Crumble the bacon and put it into a bowl with the cheese and scallions. If using the shells, put them on a baking sheet and return them to the oven to get crisp, about 5 minutes.

Reheat the bacon fat. Add the potato pieces to the pan and cook for about a minute until the potato is heated through and flavored with the fat. Remove it with a slotted spoon to the bowl. Discard any remaining fat. Toss the potatoes with the bacon, cheese, scallions and vinegar. Add freshly ground pepper to taste. Spoon the salad into the crisp potato skins and serve at once.

Serves 4.

Risotto

This creamy Italian rice dish gets its flavor from the stock and Parmesan cheese. Properly made, it takes time and a strong arm. If you have leftovers, use them to make Suppli (see recipe, page 122).

5½ cups chicken stock, approximately
2 tablespoons unsalted butter
1 medium onion, minced
2 cups arborio or long-grain rice
¾ cup grated Parmesan or other Grana

Put the stock in a pot and bring it to a boil.

In a separate heavy, 3-quart pot, melt the butter. Add the onion and cook until very soft but not brown. Add the rice and toss until coated with the butter. Cook another minute.

Ladle about ½ cup stock over the rice. With a wooden spoon, stir constantly until the rice absorbs most of the liquid. Add another ½ cup liquid. Continue in this way, adding the stock slowly and stirring constantly until the rice is creamy and just done through. Stir in the Parmesan and serve at once.

Serves 6 to 8.

Cheese-Vegetable Pancakes

These pancakes are crisp on the outside, soft in the middle. Serve them alongside pot roast.

2 carrots
6 ounces potatoes
¼ pound zucchini
¼ pound Cheddar
2 large eggs
¼ cup dry bread crumbs
¼ teaspoon kosher salt
1⁄16 teaspoon cayenne pepper
Vegetable oil

Peel the carrots and potatoes. Grate them along with the zucchini and Cheddar into a large bowl. Stir in the eggs, bread crumbs, salt and cayenne.

Heat about ½ inch vegetable oil in a 10-inch skillet. Put about ¼ cup vegetable mixture into the pan. Press down with a spatula to flatten and cook until well browned on both sides, about 2 minutes a side. Cook as many pancakes at a time as will fit in the skillet in a single layer without touching, about five. As each pancake is done, remove it to a pan or plate lined with absorbent paper to drain; keep warm. Continue in this way until all the mixture is used. Serve hot sprinkled with salt.

Makes about 12 pancakes.

Jacques Pépin's Gratin Savoyard

Potato and Cheese Casserole

Jacques Pépin, the well-known chef, author and instructor, uses a French Gruyère for this dish to reflect his national heritage; other Gruyères will also work well. Serve with roasted chicken, beef or pork.

3 pounds mealy potatoes
1 teaspoon salt
Freshly ground white pepper
Freshly grated nutmeg
½ pound Beaufort or Comté, grated
6 tablespoons unsalted butter
1¼ cups chicken stock

Heat the oven to 425°F.

Peel the potatoes and cut them into ⅛-inch-thick slices. Put them in a large bowl of cold water to remove the excess starch. Butter an 11 x 8-inch baking/serving dish.

Drain the potatoes and pat dry. Layer a third of them over the bottom of the baking dish. Sprinkle with a third of the salt, pepper and nutmeg, a third of the cheese and 2 tablespoons of the butter. Make two more layers in the same way, then pour in the chicken stock.

Place the baking dish on a baking sheet and cook in the preheated oven for about 1 hour 10 minutes. The top should be nicely browned and most of the liquid absorbed by the potatoes. Let stand for 10 to 15 minutes before serving.

Serves 8 to 10.

Marion Cunningham's Spoon Bread with Teleme Cheese

Marion Cunningham, the modern Fanny Farmer, is a native of California where Teleme is readily accessible so she uses it in her wonderful spoon bread. If you can't get Teleme, Monterey Jack or another mild semisoft cheese will work beautifully. She recommends serving the spoon bread as a side dish with a pork roast.

2 cups water
1 teaspoon salt
1 cup yellow cornmeal dampened with
    cold water
2 tablespoons butter
1 cup milk
4 large eggs, well beaten
1½ cups (about ½ pound) Teleme, cut
    into small pieces
1 cup fresh coriander (cilantro or
    Chinese parsley) sprigs

Heat the oven to 400°F. Butter a 1½-quart ovenproof casserole and set aside.

Bring the water to a boil in a 2-quart saucepan. Add the salt, then lower the heat to a simmer. Add the cornmeal slowly, stirring vigorously all the time to keep lumps from forming. Dampening the cornmeal helps to prevent the lumping. When all the cornmeal has been added, continue cooking, stirring constantly, for a minute or two. Be sure to get into the corners. The mixture should be completely smooth.

Remove the pan from the heat and stir in the butter, then the milk. When the mixture is smooth, stir in the eggs, beating well until everything is smooth and blended. Stir in the cheese.

Pour the mixture into the casserole and bake in the preheated oven for 40 minutes, or until a straw inserted in the center comes out clean. The spoon bread will be puffy, almost like a soufflé.

Arrange the coriander on top and serve hot.

Serves 6 to 8 as a side dish, 3 or 4 for supper.

Baked Potato with Cottage Cheese

This is just one of many stuffings for potatoes. It has the added appeal of being a delicious, low-calorie substitute for sour cream and chives.

2 baking potatoes, about ½ pound each
1 cup Cottage Cheese
3 tablespoons chopped chives
2 tablespoons milk
½ teaspoon kosher salt
Pinch cayenne pepper

Heat the oven to 400°F. Put the potatoes on the oven rack and bake for 45 minutes, or until done through.

Cut the potatoes in half lengthwise. With a spoon, carefully remove most of the potato from the skins, leaving shells about ¼ inch thick. Put the potato in a mixing bowl and mash well with a fork or potato masher. Add the Cottage Cheese, chives, milk, salt and cayenne. Continue mixing until everything is well blended. Spoon the potato mixture back into the shells, mounding it up in the center of each.

Place the filled shells on a baking sheet and return to the oven to bake for 10 to 15 minutes. The filling should be heated through and beginning to brown on top.

Serves 4.

Sandwiches

Cheese sandwiches come in all shapes and sizes with fillings as varied as Chèvre and walnuts; pesto and Emmentaler; Mozzarella, basil and sun-dried tomatoes. They may be eaten at room temperature, baked, even covered in sauce. The sandwiches that follow are just a few possibilities. Other combinations are mentioned throughout the cheese descriptions.

Sometimes the best sandwich is the simplest. In Italy, they eat hunks of Parmesan on bread dipped in olive oil. We love fresh pumpernickel rolls with thick slices of aged Cheddar or a fresh bagel with slices of Swiss and a little grainy mustard.

Grilled Cheese

Some people consider grilled cheese sandwiches to be ordinary fare. It's probably because they've never tasted a perfectly grilled cheese sandwich, beautifully browned in butter enclosing slices of softly melted, but still firm Cheddar cheese, not slices of processed cheese food wrapped in plastic. It isn't hard to make, but it does require care and a little patience to do it right.

First, of course, you need the proper ingredients: some firm-textured white bread; true, medium aged orange Cheddar; and plenty of unsalted butter. Next you need the right equipment: a griddle or frying pan large enough to hold the sandwich flat with room to flip it over, and a spatula. You can certainly make more than one at a time. Don't try to cook more than four; they won't get the proper attention.

Perfectly wonderful grilled cheese sandwiches have been made with whole wheat and even fancier breads. Swiss and Gruyère melt beautifully. Even Brie works. But to understand the basics, start with white bread and American (Cheddar) cheese, what's called store cheese in the country.

Cover a slice of bread evenly with the cheese so you have a layer about ¼ inch thick. Depending on the size of your piece of cheese and your skill with a knife, this may be anything from one to eight pieces. Try for the large pieces since small ones may fall out of the sandwich before they melt together. The cheese layer should be just a little bit smaller than the bread so the cheese doesn't ooze into the pan. Place a second slice of bread on top to match the first one.

Next comes the butter. After years of trying to butter the bread carefully without tearing it, we finally found the solution. Melt the butter in the pan and place the sandwich on top of it. The exact amount of butter depends on the size of the pan and the absorbency of the bread. Start with a tablespoon for each sandwich and add more as needed. Keep the heat on medium so the butter bubbles but doesn't burn.

Place the sandwich in the pan and press down firmly on the top slice of bread with the spatula. Make sure the spatula is dry and free of grease or the bread may stick to it rather than to the cheese. The goal is to have the cheese melt enough so it adheres to both slices of bread. After about 30 seconds, peek under the sandwich by lifting it with the spatula. If the bread seems dry, slip some more butter under it. Keep pressing.

When the bottom slice of bread is moist and golden, lift the sandwich out. Melt another tablespoon butter in the pan. Flip the sandwich over onto the newly melted butter. Press down with the spatula until that side is equally done.

The final masterpiece is a little greasy. We always give company a knife and fork. When no one's around, we use our hands.

Once you've mastered the basic sandwich, get as creative as you want. Fontina, Mozzarella, Emmentaler, creamy Blues can all be good. Dieters like New Holland. Combine them with other ingredients like bacon strips, Virginia ham with sweet mustard, ripe tomato slices, avocado wedges, anchovies, olives, fresh herbs, nuts. Divide the cheese so half of it is on either side and the filling is in the center. Limit the filling to a thin layer so the cheese takes precedence. The cheese will bind together over the filling, making a union of foods that still retain their own characteristics.

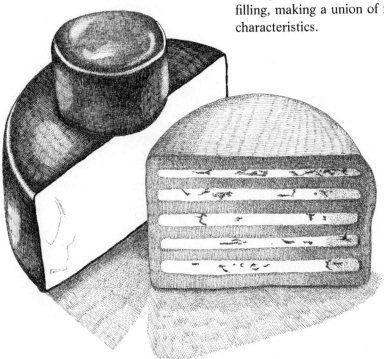

Croque Monsieur

A cross between the usual grilled cheese sandwiches and French toast, these elegant sandwiches can be filled with just about anything that works for their simpler relatives.

¼ **pound baked ham**
¼ **pound Emmentaler or other Swiss-style cheese**
8 **slices white or whole wheat bread**
3 **large eggs**
1 **tablespoon milk**
Butter

Arrange a fourth of the ham and cheese on top of each of four slices of bread. Top with the remaining bread to make four sandwiches.

Beat the eggs and milk together in a mixing bowl. Place the sandwiches in the egg mixture and let sit for a minute or so until the bottom slice absorbs the egg but isn't soggy. Turn and soak the other side in the same way.

Heat butter in a 10-inch skillet until hot. Put the sandwiches in the pan and cook, pressing on the bread, until nicely browned on the bottom. Add more butter and turn the sandwiches over to cook the other side. The total cooking time should be about 5 minutes.

Makes 4 sandwiches.

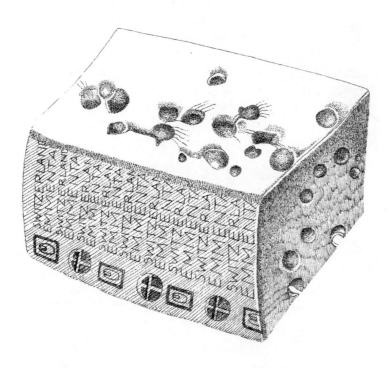

Mozzarella in Carrozza

This Italian cheese sandwich, common in Rome, is a great snack or lunch. Cut into small pieces, they make perfect finger food with cocktails. For variety, add some chopped anchovies or sun-dried tomatoes to the sandwiches.

1 loaf French or Italian bread
1 to 1½ pounds Mozzarella
4 or 5 large eggs
Salt
1 cup olive oil

Slice the bread and cheese into pieces ¼ inch thick. Trim the cheese slices so they are about the same size as the bread.

Make as many cheese sandwiches as you can, each with two slices of bread and one of cheese. There should be about thirty. The cheese scraps can be pieced together to make a slice.

Beat the eggs with some salt in a flat pan. Place the sandwiches, bread side down, in the egg for about 15 minutes. The bread should absorb the egg but not fall apart. Turn and let sit for another 15 minutes to absorb the egg on the other side.

In a 10-inch skillet, heat the oil over medium-high heat until it just ripples on the surface. Remove the sandwiches from the egg, shaking off the excess, and place in the hot oil. Cook as many at a time as will fit in the pan in one layer without touching. As they cook, press down on the tops with a spatula, forcing the cheese to adhere to the bread.

When they are brown on the bottom, about 1 minute, turn and cook on the other side, again pressing down with the spatula. Drain on paper towels and keep warm. Repeat until all the sandwiches are cooked. Serve hot, either whole or halved.

Makes 60 half sandwiches for cocktails, 30 whole for lunch.

Reuben

This standard deli item must be made as a closed, grilled sandwich to let the flavors and textures of the various ingredients—Swiss cheese, corned beef, sauerkraut and bread—work together. Many restaurants now serve open-faced Reubens, but they aren't the same.

8 slices rye bread
Mustard
½ pound Swiss cheese
¾ pound corned beef
1½ cups sauerkraut, squeezed dry
Butter

Put half the bread on your work surface and spread with mustard. Top each slice with an ounce of cheese, a fourth of the corned beef, a fourth of the sauerkraut and the remaining cheese. Top with the remaining bread.

Heat the butter in a large skillet or on a griddle. Add the sandwiches and cook, pressing on the tops with a spatula, until the bottoms are nicely browned. Add more butter, turn the sandwiches and cook the other sides. Serve hot.

Makes 4 Reubens.

Seppi Renggli's Poached Pears with Brie and Canadian Bacon

Seppi Renggli created this unusual, very satisfying lunch or supper meal. The pear, bacon and Brie make a wonderful combination of tastes and textures in the mouth.

8 slices white bread
3 tablespoons unsalted butter
8 Poached Pear halves (see recipe, page 238)
24 slices (12 ounces) Canadian bacon
1 pound Brie
Cayenne pepper

Heat the broiler until hot.

Trim the crusts off the bread and toast it. Spread each slice with some butter and set aside.

Starting at the bottom of each pear half and moving toward the stem, cut parallel slits about ⅛ inch apart. Leave the pears attached at the stem ends. Turn them slightly so they fan out.

Heat the remaining butter in a skillet. Add the bacon and sauté for a minute or two to heat through. Trim the white rind off the Brie and discard. Cut the cheese into slices ⅛ inch thick.

Put the toast, buttered sides up, in a layer on a broiler pan so they don't touch. Arrange three slices of bacon, slightly overlapping as necessary, on each piece of toast to cover. Flip the pear halves over so the curved parts are underneath. Arrange one half on each sandwich. Top each pear half with a layer of Brie. Sprinkle some cayenne on top. Put the pan under the broiler until the Brie melts and begins to bubble, about 2 minutes. Serve immediately.

Makes 8 open sandwiches.

Desserts

Say cheese and dessert—and cheesecake immediately comes to mind. We like ours very rich without any fruit toppings as the recipes show. Cheese can also be a wonderful ingredient in pastries and a filling for doughs. Cream and Cottage Cheeses are the usual choices for baking but we've been delighted with Blues, Cheddars and Chèvres for desserts.

As we mention in the cheese section, we often happily end a meal with a fine cheese and fruit—lush pears, crisp apples, seedless grapes. When we are feeling extravagant, we add a fine dessert wine or port.

Lindy's Cheesecake

The original Lindy's was a New York landmark famous for its heavy, luscious cheesecake. The restaurant is gone, but for those who believe Lindy's made the world's finest cheesecake, ourselves included, the recipe lives on. The crust is a cookie dough rather than crumbled graham crackers. It's a little more work but well worth the effort.

CRUST

1 cup all-purpose flour
½ cup sugar
Grated rind of 1 small lemon
¼ pound unsalted butter, cold, cut into
    eight pieces
1 large egg yolk

The crust can be made with a mixer, food processor or by hand. Mix together the flour, sugar and grated rind. Add the butter and egg yolk; mix until smooth. Wrap in wax paper and chill for an hour.

Heat the oven to 400°F. Butter the bottom and sides of a 9-inch springform pan. Remove the sides and set aside.

Place a third of the dough in the center of the pan bottom and roll the dough to make an even circle covering the bottom. Trim off any excess. Bake in the preheated oven for 8 minutes, or until evenly brown. Remove and let cool.

Roll the rest of the dough into a rectangle ⅛-inch thick. Cut it into strips 2 inches wide. (If the dough is sticky, roll it between sheets of wax paper.)

Reassemble the springform and place the uncooked dough strips around the sides, pressing the pieces together to make an even crust. The raw dough should just slightly overlap the baked bottom to make a complete seal. Refrigerate until the filling is ready.

FILLING

2½ pounds Cream Cheese, at room
    temperature
1¾ cups sugar
3 tablespoons all-purpose flour
Grated rind of 1 orange
Grated rind of 1 lemon
¼ teaspoon vanilla extract
5 large eggs
2 large egg yolks
¼ cup heavy cream

Heat the oven to 550°F.

Place the Cream Cheese, sugar, flour, grated rinds and vanilla in the bowl of an electric mixer. Beat until smooth, then add the whole eggs, one at a time, followed by the yolks. Finally, beat in the cream.

Pour the mixture into the prepared pan. Bake in the preheated oven for 10 minutes. Without opening the door, lower the heat to 200°F. and bake 1 hour longer. Ideally, the cake should be lightly browned on top and completely smooth. It may crack or not brown at all and will still be wonderful. It should be firm and set but not hard.

Place on a wire rack until completely cool, then remove the sides. Serve from the springform bottom.

Serves 12 or more.

Barbara Kafka's Preservative-Free Cheesecake

When Barbara Kafka first tasted preservative-free Cream Cheese, she realized this sweeter, richer cheese would make a fabulous cheesecake. Starting with Lindy's classic, she developed this version to allow for the differences in taste and texture between the new Cream Cheese and the supermarket standby.

CRUST

**See ingredients and directions for
    Lindy's Cheesecake (page 206)**

FILLING

2½ **pounds preservative-free Cream
    Cheese**
1¼ **cups sugar**
3 **tablespoons all-purpose flour**
Grated rind of 1 orange
Grated rind of 1 lemon
¼ **teaspoon vanilla extract**
5 **large eggs**
4 **large egg yolks**
½ **cup heavy cream**

Follow the same procedure and baking times as for Lindy's Cheesecake.

Pear and Maytag Blue Tart

This pretty tart shows once again the natural affinity of pears and blue cheeses.

1 recipe Pastry Dough made with sugar (see page 240)
½ cup toasted slivered almonds
6 Poached Pear halves (see recipe, page 238)
¼ pound Maytag Blue or other medium blue cheese
½ cup heavy cream
⅓ cup sugar
1 large egg

On a floured work surface, roll out the pastry dough into a 12-inch circle. Fit it into a 9-inch round quiche pan with 1½-inch sides. Trim any excess dough from the edges. Chill for 30 minutes to an hour.

Heat the oven to 400°F.

Line the dough with aluminum foil and weight it with dry beans, rice or aluminum scraps. Bake in the preheated oven for 15 minutes, or until the dough begins to set. Remove the foil and weights and bake 5 minutes longer. Prick the bottom with a fork and set aside. Lower the oven temperature to 350°F.

Sprinkle the almonds over the bottom of the crust.

Place one pear half at a time on your work surface. Working with your knife at a diagonal, slice each half crosswise into ¼-inch-wide slices. Holding the pear halves together, arrange them evenly over the almonds so the stem ends meet in the center. Gently spread them out so each one extends from the center to the edge of the crust.

Place the cheese in the work bowl of a food processor. Process until fairly smooth. Add the cream, sugar and egg. Process for about 30 seconds. The mixture should be fairly smooth but it is fine if pieces of cheese remain. Pour the mixture over the pears in the crust. Scrape the bottom of the work bowl to get all the cheese. Spread the mixture gently with a rubber spatula to make sure it covers everything fairly evenly.

Bake in the preheated oven for 35 minutes, or until set. Serve hot or warm.

Serves 6 to 8.

Pears in Gorgonzola Sauce on Puff Pastry

This is a wonderful dessert, quick to make if you have puff pastry on hand. If not, use the pear and Gorgonzola mixture in crêpes. It would also be good spooned over vanilla ice cream or sponge cake.

1¼ pounds Puff Pastry dough (see recipe, page 239)
Egg glaze (1 egg beaten with 1 teaspoon water)
2 large ripe pears
2 tablespoons unsalted butter
¼ cup sugar
⅔ cup chopped walnuts
3 ounces Gorgonzola, crumbled
Confectioners' sugar

Roll the pastry out into a rectangle about ⅛ inch thick. From it cut six even squares about 4 inches on a side. Place them on a baking sheet and chill for 30 minutes while heating the oven to 375°F.

Brush the top of each pastry with egg glaze, being careful not to let it drip down the sides. Then bake the pastry for 20 minutes, or until puffed and nicely browned. While the dough is baking, make the pear filling.

Peel the pears and remove their cores. Cut them into ¼-inch-thick slices. Halve the long slices.

Heat the butter in a skillet and add the pears along with the sugar. Cook until the pears are warmed through and soft. Over low heat, stir in the walnuts and cheese. Stir until the cheese melts into the liquid. Keep warm until the pastry is done.

When the pastries are done, remove them from the oven. With a fork, split each pastry crosswise into two pieces and pull out and discard any dough that is not cooked. Place the bottom of each pastry on a heated dessert plate. Spoon some of the warm pear mixture over it and top with the pastry tops, set at an angle. Sprinkle some confectioners' sugar over each pastry and serve at once.

Serves 6.

Cheese and Apple Bread Pudding

Apples and Cheddar cheese have a natural affinity for each other, be they paired as a thick slice of cold crunchy apple with an equally thick slice of cheese, or as a wedge of sharp Cheddar gently warmed by a slice of fresh-from-the-oven apple pie. Somehow we knew apples and cheese would do as well together in a custardy bread pudding. This is an easy dessert to make, the kind that disappears quickly as everyone takes "just a little more" until the dish is clean.

½ loaf French bread
2 McIntosh or other crisp apples
6 to 8 ounces Cheddar cheese
6 tablespoons sugar mixed with
    1 tablespoon ground cinnamon
1 cup heavy cream
1 cup milk
½ cup sugar
2 large eggs, beaten
½ teaspoon vanilla extract

Butter a 2-quart soufflé dish or similarly shaped casserole. Cut the bread into ¼-inch slices. Peel and core the apples. Cut them into ¼-inch slices. Cut the cheese into ¼-inch slices.

Place a layer of bread in the bottom of the soufflé dish. Sprinkle on some of the cinnamon/sugar mixture. Top with a layer of apples and one of cheese, using about half of each. Sprinkle with some more cinnamon/sugar. Repeat with another layer of bread, sugar, apples, cheese, sugar, bread, reserving some of the cinnamon/sugar.

In a separate bowl, whisk together the cream, milk, sugar, eggs and vanilla until completely blended. Pour over the layers in the dish. Gently press on the top layer so the bread gets soaked. Set aside for 30 minutes. Meanwhile, heat the oven to 350°F.

Just before baking, sprinkle the top with the remaining cinnamon/sugar. Bake until set, about 45 minutes. Serve hot.

Serves 4 to 8.

Rugelach

These crescent-shaped cookies are made with a wonderfully flaky Cream Cheese dough.

½ pound Cream Cheese
½ pound unsalted butter
½ cup plus 1 tablespoon sugar
2 cups (10 ounces) all-purpose flour
1 teaspoon ground cinnamon
1 cup (¼ pound) finely chopped walnuts
1 cup (¼ pound) chopped raisins
2 tablespoons melted butter

Beat the Cream Cheese and butter together until smooth, then beat in 1 tablespoon of the sugar and the flour. Turn the mixture out onto a lightly floured work surface and knead gently until smooth. Divide the dough into four equal pieces and shape each into a flat round. Wrap in wax paper and refrigerate overnight.

Heat the oven to 375°F.

Mix the cinnamon with the remaining ½ cup sugar. Have ready at your work space along with the walnuts, raisins and melted butter.

Work with one piece of dough at a time. Roll it into a circle about 12 inches in diameter. Don't worry if the edges are uneven and the circle isn't perfectly round. Brush the dough with some melted butter, then sprinkle on a fourth of the cinnamon-sugar mixture. Spread a fourth of the walnuts and raisins over that. Press down on everything with a rolling pin to help keep the nuts and raisins in place.

Using a very sharp knife, cut the circle into four even quarters. Then cut each quarter into three equal wedges. Beginning at the wide part of each wedge, roll it up toward the center, turning the dough so the tip is underneath. Gently bend the dough toward you so it curves slightly and place it on an ungreased baking sheet. Continue in this way until you have made twelve crescents, then follow the same procedure with the remaining dough and toppings.

Bake in the preheated oven for 20 to 25 minutes, or until nicely browned. Cool on a rack.

Makes 4 dozen.

Paul Kovi's Cheese Strudel

Paul Kovi, one of the owners of the famed Four Seasons restaurant in New York, learned to make strudel from his mother. She, of course, makes the dough herself. The packaged leaves, while not as delicate, are usually quite good and make this a simple pastry to prepare.

¼ pound unsalted butter
6 tablespoons sugar
1 pound Farmer Cheese, pushed
    through a sieve
2 large egg yolks
½ cup sour cream
1 teaspoon vanilla extract
Grated rind of 1 lemon
½ cup golden raisins, soaked for 2 hours
    in ¼ cup brandy
10 sheets (about ½ pound) strudel or
    filo dough
¼ pound unsalted butter, melted
¼ cup fine bread crumbs

Heat the oven to 400°F. Lightly grease a baking sheet and set aside.

In the bowl of an electric mixer, cream together the butter and sugar until smooth. Add the cheese and beat until well mixed. Add the egg yolks, sour cream, vanilla and lemon rind and beat again. Finally, stir in the raisins and any remaining brandy.

Spread a clean dish towel on your work surface. Place one sheet of strudel dough on it and brush it carefully with some of the melted butter. Sprinkle on some bread crumbs. Top with another sheet of dough, adding butter and bread crumbs in the same way. When you have five sheets of dough so stacked, spoon half the cheese mixture along the short side, leaving a two-inch border on one side and both ends. Brush more butter around the border. Fold the ends over the filling and roll up, using the towel to help you move the roll. Carefully transfer the filled pastry to the prepared baking sheet.

Repeat with the remaining strudel and filling. Brush the tops of the strudels with the remaining melted butter. Sprinkle some crumbs on top.

Bake in the preheated oven until nicely browned, about 20 minutes. Serve hot or at room temperature.

Serves 12.

Tiramisu

This Italian dessert, literally "pick me up," is becoming a standard at new Italian restaurants. It makes excellent use of the richness of Mascarpone.

16 ladyfingers
3 egg yolks
2 tablespoons sugar
½ pound Mascarpone
1 tablespoon triple sec or Cognac
¾ to 1 cup espresso or strong coffee, at room temperature
3 ounces semisweet chocolate, chopped (or use miniature chips)
1 ounce chopped toasted almonds (about ⅓ cup)

Heat the oven to 250°F. Split the ladyfingers and spread them in a single layer on a baking sheet. Bake for about 5 minutes a side until crisp and light brown. Set aside.

Beat the egg yolks and sugar together on high speed until very thick and pale yellow, about 5 minutes. Add the Mascarpone and triple sec and beat until smooth.

Have ready a serving platter about 6 x 16 inches or one that half the ladyfingers will almost completely cover in a single layer. Put the coffee in a bowl.

Dip the ladyfinger bottoms briefly into the coffee so they soak up some coffee but do not become soggy. Arrange half the ladyfingers, bottoms down, on the platter. Spread half the Mascarpone mixture on top to cover the ladyfingers. Sprinkle half the chocolate and almonds over the Mascarpone. Top with the remaining ladyfingers, dipped side down, the Mascarpone, chocolate and almonds. Cover loosely with foil and refrigerate five hours or overnight.

Serves 4 to 6.

Mascarpone-Filled Crêpes

Mascarpone is a luscious but delicate cheese. It separates when exposed to heat so the sweetened filling is spooned cool into its crêpe wrapper and gently warmed for a simple elegant dessert.

1 pound (2 cups) Mascarpone
¼ cup sugar
1 teaspoon vanilla extract
1 tablespoon Grand Marnier or other orange liqueur
16 Crêpes (see recipe, page 241)
Butter
Raspberry Sauce (see recipe, page 238)

Put the Mascarpone in a bowl and stir in the sugar, vanilla and Grand Marnier.

Working with one crêpe at a time, place it browned side up on your work surface. Put 2 tablespoons Mascarpone filling on the crêpe about a third of the way up from the bottom. Fold the sides in over the filling, then roll up the crêpe like an egg roll. Continue in this way until all the crêpes are filled.

Heat some butter in a large skillet over medium heat. Add as many filled crêpes as will fit in one layer and cook to barely warm, about 20 seconds on a side. Repeat with the remaining crêpes. As the crêpes are done, remove them to heated serving plates, allowing two crêpes per person. Spoon some Raspberry Sauce over each crêpe and serve the rest on the side in a bowl.

Serves 8.

German Pancakes

German pancakes, an easy oven-baked dessert that puffs like Yorkshire pudding, is usually made with a cheeseless batter. We like the tartness added by the goat cheese. Traditionally, these are served hot with sautéed apple slices. Try it that way in the winter. When fresh berries are available, toss blueberries, strawberries and raspberries together with a touch of Cointreau and spoon over the hot pancake.

¼ cup (scant 2 ounces) soft, young goat
    cheese
¼ cup milk
½ cup all-purpose flour
3 large eggs
1 tablespoon sugar
¼ teaspoon kosher salt
3 tablespoons unsalted butter

Heat the oven to 400°F.

Put the cheese, milk, flour, eggs, sugar and salt in the work bowl of a food processor or in a blender and blend until smooth. Set aside.

Melt the butter in a 10-inch ovenproof skillet, preferably a well-seasoned cast-iron pan. Pour in the batter and place in the oven to bake for 25 minutes, or until the sides are puffy and the top is brown.

Either bring the pancake to the table in its pan or slide it onto a serving plate. Top with the fruit and serve at once.

Serves 6.

Coeur à la Crème

This simple dessert is perfect for Valentine's Day and other romantic occasions. Traditionally, fresh white cheese was put into heart-shaped baskets to drain, then turned out and served with a red berry sauce. An excellent substitute for the white cheese is given in Jacques Pépin's Fromage Blanc à la Crème on page 115. Line a heart-shaped porcelain mold with holes or a reed basket with cheesecloth and fill it with the cheese mixture. Let drain overnight, then unmold and serve with fresh berries or Raspberry Sauce (page 238).

Breads

Cheese and bread are an obvious pair. Cheeses added to bread dough can be equally wonderful. They usually lose their identity but leave their mark, changing the texture, adding flavor to the bread. Many basic recipes will work with a little shredded cheese folded in, as we found when making cornbread and popovers. In other recipes, we leave the cheese in a layer inside the dough, baking the two together. The cheese remains distinct and we have something like a baked sandwich, best served warm or hot. With some lightly dressed greens, these make a lovely lunch.

Gruyère-Nut Muffins

Warm muffins fresh from the oven are wonderful any time. These make a nourishing breakfast but we like them even better with a hearty soup or salad. The cayenne pepper gives a soft spicy taste. Should you have extras, freeze them wrapped in foil. Reheat in the foil in a 350°F. oven for 20 to 30 minutes.

2 cups all-purpose flour
2 teaspoons baking powder
1 teaspoon kosher salt
¼ teaspoon cayenne pepper
2 large eggs
¾ cup milk
4 tablespoons unsalted butter, melted
6 ounces (about 1½ cups) minced
    Gruyère
½ cup (2 ounces) finely chopped
    walnuts

Heat the oven to 400°F. Grease twelve ⅓-cup muffin tins and set aside.

Sift the flour, baking powder, salt and cayenne into a large mixing bowl. In a separate bowl, beat the eggs just to combine the yolks and whites. Stir in the milk and butter. Pour over the flour mixture along with the cheese and nuts.

Stir quickly and vigorously just until the dry ingredients are all moist and mixed in. The batter will be quite thick. Divide it evenly among the muffin tins.

Bake in the preheated oven until nicely browned, 20 to 25 minutes. Serve warm.

Makes 12 muffins.

Pepper Jack Popovers

Just about any semisoft cheese will work well in this recipe. We like the spiciness of the jalapeño peppers.

1 cup all-purpose flour
1 cup milk
1 tablespoon unsalted butter, melted
½ teaspoon kosher salt
2 large eggs, at room temperature
¼ pound (generous ½ cup) minced
    Pepper Jack

Heat the oven to 425°F. Grease ten ⅓-cup muffin or custard cups.

In a mixing bowl, whisk the flour, milk, butter and salt until smooth. Add the eggs and whisk again until smooth. Spoon a thin layer of the batter into each greased cup just to cover the bottom. Add a scant tablespoon cheese, then add more batter so each cup is about two-thirds full.

Bake in the preheated oven for 30 to 35 minutes. The popovers should be puffed and brown. Serve hot.

Makes 10 popovers.

Goat Cheese Biscuits

These are at their best served fresh at just about any meal or for breakfast with orange marmalade.

¼ pound young goat cheese
⅓ cup milk
2 cups all-purpose flour
1½ teaspoons baking powder
½ teaspoon baking soda
1 teaspoon kosher salt
4 tablespoons unsalted butter, cut into
    eight pieces

Heat the oven to 450°F. Mix the goat cheese and milk together until smooth. Set aside.

Mix the flour, baking powder, baking soda and salt together in a bowl. With your fingertips, quickly mix in the butter until it is the size of small peas. Pour in the goat cheese and milk and mix until it is absorbed.

Turn the dough out onto a lightly floured board and knead quickly until smooth. Roll the dough out until it is ¼ inch thick. Using a 2¼-inch biscuit cutter, cut rounds from the dough. Place them on an ungreased baking sheet, leaving at least ½ inch between them. Knead the excess dough together, roll again and cut more biscuits.

Bake in the preheated oven for 12 minutes, or until nicely browned.

Makes about 16 biscuits.

Brioche-Cheese Spirals

These are beautiful loaves for a brunch with scrambled eggs or at a supper with salad or soup. The fillings—baked ham and Cheddar or goat cheese and Greek olives—are both enhanced by the buttery brioche dough. The cheese and olives are reminiscent of the cream cheese and black olive sandwiches of our childhood.

The brioche dough is enough for one loaf with each filling. If you want them both the same, double that recipe's filling ingredients.

BRIOCHE DOUGH

1 recipe Brioche Dough (see page 241)

Make the dough as directed in the recipe and let rise until double in bulk.

CHEDDAR-HAM FILLING

3 ounces Cheddar, roughly chopped
3 ounces baked ham, roughly chopped
4 tablespoons unsalted butter
½ cup parsley sprigs, stems removed
Pinch cayenne pepper

Put the cheese and ham in the work bowl of a food processor and process, first with pulses, until finely chopped. Add the butter, parsley and cayenne. Run until very smooth. Do not refrigerate or it will get too firm to spread.

GOAT CHEESE-OLIVE FILLING

½ cup Kalamata (black Greek) olives, pits removed
3 scallions, chopped
6 ounces Bucheron or other flavorful goat cheese, crumbled
4 or 5 drops red pepper sauce

Place everything in a food processor and run, first with pulses, until the mixture is a smooth purée. Do not refrigerate or it will get too firm to spread.

ASSEMBLY

Brioche Dough
Cheddar-Ham Filling *and* **Goat Cheese-Olive Filling**

Butter two 4 x 8 x 2-inch loaf pans. Set aside.

After the brioche dough has risen, punch it down and cut in half. Cover one half and set aside. Roll the other half into a thin rectangle about 8 x 20 inches, so the short end is at the bottom. Spread half the filling over the dough, leaving a ¼-inch border along the sides and bottom and a ½-inch border at the top. When the filling is even, roll the dough up into a tight jelly roll, starting with the bottom. Pinch the edges together to seal and place seam side down in a prepared pan. Repeat with the remaining dough and filling. Cover and let rest 20 to 30 minutes while the oven heats to 350°F.

Bake for 30 minutes. Remove from the pans to a cutting board. Slice and serve while still hot.

Makes 2 loaves, enough for 10 to 12.

Paula Wolfert's Camembert in Brioche

Paula Wolfert is one of the most exacting, diligent cooks we know. Always on the lookout for new recipes, she found this one from a young chef in France and adapted it to the American kitchen. She serves it with soup or salad to make a simple meal quite special. Aside from the time involved in making the brioche, this is a surprisingly easy recipe. The one pitfall is that the cheese may leak out the bottom. To avoid this, Ms. Wolfert uses the egg glaze as a seal. She also suggests baking it in a dish you can use for serving so no one will notice the leaking cheese.

1 recipe Brioche Dough (see page 241)
1 not-too-ripe French Camembert (8 ounces)
1 egg mixed with 1 teaspoon cream or milk for glaze

Make the dough a day in advance to let it ripen in the refrigerator.

With a small sharp knife, cut all the white rind away from the cheese so it is completely ivory/yellow. Keep wrapped in the refrigerator until ready to use.

Place the dough on a well-floured surface and roll it into a 12-inch square or round. Place the cheese in the center of the dough and bring up the sides to completely cover the cheese, using some of the glaze to seal the edges. Pinch them together to make a tight seal, then invert onto a lightly buttered, shallow baking/serving dish. Cover it loosely with buttered foil and let rest in a warm, humid place for 1½ to 2 hours. The dough should be light and springy.

Heat the oven to 425°F. and adjust the rack to the lower middle level. Set a baking sheet on the rack to get very hot. Put the baking dish on the hot sheet and bake for 10 minutes. Lower the temperature to 350°F. and bake 10 minutes longer. Cut into wedges and serve warm.

Serves 6.

Kielbasa-Provolone Rings

This spicy bread is a sandwich in itself. Enjoy slices plain or buttered. Use them for sandwiches with sliced Provolone and tomatoes or roasted peppers.

1½ cups warm water
1 package dry yeast
3½ cups all-purpose flour
½ cup whole wheat flour
1 tablespoon kosher salt
1 tablespoon olive oil
2½ ounces Provolone, cut into ¼-inch cubes
2 ounces cooked, peeled kielbasa, minced

Stir the yeast in the water and set aside to let it dissolve. Put the flours and salt in the bowl of an electric mixer fitted with the dough hook. Stir the yeast mixture and pour it and the olive oil into the flour. Knead until smooth, about 5 minutes. Remove to a floured board and knead a minute or two longer.

Place the dough in a greased bowl, cover with a clean towel and set aside to rise in a warm place for an hour, or until double in bulk.

Punch down the dough and put it on a floured board. Sprinkle the cheese and kielbasa on the board and gradually work them into the dough until they are spread fairly evenly through it. Return the dough to the bowl, cover and let rise for about 30 minutes in a warm place.

Punch down the dough and divide it in half. Shape each half into an 18-inch rope, then shape the ropes into rings. Place them on an ungreased baking sheet, cover and let rise for another 30 minutes. While the dough is rising, heat the oven to 475°F.

Just before baking, brush the rings with water. Bake for 15 minutes, then lower the heat to 375°F. and bake 15 minutes longer. The rings should be brown on the top and bottom. Cool slightly before serving.

Makes two ring-shaped loaves.

Richard Sax's Red Pepper and Cheese-Stuffed Bread

Richard Sax, author of several cookbooks and numerous articles, makes this incredible stuffed bread as an hors d'oeuvre to serve hot with a glass of wine or cold at a picnic.

BREAD DOUGH

4 teaspoons dry yeast
1½ cups lukewarm water, or more if needed
2⅔ cups all-purpose flour, plus more if needed
1 cup whole wheat flour
1 tablespoon cornmeal
2 to 3 teaspoons kosher salt
1½ tablespoons olive oil
2 tablespoons chopped parsley
1½ teaspoons chopped fresh rosemary, or ½ to ¾ teaspoon dried

Dissolve the yeast in the lukewarm water. Set aside for 10 minutes.

Meanwhile, place the flours, cornmeal and salt in the work bowl of a food processor and mix with a few pulses. When the yeast is ready, stir the olive oil into it. With the processor running, pour most of the liquid into the flour. The dough should be soft but cohesive and slightly sticky. If necessary, add more of the yeast mixture, a bit more water, or some all-purpose flour. Process the dough a minute longer, adding the parsley and rosemary in the last few seconds.

Turn the dough out onto a floured board and knead for about 2 minutes, until smooth and elastic, kneading in a bit more flour until the dough is no longer sticky.

Lightly oil a bowl and put the dough in it, flipping it over so the top is greased. Dip a kitchen towel in hot water and wring it out, then use it to cover the bowl of dough. Let stand in a warm place until the dough has doubled in bulk.

FILLING

4 red bell peppers, or 2 red and 2 yellow bell peppers
2 tablespoons olive oil
¾ to 1 pound onions, quartered lengthwise, then sliced
3 tablespoons chopped parsley
Salt
Freshly ground black pepper
6 ounces fresh goat cheese (Chèvre Frais or Fromage Blanc), or other soft cheese (e.g., Ricotta, homemade Fromage Blanc or Mascarpone)

While the bread dough is rising, roast the peppers on a grill or under a hot broiler. Turn with tongs to let each side, top and bottom get black. When the peppers are completely charred, remove them to a plastic or paper bag and close tight. The steam in the bag helps loosen the skins. Set aside until the peppers are cool enough to handle.

Meanwhile, heat the olive oil in a skillet and add the onions. Cook over moderate heat until softened but not browned, about 10 minutes. Remove them from heat.

When the peppers are cool, pull away and discard the charred skins. Cut out the stems and discard along with the seeds inside. Cut the peppers in half crosswise, then

Milk or cream, if needed
1 garlic clove, finely minced
3 tablespoons chopped parsley,
    rosemary, thyme, chives and/or
    basil
Cornmeal
1¼ pounds Mozzarella, thinly sliced
1 egg yolk beaten with 1 teaspoon cold
    water for glaze

into wide strips. Pat dry, then add them to the onions. Stir in the parsley and salt and pepper to taste.

Place the fresh cheese in a small bowl and beat it lightly with a fork. If it is not liquid and quite fluid, stir in some milk or cream to make it looser. Then stir in the garlic, herbs and salt and pepper to taste.

When ready to assemble the bread, rub an 11-inch porcelain quiche pan or similar baking dish with olive oil, then sprinkle the bottom with a little cornmeal.

Punch down the dough and divide it into two unequal pieces. Flour your work surface and roll the larger piece into a circle 2 inches larger than your pan. The edges of the dough should be quite thin. Fit the dough into the pan so about an inch of dough hangs over the sides.

Arrange half the Mozzarella slices over the dough, slightly overlapping. Gently spoon about half the pepper and onion mixture over that. Carefully spoon the seasoned cheese mixture on top. Cover with the remaining pepper mixture, then the rest of the Mozzarella slices. Roll the smaller piece of dough into a circle the size of your pan, rolling the edges quite thin. Lay it gently over the Mozzarella slices. Bring the overhanging dough up to meet the top dough and pinch to seal well. Brush the egg glaze over the top for the dough, then cut symmetrical curved lines into the top of the dough, starting near the center and going out toward the edge. Let the dough rest for at least 10 minutes while you heat the oven to 400°F.

When the oven is hot, bake the bread for 40 to 50 minutes, until it is golden brown and sounds hollow when tapped. Cool 15 to 20 minutes on a rack before serving.

Makes one 11-inch round loaf, enough for 10 to 16 wedges.

Alsatian Muenster Rye Bread

Hearty rye breads are perfect foils for strong cheeses like Alsatian Muenster. When the cheese is used in this rye bread, however, it is absorbed into the dough, making a pleasant crusty bread that is surprisingly mild. Try using it for sandwiches with the uncooked Muenster, some smoky ham and mustard.

2 packages dry yeast
2 cups warm water
6 tablespoons molasses
¼ cup vegetable oil
1 tablespoon kosher salt
2 cups rye flour
2½ cups whole wheat flour, or more if
    necessary
6 ounces Alsatian Muenster, cut into
    small pieces, rind on
2 tablespoons caraway seeds
2 cups all-purpose flour
Cornmeal

Dissolve the yeast in ½ cup of the warm water. Place the molasses, remaining 1½ cups water, oil and salt in the bowl of an electric mixer with a dough hook. Add the dissolved yeast and stir to mix.

A cup at a time, beat in the rye flour and 2 cups of the whole wheat flour. Beat in the cheese and caraway seeds, then the all-purpose flour, ½ cup at a time. Sprinkle in more whole wheat flour until the dough comes together and cleans the sides of the bowl. Then knead for 5 minutes longer.

Oil a large bowl and add the dough. Turn it over so the top is oiled. Cover loosely with a clean cloth and let rise in a warm place until double in bulk, about 1½ hours.

Punch down the dough and divide it in half. Shape each half into a round. Sprinkle a baking sheet with cornmeal and arrange the loaves on it so they don't touch and have enough room to rise. Cover and let rise again for 30 minutes. Meanwhile, heat the oven to 375°F.

Just before baking, gently brush the tops of the loaves with water. Bake for 40 minutes. The loaves should be firm and sound hollow when thumped on the bottom. Cool on a rack.

Makes two 1¾-pound loaves.

Spicy Corn Bread

The cheese and peppers added to the basic corn bread turn it into a special dish to serve with barbecued brisket or scrambled eggs. For Thanksgiving, cube it and dry it out for a delicious stuffing.

2 tablespoons unsalted butter
1 jalapeño pepper, cored, seeded and minced
¾ cup cornmeal
1 cup all-purpose flour
2 tablespoons sugar
½ teaspoon kosher salt
1 tablespoon baking powder
¼ pound Monterey Jack, cut into ¼-inch cubes
1 large egg
1 cup milk

Heat the oven to 425°F. Butter a 9-inch square baking dish and set aside.

Melt the butter in a small skillet. Add the jalapeño pepper and cook for 2 minutes. Set aside.

Put the cornmeal, flour, sugar, salt and baking powder in a mixing bowl. Stir to blend. Add the cheese, tossing it with the flour mixture so the pieces stay separate.

Beat the egg into the milk and pour the mixture into the bowl along with the butter and jalapeño pepper. With a wooden spoon, blend everything quickly, stirring just until all the dry ingredients are wet.

Spoon the mixture into the prepared pan and bake in the preheated oven for 25 minutes. Serve hot.

Makes nine 3-inch squares corn bread.

Basic Recipes

There are certain recipes for sauces and doughs that we use over and over as part of other dishes. We needed them for recipes in this book and are sure to continue to do so. Although they are a diverse lot, we've grouped them together. The only ones that contain any cheese are the pesto, a thick basil sauce usually tossed over pasta, and the salad dressings, meant for basic bowls of mixed greens for which there is no recipe, or your favorite composed salad with poached fish or flaky tuna.

Basic Tomato Sauce

In the summer, when beautiful, red, flavorful tomatoes are available, we use them for sauce. The rest of the year we are happy with canned Italian plum tomatoes.

1 tablespoon olive oil
1 large garlic clove, minced
1 small onion, minced
1 can (28 ounces) Italian plum tomatoes
2 tablespoons red wine vinegar
1 teaspoon kosher salt
Freshly ground black pepper

Heat the olive oil in a saucepan. Add the garlic and onion and cook over medium-high heat for 2 minutes, or until the onion is soft but not brown. Add the tomatoes with their liquid, crushing the tomatoes with your hands or a spoon. Simmer over medium heat for about 10 minutes, stirring from time to time to keep the sauce from sticking. Add the vinegar and simmer 20 minutes longer.

Put the sauce through the fine blade of a food mill and season to taste with salt and pepper.

Makes about 2¹/₂ cups.

Creamy Tomato Sauce

This quick, creamy sauce is excellent with the Shrimp and Fennel Ravioli (see page 138). Try it, also, with sautéed scallops.

1 can (14 ounces) Italian plum tomatoes
1 cup heavy cream
1 teaspoon kosher salt
Pinch cayenne pepper

Put the tomatoes through a food mill or sieve into a non-aluminum saucepan. Bring to a boil and simmer for 5 minutes to thicken. Add the cream, salt and cayenne. Cook until heated through and slightly reduced. Taste and add more salt and pepper if needed.

Makes about 1¹/₄ cups.

Tomato Mushroom Sauce

We use this sauce in the Vegetarian Lasagne (see page 137) and with the Deep-Fried Goat Cheese (see page 129), but it also goes well with sliced zucchini or baked scrod.

2 tablespoons olive oil
2 large garlic cloves, minced
1 large (6 ounces) onion, chopped
1 can (35 ounces) plum tomatoes
Kosher salt
Freshly ground black pepper
2 tablespoons unsalted butter
½ pound mushrooms, sliced through the
    caps
1 tablespoon fresh minced marjoram, or
    1 teaspoon dried

Heat the olive oil in a deep 10-inch skillet. Add the garlic and cook for a minute to soften. Then add the onion and cook for about 5 minutes, until the onion is soft but not brown. Add the tomatoes with their liquid, crushing them with a spoon or your hand. Let simmer for about 10 minutes, then put the mixture through a food mill fitted with the medium blade. Season to taste with about ½ teaspoon salt and some freshly ground pepper. Set aside.

Melt the butter in another skillet. Add the mushrooms, marjoram and ½ teaspoon salt. Cover and cook over medium heat for about 5 minutes. The mushrooms should be soft. Add them with their liquid to the tomato sauce.

Makes about 4 cups.

Bolognese Sauce

This thick sauce is excellent over pasta with grated Parmesan sprinkled liberally on top at the table.

1 tablespoon olive oil
1 medium onion, chopped
2 garlic cloves, minced
1 carrot, minced
½ pound ground pork
½ pound ground beef
2 cans (35 ounces each) Italian plum
    tomatoes, drained
1 teaspoon kosher salt
2 tablespoons chopped fresh basil, or 2
    teaspoons dried
1 tablespoon chopped fresh marjoram,
    or 1 teaspoon dried
Freshly ground black pepper

Heat the oil in a 3-quart saucepan. Add the onion and garlic and cook until soft but not brown, about 1 minute. Add the carrot and cook for 30 seconds. Break the beef and pork into chunks and add to the pan, stirring until it is all brown.

Put the tomatoes through a food mill with a coarse blade and stir them into the pot. Season to taste with the salt, basil, marjoram and pepper. Simmer for 30 minutes.

Makes about 6½ cups.

Pesto

This popular basil sauce has Parmesan in it. Italians never add more cheese at the table. The sauce should just barely coat the pasta, never drown it, so a little sauce goes a long way. Leftovers freeze well, however, and can be added to vegetable soups or spooned over grilled fish. Since you need only small amounts at a time, freeze the sauce in individual ice cube holders, pop them out when frozen and keep in a plastic bag.

¼ cup pine nuts
1 large garlic clove
1 packed cup fresh basil
½ cup Italian flat-leaf parsley
6 tablespoons (1 ½ ounces) Parmesan
6 tablespoons fruity olive oil
Freshly ground black pepper

Put the pine nuts in a small dry frying pan and cook over medium heat, shaking the pan frequently, until the nuts are nicely browned.

Mince the garlic in the work bowl of a food processor fitted with the metal blade. Add the basil and parsley and process with pulses until finely chopped. Add the cheese and pine nuts and run until fairly smooth. With the machine running, pour in the olive oil. Add freshly ground pepper to taste.

If the sauce is too thick, stir in some of the cooking liquid from the pasta or water.

Makes about ¾ cup.

Green Salsa

This uncooked sauce is delicious with all kinds of Mexican or Tex-Mex preparations. Make it as hot or mild as you want by varying the strength and number of the peppers. Always be careful when handling hot peppers. The oils will remain on your fingers and can burn anything else you touch, especially eyes and lips. The seeds are the hottest of all, so always remove them.

2 garlic cloves
1 medium (¼ pound) white onion
1 fresh jalapeño pepper or more to taste, core and seeds removed (if jalapeño peppers are not available, use other fresh, small hot peppers, or if necessary, canned)
1 can (15½ ounces) green tomatoes (tomatillos), drained and rinsed
1 teaspoon kosher salt
1 tablespoon fresh minced coriander (cilantro or Chinese parsley)

Place the garlic, onion and pepper in the work bowl of a food processor and process until finely minced. Add the green tomatoes, salt and coriander. Process until fairly smooth. Adjust seasoning to taste with more salt, coriander or hot pepper.

Makes about 1½ cups.

Bell Pepper Sauce

Jane Joseph made this sauce to serve with her Cheese Roulade (see page 158), but we also serve it with Rolled Eggplant (see page 163) and broiled fish. If you make the sauce ahead, refrigerate and reheat slowly.

5 tablespoons unsalted butter
¼ cup chopped onion
1 teaspoon minced garlic
6 cups coarsely chopped red bell
    peppers (4 or 5 large)
1¾ cups chicken stock
½ cup dry white wine
3 tablespoons all-purpose flour
1¼ teaspoon salt
1 teaspoon fresh lemon juice
¼ teaspoon freshly ground black pepper
⅛ teaspoon ground cayenne pepper

Heat 2 tablespoons of the butter in a 3-quart saucepan. Add the onion and garlic and cook for 1 minute. Add the red peppers and stir to coat. Pour in the stock and wine. Bring the liquid to a boil, lower the heat so it simmers, cover and cook for about 20 minutes, until the peppers are very soft.

Let the peppers cool a bit, then remove them with a slotted spoon to the work bowl of a food processor. Depending on the size of the bowl, you may have to work in batches. Run the machine until the peppers are a fine purée. Pour the mixture through a fine strainer into a clean saucepan, pressing on it with a wooden spoon to get all the pulp. Pour the reserved pepper liquid through the strainer as well. When you have only a small amount of solids, mostly skin, left, stop and discard the solids. Return the saucepan to the stove and bring to a boil.

While the sauce is heating, work the flour and remaining 3 tablespoons butter together with a fork or your fingers to make a paste called beurre manié. When the sauce starts to boil, start whisking the beurre manié into it, ½ teaspoon at a time. When it has all been added, let the sauce boil gently for a minute.

Off the heat, season with the salt, lemon juice and the peppers. Taste and adjust the seasonings if needed. Serve hot.

Makes about 3 cups.

Red Chile Sauce

Serve this sauce when you want to give a dish a Mexican touch. It can be used as is or heated.

1 chile pasilla (dried chile chilaca)
2 garlic cloves
1 medium (¼ pound) onion
1 can (28 ounces) plum tomatoes, drained
1 tablespoon kosher salt
¼ teaspoon red pepper sauce

Remove and discard the seeds and core from the chile. Place the flesh in a bowl and add boiling water to cover. Let sit for about 30 minutes, until very soft.

Drain the chile, reserving some of the liquid, and place it in the work bowl of a food processor. Process until finely chopped. Add the garlic and onion and process until well chopped. If the mixture is very thick, add a tablespoon or two of the reserved soaking liquid.

Add the drained tomatoes and process until smooth. Season to taste with salt and pepper sauce.

Makes about 2 cups.

Blue Cheese Dressing

2 tablespoons fresh lemon juice
½ cup olive oil
2 ounces Danish Blue, crumbled
Cayenne pepper

Mix the lemon juice and oil together. Add the cheese and mix well. Season to taste with cayenne.

Makes about ⅔ cup.

Goat Cheese Dressing

This dressing is our choice for salads of mixed greens with croutons and avocados, over poached chicken and grilled salmon. If you leave out the milk, it makes a delicious dip for raw vegetables.

2 garlic cloves
¼ cup minced onion
¼ cup parsley
¼ pound flavorful, young goat cheese
½ cup mayonnaise
½ cup milk
¼ teaspoon dried oregano
¼ teaspoon dried thyme
½ teaspoon kosher salt
⅛ teaspoon freshly ground black pepper
2 drops red pepper sauce

Put the garlic, onion and parsley in a food processor and process until finely chopped. Add the remaining ingredients and run until smooth and well blended.

Makes 1⅓ cups.

Raspberry Sauce

1 package (10 ounces) frozen
    raspberries, defrosted
Juice of ½ lemon

Put the raspberries in a food processor or blender and process until smooth. Add the lemon juice. If you want a more delicate sauce, press it through a sieve to remove the seeds.

Makes about ¾ cup.

Poached Pears

Pears are one of the few reliable winter fruits, good for poaching even if they are underripe. They are fine by themselves or as ingredients in other recipes like Seppi Renggli's Poached Pears with Brie and Canadian Bacon (see page 203) and Pear and Maytag Blue Tart (see page 208).

4 firm, ripe pears
2 cups dry white wine
2 cups water
1½ cups sugar

Peel the pears, halve them, and remove the seeds and cores. Heat the wine, water and sugar in a 10-inch skillet until the liquid boils and the sugar dissolves. Add the pears. Simmer for 5 minutes, then turn the pears over and simmer 5 minutes longer, or until just soft when pierced. Drain. Serve hot, cold or at room temperature. If you are using them for another recipe, you can make them a few days ahead and refrigerate.

Makes 8 pear halves.

Puff Pastry

Puff pastry is an incredibly flaky dough made of dozens of layers of dough and butter. Not the place for a beginner to start, to be sure, but it is not as difficult as many bakers infer. It takes time from start to finish, although much of that is to let the dough rest. The results are worth it.

3 cups (about 15 ounces) all-purpose flour
1 teaspoon kosher salt
¾ pound plus 2 tablespoons unsalted butter
1 tablespoon lemon juice
¾ to 1 cup ice water

Place the flour and salt in the work bowl of a food processor with the 2 tablespoons of the butter. Process with pulses until the mixture resembles coarse meal. With the machine running, pour in the lemon juice followed by the water. Add just enough water for the dough to come together. It should not be too sticky.

Turn the dough out onto a lightly floured board and knead for a few minutes, until the dough is smooth. Wrap it in wax paper and refrigerate for 1 hour.

Take the remaining ¾ pound butter and work it into a 6-inch square by placing the sticks between two sheets of wax paper and beating them with a rolling pin until they are soft enough to blend together. Press against the wax paper to shape the square. Refrigerate until the dough is ready. Both butter and dough should have similar textures, neither being too cold so they roll smoothly together.

When the dough has chilled, place it on a floured board and roll into a 12-inch square. Place the butter square on top. Fold the top and bottom of dough over the butter, then fold in the sides. Pinch the edges of the dough together to make a sealed package around the butter.

Roll the dough out into a rectangle 18 inches long. Fold the top third of dough down over the rest. Then fold the bottom up (much as you would fold a business letter). Rotate the dough so the open end is to your right. Roll the dough again until it is 18 inches long. Repeat the folding.

Wrap the dough carefully in a kitchen towel, then place in a plastic bag and refrigerate for 30 minutes. Repeat the rolling and folding two more times. Wrap and refrigerate 45 minutes longer, then roll and fold twice more, for a total of six turns. The dough is now ready to use in specific recipes.

Makes 2¼ pounds.

Basic Bread/Pizza Dough

1 teaspoon dry yeast
1 cup warm water
2 to 2½ cups all-purpose flour
1½ teaspoons kosher salt
1 tablespoon olive oil

Dissolve the yeast in the warm water. Set aside. Place 2 cups of the flour and the salt in a mixing bowl. Add the dissolved yeast and liquid along with the olive oil. Mix until the liquid is all absorbed, then turn the dough out onto a floured board and knead until smooth, adding more flour as necessary. You can also knead the dough in an electric mixer with a dough hook or in a food processor.

Place the dough in a greased bowl. Flip it so the top is greased. Cover and let rise in a warm place until double in bulk, about 1 hour, before using. If made ahead, wrap in plastic and refrigerate or freeze.

Pastry Dough

This versatile dough can be made in a food processor, electric mixer, or by hand. Try to handle the dough as little as possible or your crust will get tough. The exact amount of water needed varies from day to day but the less you add, the less the crust will shrink, so pour slowly and stop before you think you've added enough. The same recipe works for both savory and sweet pies, but for the sweet version, we usually add a little sugar.

1½ cups all-purpose flour
2 tablespoons sugar (for sweet dough)
Pinch salt
¼ pound unsalted butter, chilled, cut into 8 pieces
4 to 5 tablespoons ice water

Place the flour, sugar (if using) and salt in the work bowl of a food processor. Process for 10 seconds to mix. Add the butter and process with pulses until the mixture resembles coarse meal. With the machine running, pour in the water. Stop the moment the dough starts to come together. Remove the dough to your work surface and shape quickly into a ball. Flatten the ball into a disk and wrap in wax paper. Chill for at least an hour before using.

Brioche Dough

1½ teaspoons (less than 1 package) dry
    yeast
1 tablespoon sugar
6 tablespoons lukewarm (105° to
    110°F.) milk
1 pound (about 3 cups) all-purpose flour
¼ pound unsalted butter, cut into eight
    pieces
3 large eggs
½ teaspoon kosher salt

Dissolve the yeast and sugar in the warm milk. Set aside for a few minutes until frothy.

Put the flour in the bowl of an electric mixer with a dough hook. Add the butter, eggs, salt and yeast mixture. Knead the dough until it is completely mixed and smooth, 5 to 10 minutes. If the dough is very sticky, add a little more flour. If you don't have a powerful electric mixer, mix the dough in a food processor.

Place the dough in a large buttered bowl. Turn the dough over so it is completely buttered. Cover with a clean cloth and leave to rise in a warm place until double in bulk, 1 to 1½ hours.

Use as directed in the recipes for Brioche-Cheese Spirals (see page 220) or Camembert in Brioche (see page 222).

Crêpes

1 cup all-purpose flour
2 large eggs
½ cup milk
½ cup water
3 tablespoons unsalted butter, melted
1 teaspoon sugar (if dessert crêpes)
¼ teaspoon kosher salt
Vegetable oil

Put all the ingredients except the oil in a food processor or blender and process until completely smooth. Cover and refrigerate at least 6 hours before using.

Rub the bottom of 6-inch crêpe pan with vegetable oil just to coat. Heat the pan until hot. Pour in 2 tablespoons batter and swirl it around to coat the bottom of the pan evenly. Cook over medium-high heat until the edges begin to curl, meaning it is cooked on the bottom. Peek underneath to see if the crêpe is golden brown throughout. When it is, lift it up with your fingers or a spatula and turn to cook for a moment on the other side. The second side will not be as evenly brown as the first.

Turn the cooked crêpe out onto a plate or board and continue to cook the other crêpes in the same way until all the batter is used. It may be necessary to add a little more oil to the pan from time to time.

Makes about sixteen 6-inch crêpes.

Mail-Order Sources

Ideal Cheese Shop Ltd.
1205 Second Avenue
New York, NY 10021
(212) 688-7579
    Will ship full range of domestic and imported cheeses. Catalogue available.

Cabot Farmers' Co-Op
Cabot, VT 05647
(802) 563-2231
    Raw milk aged Cheddar

Caleb's Farm Cheese
R.D. 3
Bingham Farms
Wellsboro, PA 16901
(717) 724-3959
    Boerkäse Gouda; Double Cream Gradost; low-fat, low-salt Chalet, Colby

Crowley Cheese
Healdville, VT 05758
(802) 259-2340
    Colby

Gethsemani Farms
Trappist, KY 40051
    Trappist Cheese

the Goat Works inc.
R.D. 1, Box 57
Washington, NJ 07882
(201) 689-6899
    Goat cheeses

Hawthorne Valley Farm
Box 225A
R.D. 2
Ghent, NY 12075
(518) 672-7500
    Swiss-style cheese, plain, with caraway, smoked

Kendall Cheese Company
cheeses available through:
California Sunshine Fine Foods
144 King Street
San Francisco, CA
(415) 543-3007
    Goat cheeses

Marin French Cheese Company
7500 Red Hill Road
P.O. Box 99
Petaluma, CA 94953
    Rouge et Noir Brie, Camembert, Schloss, Breakfast Cheese

Maytag Dairy Farms
Rural Route 1
Box 806
Newton, IA 50208
(800) 247-2458 outside Iowa
(515) 792-1133
    Maytag Blue cheese

North Pack Cheese
Route 1
Box 79
South Lyndeboro, NH 03082
(603) 547-2029
    Raw milk semisoft cheese

Shelburne Farms
Shelburne, VT 05482
(802) 985-3222
    Cheddar

Vella Cheese Company
P.O. Box 191
Sonoma, CA 95476
(707) 938-3232
    Dry Jack

Index

COPYRIGHT ACKNOWLEDGMENTS